A
TOUR

THROUGH PART OF

NORTH WALES,

IN THE YEAR 1798, AND AT OTHER TIMES;

Principally Undertaken with a View to

BOTANIAL RESEARCHES

In that Alpine Country:

INTERSPERSED WITH OBSERVATIONS

ON ITS

SCENERY, AGRICULTURE, MANUFACTURES,
CUSTOMS, HISTORY, AND ANTIQUITIES

by

THE REV. J. EVANS, B. A.

LATE OF JESUS COLLEGE, OXON.

London
Hounskull Publishing
2024

HOUNSKULL PUBLISHING
BM Box Hounskull
London WC1N 3XX

A Tour through Part of North Wales in the Year 1798,
and at Other Times; Principally Undertaken with a View to
Botanical Researches in that Alpine Country: Interspersed
with Observations on Its Scenery, Agriculture, Manufactures,
Customs, History, and Antiquities

Originally published in 1800

First Hounskull edition published 2024
© Hounskull Publishing 2024

ISBN 978-1-910893-27-2

British Library Cataloguing-in-Publication Data:
A catalogue record for this book is available from the British Library.

"Tu nidum servas; ego laudo ruris amœni
Rivos & musca circumlita saxa nemusque.
Quid quæris? vivo, & regno, simul ista reliqui
Quæ vos ad cælum effertis rumore secundo."
HOR. EPIST. X. LIB. I.

———————

"O Nature, how, in every charm supreme,
    Thy votaries feast on raptures ever new!
Oh for the voice and fire of seraphim,
    To sing thy glories with devotion due!
    Blest be the day I ' scap'd the wrangling crew
From Pyrrho's maze and Epicurus' sty;
    And held high converse with the god-like few,
Who, to th' enraptur'd heart, and ear, and eye,
Teach Beauty, Virtue, Truth, Love, and Melody."
BEATTIE.

TO THE RIGHT HONOURABLE

RICHARD PENNANT,

BARON PENHRYN, OF PENHRYN;

THESE LETTERS,

ON A COUNTRY,

THE SUBJECT OF HIS LORDSHIP'S ADMIRATION,

And to which he is so Liberal

A BENEFACTOR,

ARE,

With a Propriety not usually adopted in Dedications,

INSCRIBED,

WITH THE MOST PROFOUND

RESPECT AND ESTEEM,

BY
HIS LORDSHIP'S
MOST OBEDIENT
HUMBLE SERVANT,

J. EVANS.

Table of Contents

TABLE OF CONTENTS

Note on This Edition

The present volume is based on the 1800 edition published in London by J. White. The text has been reproduced in its entirety.

The spelling and punctuation remains as in the original. Capitalisation of certain words, e.g., Christianity, has been harmonised. Latin passages have been consistently italicised, as have the titles of works referred to in the text. Geographical names, sometimes inconsistently spelt, and those of historical figures, have been left unaltered, but indexed as per current spelling, except where no other reference could be found. Extensive quotes have been taken out of quotation marks and long passages between quotation marks have been set as block quotes.

Where bibliographical footnotoes have been expanded, the expanded information appears in square brackets, and titles put in Italics, as per modern convention.

A number of editorial footnotes have been added and identified as such, to distinguished by the author's.

Preface

The following observations, on the manners of a people and appearances of a country, nearly connected with our own, were made *at different times*, but more particularly in the summer months of 1798.

As several publications have, of late, appeared under the title of "A Tour in Wales", &c. the present may seem to have little claim to attention, and an apology may be thought necessary, for intruding upon the public any thing further respecting a subject, which will, by some perhaps, be considered as already exhausted.

It may be observed, that the life of man is of short duration; but a day, compared with the time necessary for thoroughly surveying the multiplicity of objects around him; the brevity of life, therefore, stamps a value upon ideas otherwise unimportant, and raises into consequence descriptions that would otherwise be disregarded.

Every traveller sees, or fancies that he sees, some thing unobserved before, and that he is capable of communicating knowledge not obtained or imparted by others. Curiosity produces an accuracy and industry of research; and the desire of relating what was pleasant to behold or difficult to obtain, induces him to conclude, that whatever was important to himself must be important to mankind.

It will be admitted, that even in the same route different objects will strike different minds; and that the same objects will not appear of equal importance in the eye of every observer. To examine the elevations of Snowdon a Botanist would esteem weeks well employed; while, to the superficial traveller, who looks upon a country merely as a landscape, for the gratification of the eye of taste, the pursuit of Botany would be considered as the vagaries of enthusiasm; as the minute investigations of the Antiquarian are the subject of ridicule to the fashionable Tourist, whose pursuits might, in their turn, be regarded by some as the mere energies of folly.

A country like North Wales, almost inaccessible in many of its parts to the traveller, and, till very lately, but little frequented by the votaries of Science, must yet remain, in a great measure, unexplored. It affords, therefore, to the lovers of Natural History, ample room for speculation and research; an extensive field both above and beneath the surface offers itself to the eye of curiosity, and solicits the investigations of Science,

A Journey, undertaken for Botanical purposes, and with a view of publishing, at some future period, a *Flora Cambrica*, cannot be expected to abound with learned Remarks upon the remains of Arts and Institutions; nor with those profound observations upon life and manners which would adorn the pages of the Moralist and Politician; yet, it would be impossible for the man of feeling to pass through a country considered as part of his own, but to which the manners and customs of its inhabitants, form so great a contrast, without taking some notice of its peculiarities.

If it should be objected as derogatory to the dignity of a writer, that, in the course of this little Work, too much attention has been paid to humble circumstances, to "The short and simple annals of the poor," I must apologize in the words of a celebrated Author:

> Let it be remembered, that life consists, not of a variety of illustrious actions or elegant enjoyments; the greater part of our time passes in compliance with necessities: in the perfor-

mance of daily duties in the removal of small
inconveniences: in the procurement of petty
pleasures: and we are well or ill at ease as the
main stream of life glides on smoothly, or is
ruffled by small obstructions and frequent interruptions. *The true state of every nation is
the state of common life.*

These Letters, addressed to a friend, were not
originally intended for publication; they consisted merely of diarian memoranda on such objects
as appeared singular or striking; with cursory remarks on the inaccuracies and erroneous statements of former travellers interwoven with historic facts and allusions to ancient usages, and
the customs of other nations. They have been, in
consequence of the solicitations of friends who
had seen them, prepared for the press; and the
Author has thought proper to avail himself of a
few observations of others, to correct or illustrate
his own; here he acknowledges himself obliged to
the ingenious *Aikin*, and the laborious *Pennant*,
whose volumes are as remarkable for accuracy of
description, as for the nature of their contents.

The Writer of these Letters entertains no
high expectations: he forms no sanguine views.
If from his pages the reader should derive any
amusement, the Author will have the satisfaction
to reflect that it has been afforded without recommending folly or administering to vice; and if he
has added another volume of what is called light
reading, to the many already before the public,

it is one at which Modesty will have no cause to blush, nor Morality to frown. Such as it is, it is presented to the Public: the Author is answerable to the guardians of the public taste; on its merits or demerits it is for them to decide; and by their decision let it justly stand or fall.

Si quid amicum ergà bene feci aut consului fideliter;
Non videor meruisse laudem, culpâ caruisse arbitror.
Plaut. *Trinum.* Scen. ult.

Letter I

DEAR SIR,

o apology is necessary for addressing you upon a subject that mutually interested us both at an early period of our lives: the romantic scenery, rare productions, and peculiar manners of a country, which for ages was the asylum of Religion and Liberty, and for a series of years hurled defiance at the ambitious usurpation of the English Monarchy, and checked the tyrannical oppression of its votaries. The estimates, my Friend, of human existence, and human power, are generally made upon imaginary data. Few consider that thought is an energy of the mind, while action is only an effort of the body. The multiplicity of plans that are formed without being realized, convince us it is easier to project than to execute; and while it demonstrates the very limited power of man, it furnishes an unanswerable argument for the Immortality of the Soul.

The scheme we had long in view of traversing these scenes together, from circumstances well known to you, was frustrated; and the alternative was left to me to undertake the journey without the valuable company of so intelligent a Friend, or to give up those expectations which had been raised to a higher pitch by the recurrence of disappointment.

In the Summer of 1798, accompanied by persons calculated to give assistance to inquiry, and stimulus to research, I entered on a journey that promised to open new sources of information and delight; and it is with conscious pleasure I am able to say, that my most sanguine hopes were realized. I experienced pleasures, the recollection of which will tend to sweeten many an otherwise irksome hour, and made reflections on men and manners still more essentially useful in a moral and religious view. Reflections which I hope will make me more humble in myself, liberal towards others, and grateful to him who is the Author of every distinction, and every good in society.

Early in the month of June we arrived at the ancient town of Shrewsbury, which is too well known for a description of it to be interesting. Leaving the Oswestry road on our right, we directed our course westward, and took the road for Poole.

The first place that claimed our attention, was a small village near the Severn, named Buttington, over which is an old stone bridge, remarkable for having been the place where the English obtained a decisive victory over the Danes, under their leader Hesten, A. D. 894. After having over-run great part of England, they were surrounded here by the Generals of the brave Alfred, who so closely blockaded the Pagans, that they were obliged to feed upon their own horses. At length reduced to despair by famine, attempting to cut their way through the Saxon Army, a terrible slaughter ensued, and scarcely sufficient were left alive to inform their countrymen of the disaster. By the road side grows in abundance, the ARTEMISIA ABSINTHIUM, It is used by the country people, instead of hops, and has the peculiar property of destroying acescency in beer, grown hard for want of them. A property mentioned by Dr. Stokes,[1] renders this a valuable plant. The leaves steeped in boiling water, and repeatedly applied to a recent bruise, remove the pain, and prevent the swelling and discoloration of the part. We reached Poole about eight

---

1   Jonathan Stokes (c. 1755 – 1831). —Ed.

3

o'clock in the evening, and were pleased to find, though we had quitted England, we had not bade adieu to the comforts and civility for which its inns are famed. At the Royal Oak the accommodations are good, and the charges moderate. We sat down to a pleasing repast, well served up, and for the first time met with a fish called a Salmon Mort,[2] somewhat like a Salmon Trout, good eating, and in great plenty through most parts of North Wales. When at an inn I generally bespeak civility from the attendants, by taking an early opportunity of paying them a compliment. The waiter could scarcely speak English. I observed that he was a good-natured fellow, and partook of the civility of his country. But I received a smart retort courteous, assuring me he was not a Welshman, which convinced me I was not yet far enough West to lay hold of the partialities of the country. On inquiry, I learnt that our waiter was born in Clun, a village, part in Shropshire and part in Radnorshire . . . WELCH POOLE, as it is generally called, is a good town, a little West of the Severn, is the principal of five boroughs in Montgomeryshire, whose joint suffrage sends one Member to the British Senate. It is governed by a Mayor, Burgesses, Common Council, Recorder, &c. But I was sorry to observe in this, as

---

2   This is a young salmon in its 3d year of growth; the 1st year they are called smelts; the 2d, sprods; the 3d, morts; the 4th, fork tails; 5th, half fish; and the 6th, are dignified with the name of salmon.

in most other places in the principality, order is preserved more by the influence of petty-fogging Attornies, than the veneration for Corporate Bodies; and security is derived rather from the dread of Common Law, than the regulations of Municipal Legis lature. This place, probably derived its present name from a deep pool now within the inclosure of Powis Park, denominated from the dark appearance of its water, Llundy Pool. In ages of ignorance, it was considered unfathomable, or, as the people term it, without a bottom . Various attempts have been made to ascertain its depth, the result of which will allow it to be about 300 feet; but from the great variation in the depth, it is not an improbable conjecture that there is an intercommunication between the waters of the Poole and those of the Severn; yet notwithstanding the average depth has been ascertained, so fond are mankind of the marvellous, that the line of actual admeasurement has not yet exploded the line of superstition.

The town is decently built, the houses consisting chiefly of brick, form one long and handsome street, in the centre of which stands a new County Hall, erected by subscription, comprising apartments above for the purposes of justice and amusement; and below for the accommodation of trade. It has an elegant front, with colonnades, and pilasters of stone, and forms a public ornament to the town, giving a favourable idea of the spirit and liberality ofthe county.

The principal manufacture carried on here, and at the adjacent villages, is flannel, and it is the mart for this article, and other coarse woollen goods, made by the little farmers in the hill country, which are bought up for ready money by the dealers of Liverpool and Shrewsbury.

We were pleasingly struck with the life and spirit that pervades this little place on the occasion. The show of native and unvarnished beauty is very great; for the business of buying and selling is chiefly conducted by women here, and through all the markets of North Wales.

A reflection naturally arose on the superiority which these females acquired, in the scale of utility and respect, over the English fair, by conducting an important part, of the staple manufactures of their country.

These women, said I, are useful as well as pleasing; while they administer to the happiness of man, they contribute to his wealth. They prove themselves worthy the honourable station they fill as mothers, by affording such essential assistance to the support of a family, and rise into importance by the considerable portion they perform of the duties in society. The common bar to matrimony, incompetence to maintain a family, does not exist here. Educated for the intended situation, and habituated to those active employments, necessary to domestic comfort and prosperity, a wife is deemed a valuable helpmate, and a numerous family an increasing blessing. "What! (still rivetted

to the spot) said I, is the genius of domestic happiness asleep, or is he driven away by luxury and
dissipation, that my fair country-women receive
an education which only fits them for the theatre
or the ball-room, and incapacitates them for every
thing venerable attached to the name of wife, or of
mother!! Taught to consider the external accomplishments of the body as comprising every thing
amiable or important, the modern fair one points
all her attention to the graces of her person, while
all that would qualify her to soften the asperities
of life, to soothe her partner's cares, to assist in
providing for the increasing demands of a rising
family, and enable her to educate her children in
the same habits of industry and economy is neglected and despised. The daughters of Athens and
of Rome were the children of usefulness; and let
Christain parents blush to hear they fall far short
of the poor benighted Pagans in estimating the
importance, and attending to the business of education. In those times no citizen of note appeared
in public in any dress that was not manufactured
by the female part of his family; and, permit me to
ask, have the fair been more respected by the other sex, or has their happiness been increased since
that period of our history, when every woman appeared at market and at church in a dress that was
spun by his wife or his daughters?"

While thus strongly impressed with the fatal
system of modern fashionable education, and
anticipating its pernicious effects to society, my

attitude and gestures had attracted the attention of a crowd of spectators, who, though puzzled to account for my extraordinary appearance, could not possibly conjecture I was making a comparison in their favour. The downcast look of many of the senior part, indicated that their sympathy was excited, and that they supposed my head was affected, while the significant giggle of some of the junior part, and the loud broad laugh of others, as clearly proved they entertained a more favourable opinion of my case. I added my smile on the occasion, and bowing respect fully, left them. The church is an old gothic structure, not remarkable for its elegance. Belonging to its ornaments, is a beautiful chalice of pure gold, containing by measure a wine quart, The idle story told by the sexton, of its having been the donation of a transported felon, who had been successful, is refuted by the inscription it bears, which informs the classic reader it was the gift of Thomas Davies, who held the office of Governor-General ofall the English Colonies on the Western Coast of Africa. That this vessel, formed of *Guinea Gold*, to the value of 168l. he bestowed upon the church of Poole, as a sacred and grateful offering for the honour of GOD, in commemoration of his life having been preserved in that unhealthy climate through the Divine Mercy. A singular appeal is made to heaven upon any sacrilegious attempt to alienate this sacred property.

The Severn is navigable for small barges, up to a place called the Poole Stake, about three quarters of a mile from the town, where it is joined by a rivulet, called Gledding. Hence taking a North easterly direction, and enlarged by the tributary rivers, the Virnwy and the Tanad, it waters the counties of Salop, Worcester, and Gloucester, and empties itself into the Channel below Bristol. But though furnished with this admirable means of conveyance, a new canal is now making; a branch of the Elesmere joining it, at a right angle near Hordly, passes through Llanymynech, Poole, and Berhiw to Newtown. By this a communication will be opened to the collieries and other mines in Denbigh shire; and, by its junction with the Elesmere Trunk, to Chester and Liverpool.

The work was now at a stand from a supposed scarcity of water, arising evidently from ignorance how to apply what was in the hands of the proprietors, to the best advantage, rather than from a real deficiency. The prejudice of the neighbourhood was strongly against the undertaking, and a powerful opposition of the Land-owners attended every step of the concern. Notwithstanding, perhaps, what we term prejudice, may in the issue prove to be the result of sterling sense and accurate reasoning. The passion for these artificial rivers has of late broken out in paroxysms of epidemic rage; and because one set of aquatic speculators have discovered a new mode to acquire wealth, the whole country must be laid under contributions to support the vanity or rashness of future adventurers.

Much has been advanced on the probable advantages and disadvantages of an extensive inland navigation, and probably the decision of the question must be left to the judgment and experience of future generations.

The partizans of canals have not failed to adopt a mode of reasoning, more specious than solid, by adverting to the advantages of this kind of communication between the extreme parts of the vast and populous Empire of China, and the swampy morasses of Holland, which, without drains, would not only be impassable, but absolutely *uninhabitable*. Neither of which are apposite cases to make deductions from, for this island, the remotest parts of which from the sea are so small a distance, that with the assistance of its navigable rivers, land carriage becomes a small object in the value of its exports or imports.

The very idea of a navigable river, the expences and the profits of which are to be defrayed out of the incumbent trade, pre-supposes much to be brought in, and much to be carried out, and consequently includes not only produce, but population.[3] It might be therefore reasonable ground for hesitation, whether the benefit of a partial

3   This remark has been justified in the canal cut through the heart of Herefordshire from Leominster, forming a junction with the Severn at Stourport, in the county of Worcester, which has not paid the proprietors 1 & ½ per cent.

water carriage, in an inland part of the kingdom, where the produce and the consumption preserve nearly an equal pace with each other, will compensate for the loss of thousands of acres of the most valuable land thus rendered useless for the purposes of agriculture, and the multifarious injury done to the adjacent meadows by the oozing of the water through the banks; not to mention the abundance of depredations to which all kinds of property in the vicinity of a canal is obviously and unavoidably exposed.

To a few individuals, whose extensive manors are covered with timber advantage will accrue, from the easy conveyance it affords for this heavy article to a market, and the increased demand and advance in the price. But an advantage of this kind must be partial in the extent, confined in its continuance, and at the same time operate as a bar to improvement among the less opulent Landholders. One fourth of the money thus expended, laid out upon the roads of a country, would have a far greater tendency to improve the soil, and ameliorate the condition of its inhabitants. Every man possesses some portion of ambition, and not less perhaps is possessed by the class of people denominated Farmers, than any other.

Ambition produces rivalry. Every man is proud of exhibiting a good team or plough on the road; this encourages a good breed of cattle and horses, by which the labours of agriculture are performed; and it requires very little science to know, that to possess the power of performing labour, is proportionate wealth, and by which alone its relative value is diminished or increased. This place acknowledged the same Lord with the adjoining Castle of Powis, (as we learn from Powel, page 300,) when the Prince of Wales came to Chester, 29th of Edward's reign, A. D. 1301, to receive fealty of all the principal Freeholders of Wales; among those who did homage was Gryffydd, Lord of Poole, for the Lordship of Powis.

A pleasant walk of a mile brought us to POWIS CASTLE. This venerable pile is built, in the castellated form, of red sand-stone, upon the ridge of a rock of very small extent. Its plan, a mixture of Castle and Mansion. The entrance is by an ancient gateway, between two massy round towers, into the area. Several other towers are still standing, flanked with semi-circular bastions. The inside exhibits nothing worthy of notice, save a long gallery, 117 feet by 20. It was once much longer, but an apartment has lately been taken from it. The hanging gardens, composed of terrace upon terrace, are ascended by flights of steps cut out of the solid rock; the clipped shrubs, and the remains of water works, discovering the imitations of the wretched taste displayed at St. Germains en Laye, which the late possessors had unfortunately too great an opportunity of copying, are removed.

We discovered on the walls, profiting by the negligence of the owner, the DIANTHUS ARMERIA;

D. DELTOIDES; COTYLEDON LUTEA; and PARIETAR-
IA OFFICIALIS, in great profusion. It would appear
sanguine to acquiesce with Lord Lyttelton, that
3000l. judiciously laid out, would make Powis
Castle the most august place in the kingdom; yet it
must be allowed, that the building is magnificent,
and the situation delightfully grand. The devotee
of nature would not, I am sure, refuse to ride a
hundred miles to obtain a view from the terrace.
The situation is peculiarly commanding. To the
North, rises abruptly from the vale, Moel y Golfa,
Breddyn, and Cefn Castyl, the trifid summits of a
rock more than 1000 feet in height. On the highest peak the loyalty and gratitude of the country
has erected an obelisk, in commemoration of the
important victory obtained by Rodney over the
French fleet in 1781: The advantageous ground
upon which this column stands, renders it a striking object to the traveller for a great extent.

Beneath lie the vales of Montgomery and
Shrewsbury, through which the Severn winds her
placid stream, and, seen in different places inter-
rupted by the meadows, heightens the pleasing
scene. The distant views are peculiarly fine, the
Wrekin, like a sugar loaf, rising solitary in the
Plain of Salop; the extensive chain of the Freidden
Hills; to the North, the summits of Snowdon; and
Westward, the Giant Cader Idris mingling with
the clouds, terminates the prospect.

The park is formed of spacious and verdant
lawns, with swelling hills, well clothed with

wood. The venerable oak, wide-spreading beech, and ornamental chesnut, diversify the views in rich variety, and highly contribute to render Powis Park an enviable place to the lovers of forest scenery.

The first mention of this place is A. D. 1108, when Cadwgan ap Cynvyn, flying from the persecution of his relation, Madwc, came to a place called Trallwng, (now Poole,) and having begun to erect a castle, intended to make it his constant residence. But such was the spirit of revenge and treachery in Madwc, that with a desperate party he lay in ambush for him, and slew him. In 1191, it was besieged, and taken by Hubert, Archbishop of Canterbury. It was then the property of Gwynwynwyn, and stiled his Castle at the Poole. In 1233, Llewellyn ap Jorwerth overthrew this fortress, which now as sumed the name of Castell Coch. Hence the conjecture is probable, that Gryffydd had joined the English, or refused the usual and legitimate submission to Llewellyn, out of courtesy to the English Monarch. This victory, like most others of the same period, was only temporary, as we find Owen, the grandson of Gryffydd, in possession of the place. By the marriage of his daughter, Hawys, it came to John de Charlton, styled Valectus Domini Regis. In his posterity it continued several generations. By the marriage of the eldest daughter of Edward Lord Powis, it was conveyed to Sir John Grey. In this family it remained till the time of Henry

VIII. The title then became extinct. In the reign of Elizabeth, Sir William Herbert, second son of the Earl of Pembroke, obtained it by purchase, and was created Lord Powis.[4]

In 1644, under Piercy Lord Powis, it held out for the King, but was soon obliged to surrender to Sir Thomas Middleton. The place was pillaged, and his Lordship remained a prisoner.

The present owner is George Earl of Powis, in right of his mother, Barbara, daughter and sole heiress of Lord Edward Herbert, brother to the last Marquis of Powis. Though little of its ancient greatness of demesne remain, yet seventeen manors are still dependent upon this Lordship.

This venerable castle is going fast to decay. The buildings are in a state of dilapidation; the garden and grounds are neglected, and the pride and ornament of the park is being removed for the sake of the timber. What the hand of time is doing for the one, the hand of avarice is doing for the other; so that at no very distant period the beauty and magnificence of Powis will be no more, and some poor drivelling boy will have to shew the passing traveller the spot where brave Cadwgan lived, and Bleddyn's royal race.

---

4   *Vide* [William] Dugdale[, *The baronage of England, or, An historical account of the lives and most memorable actions of our English nobility in the Saxons time to the Norman conquest, and from thence, of those who had their rise before the end of King Henry the Third's reign deduced from publick records, antient historians, and other authorities*] Vol. II.

A small distance from Poole is the pleasant valley of Cyveiliog; at the foot ofthe Breddin are the ruins of the Cistertian Monastery, called Strata Marcella, or Ystrad Marchell, founded by Owen Cyveiliog, A. D. 1170. It was richly endowed byGwynwynwyn, in 1201, with the whole pasturage of the district of this name, for the express purpose of inducing the Monks to pray for the repose and safety of that Prince's soul. It acquired some additional grants from Madwc ap Gryffydd, in the reign of Edward III. When the recluse amongst the Welch were removed to English abbies, and replaced by English Monks, this house was placed under the controul, and subject to the visitation of Buildwas Abbey, in Salop. At the dissolution, the revenues, according to Speed, amounted to 731. 7s. 3d.[5] In this neighbourhood the Botanist will find, CRATEGUS ARIA, PTERIS CRISPA, COTYLEDON LUTEA, SEDUM RUPESTRE, PAPAVER CAMBRICUM, CHLORA PERFOLIATA.

It was our intention from this place to visit the vicinity of Montgomery, but being informed that the ride from Llanvair, by a new road, to Newtown, was very much admired, and that we could take Montgomery on our way, we preferred this to taking the direct road. Passing a hilly country, and for Wales in a high degree of cultivation, (the culture of turnips, and sheep-folding being well understood,) we soon arrived at the little town of

---

5   *Vide* [Thomas] Tanner, [*Notitia Monastica* (Oxford: A. and J. Churchill, 1695.]

LETTER I

LLANVAIR, Situated between hills, on the banks of
the wide-flowing Virnwy. This river abounds with
such a quantity and variety of fish, as justly to entitle it to the classical name of Amnis Piscosus.[6]
These finny tribes not only add life to its widely diffused waters, but afford a very profitable
amusement to the inhabitants, who are peculiarly dexterous in the use of the harpoon, or spear.
Under this name there are two instruments, very
different in their structure, but used for the same
purpose. The single and double spear. The first is
a narrow piece of steel, about one foot long, with
a barb at the end, placed in a short handle, with a
small rope at the end to draw it back to the spear-
man. The other consists of a handle, six feet in
length, armed at the lower extremity with three
broad flat pieces of well-tempered steel, parallel
to each other, and united at the handle, similar to the three tined forks used by the London
gardners to get up potatoes, with the addition of
barbs at the end of the tines, exactly like the tri-
dent with which Neptune is fabled to be armed
by the Poets. With these they proceed to the stations. At high water the fish come up towards the
springs: the water suddenly subsiding, they are
left in what are called pools, which are deep excavations, formed by the mountain torrents in the
rocky bed of the river. Here they are entrapped,

6   Salmon, trout, samlet, grayling, minnow, perch, rough or
     pope, carp, tench, shad, roach, dace, gudgeon, bleak, chub,
     loach, bull-head, eel, lamprey, flounder.

and fall an easy prey to their wary pursuers. The spearmen stand upon the broad flat stones by the sides of these pools, and striking at the fish, if large, with the single, and if small, with the double spear, generally brings the prize to shore.

It is highly pleasing to see with what dexterity they perform these piscatory manoeuvres. Sometimes the salmon are pursued in the night by an animated chace, the spearmen being directed to the fish by whisps of lighted straw or torches, which the fish taking for the light of the sun or moon, advance, and fall an easy prey to this ungenerous treachery.

Finding nothing remarkably interesting in the town, I walked alone to the church, which stands at a small distance. On entering the church-yard, I was particularly struck (because it was here I first observed it,) with the remarkable custom that prevails over North Wales of planting the graves of departed friends with various evergreens, and all the choicest gifts of Flora's hand. Box, thrift, and other plants fit for edging, are planted round in the shape of the grave for a border, and every flower that adorns the smart parterre, is placed within, so that the taste of the living may here be known by the manner of embellishing these mansions of the dead. The snowdrop, violet, and primrose, harbingers of spring, denote the infant dust; the rocket, rose, and woodbine, shew maturer years; while tansey, rue, and star-wort, mark declining life. Each has

its little evergreen, fond emblem of that perennial state where change is known no more.[7] Nor
are they, once planted, left to be over-run by the
luxuriancy of less delicate neighbours, but constantly weeded and cherished by the hands of the
nearest friends of the deceased, who appropriate
every Saturday afternoon for this amiable weakness, or rather pious remembrance of departed
worth.[8] It was now Saturday, and several persons
were busily employed in these pleasing offices of
respect and love. I thought it inhuman to disturb
them, and I was just going softly to retread my
steps, and retire from the scene, but perceiving
I was noticed, my curiosity got the better of my
veneration. Seeing a person, whose youth and

---

7   Shakspeare sweetly alludes to this custom in his Cymbeline:

       With fairest flowers, lass,
I'll sweeten thy sad grave; thou shalt not lack
The flower that's like thy face, pale primrose, nor
The azure hare bell, like thy veins. No, nor
The leaf of eglantine, which, not to slander,
Outsweeten'd not thy breath.

8   Still when the hours of solemn rites return,
The village train in sad procession mourn;
Pluck every weed that might the spot disgrace,
And plant the fairest field-flow'rs in their place.
Around no noxious plant or flowret grows,
But the first daffodil, and earliest rose;
The snowdrop spreads its whitest blossom here,
And golden cowslips grace the vernal year:
Here the pale primrose takes a fairer hue,
And every violet boasts a brighter blue.
                    BLEEDING ROCK.

beauty, as well as profound attention, would have attracted the notice of eyes less curious than my own, I approached her with respect; I ventured to ask her the nature and meaning of the custom, but she eluded my inquiries, and went on removing the obtrusive weeds. Finding, however, that I was importunate, she turned her head, and shewed a beautiful countenance, still more interesting from grief; the tears trickled down her cheeks, and with a voice that rebuked my intrusion, she said, "I come, Sir, here every Saturday to pluck these weeds, and to weep over my dear brother—I had but one—he was a brother —but he was too good to remain here—I would I had gone in his stead!!" After an interval of silence, that it would have been long before I could have broken, she added, "I don't know whether I am wrong, Sir, but I frequently pray that my dear brother may flourish in paradise as this rose on his grave: I have been told, that I ought not to pray for the dead,[9] but I find my heart better after it, and I feel a stronger desire to be holy, that I may be the sooner fit to go to him."

My sympathy I found was strongly affected, and the piety of the sentiment disarmed me of all power to demonstrate the fallacy of the doctrine.

---

9   Whatever may have been said by able writers upon this subject, yet it requires no subtlety of reasoning to prove it an erroneous doctrine. A strict adherence to the plain representation of scripture will furnish the unlettered Christian with an invincible and decisive argument against it. Rev. chap. xxii. v. 10, 11.

A little further appeared one that had been recently dressed, and the friend lately gone. There was a peculiar degree of neatness about this grave; within the outer inclosure was an inner one, the size of a young child's; on inquiry, I found that a female was interred here, who, in the act of giving life, had lost her own. She had died in child-bed, and her offspring living but a few hours after the mother, was placed in the same coffin, and buried in the same grave. Here, in a representation of aromatic flowers, the infant was lying on her breast. The husband, still a widower, had just been to perform this sadly pleasing task, returning home doubtless satisfied that he had done all for the friend of his bosom that distance and separation allowed him to do; and evincing to the surviving friends, that the virtues of her who had left them were still dear in his remembrance, and that they still lived in his affections.

To live in the remembrance of those we love, is an instinct connate with our very Being; and this posthumous attention to our departed friends, while it cherishes that principle which is the soul of society, and the sweetner of life, impresses upon our recollection the virtues which through life we had forgotten to appreciate, urges them strongly to our imitation, and calls our attention to that Great Day of Inquisition which they have already seen, and we shall soon be summoned to behold! The gay and dissipated may cast a sneer, and the philosophically morose may heave a sigh over the prevalence of this antiquated, and as they may term it, superstitious custom; but to me, who scorn all participation with these characters, it appeared in a sacred point of view, and the tear of sympathy has often stolen down my cheek while I beheld it. On the whole, I cannot but be strongly inclined to think, that whatever tends to cherish the remembrance of departed virtue, and to solicit our attention to a future world, must be consistent with the highest reason, and ultimately productive of essential good. With such sentiments so congenial to your own, and in the sincerity of friendship,

I remain yours, &c.

Letter II

Dear Sir

In the morning of life the mind is elated with hope, because yet unacquainted with its delusions; and is sanguine in its views, because it has not experienced the bitterness of disappointment. The body, unwearied with reiterated fatigue, attends a willing and agile associate in the pursuit of happiness every object around wears a correspondent tint of gaiety; and the distant prospects in the horizon of life fill the imagination with fascinating dreams of ideal and inexpressible pleasures.

We left Llanfair just as the beauteous orb of day was darting his golden beams from behind a lofty mountain on our left: while the grey mists of morn were fast retiring towards the ocean. His brilliant rays threw a lustre over the umbrageous woods, and the dew drops, like sparkling gems, stood tiptoc on the waving foliage. The feathered tribes were chanting their matin song of gratitude; and the hills in distant whispers echoed these warbling notes of praise. Every thing conspired to excite the most pleasing sensations, to stimulate exertion, and inspire hope.

Hitherto we had experienced little difficulty, and our labour had been amply rewarded by the pleasure we had received. Highly gratified with the past, we were disposed to look favourably to the future; and, in defiance of the many obstacles thrown in our way, to take within this excursion *the source of the Severn*. Our road lay through a country consisting of vales and moderately rising hills; their bases skirted with woods, their sides cultivated far up, and their tops adorned with numerous flocks. The intermediate risings were now covered with the golden grain, and the meadows rich in luxuriant pasturage:[1] the country well wooded, and the different streamlets meandering in gentle murmurs by to join their waters with the Severn, gave life to the pleasing scenery.

---

1   By the road side we found the ORNITHOGALUM LUTEUM and CARDUUS ERIOPHORUS.

In passing the Castle of Caereinéon, a Roman Fortress, few remains of which are left, and of those it may be said, "*Etiam periere ruina*,"[2] we came to the small village of BERHIW: where the handsome little church and parsonage, the neat appearance of the whited cottages, and highly cultivated farms, gave us an idea of content and plenty; and brought to our recollection Goldsmith's description of Auburn in its prosperous state, with which he commences his elegant Poem *The Deserted Village*:

> Sweet Auburn! loveliest village of the plain,
> Where health and plenty chear'd the labouring swain;
> Where smiling spring its earliest visits paid,
> And parting summer's ling'ring blooms delay'd.
> Dear lovely bowers of innocence and ease,
> Seats of my youth, when every sport cou'd please,
> How often have I loiter'd o'er thy green,
> Where humble happiness endear'd each scene!
> How often have I paus'd on every charm,
> The shelter'd cot, the cultivated farm,
> The never-failing brook, the busy mill,
> The decent church, that topt the neighbouring hill,
> The hawthorn bush, with seats beneath its shade,
> For talking age, and whispering lovers made!

A venerable mansion rose to view at the end of an avenue of aged trees, the seat of the late Arthur Blaney, Esq. a descendent from Brochwel Ys Chythrog. An elder branch of the family was ennobled in Ireland, in the year 1620, by the title of

---

2   Latin: 'Even the ruins have perished.' —Ed.

Lord Blaney, of Monoghan. On inquiring into the character of this gentleman, we soon discovered the great cause of all the neatness and chearfulness we admired. He had lived near three generations on his own estate, amidst the smiles of an indulged and happy tenantry, in the old British style of dignified hospitality. Though possessed of an immense landed property, Mr. Blaney was virtually his own steward. No tenant of his was ever ruined or oppressed by the petty tyranny of an agent. He who received the rents, and he who paid them, were confronted together at the table of this truly great man. He entered with paternal attention into all their little concerns, redressed their grievances, and supplied their wants. He knew their profits and their losses; the one received a smile of approbation, the other he commiserated and relieved. Virtuous industry, if unfortunate, always found in him a sympathizing friend: it gave him pleasure to see a family rising into a state of comfort and consequence from the produce of that soil, which, exclusive of this just reward of labour, yielded him so affluent a portion. A respectable yeomanry and happy peasantry, he used to observe, were the pride and support of a country. As the language of Timoleon was his, the wish of Timoleon should have been his motto, "*Maluit se diligi quam metui.*"[3] Cor. Nep.

This was the character of the proprietor of Berhiw Park in one relative duty; and in every other

3   Latin: 'He preferred to be loved rather than feared.' —Ed.

he acted consistent with himself. He is gone! and fearful lest they should never see his like again, the land laments and mourns. Happy would it be for the welfare of kingdoms, if those in power did but practically adhere to the solid maxims of this able politician.[4] Luxury may administer food to vanity, and wealth may add insolence to pride; but it must be by a proper balance of importance amidst the different relations of society, that the safety of a State can be secured; and on the strength of the component parts, its welfare and stability must depend. When a due equilibrium is preserved of stimulus and sensorial power in our corporeal system, the body remains in a state of health; but the least departure from this, is approximation to disease: only destroy this equilibrium, let the vital fluids flow unequally, the body becomes weak, the solids debilitated, the functions of life gradually cease, and a continuance of the same fatal causes produces dissolution and death. A wretched peasantry is the body politic, paralysed at the extremities; and an oppressed and over-burthened yeomanry, the solids of the country in a state of gangrene.

Crossing the Severn over a wooden bridge we arrived at MONTGOMERY. Having ideally supposed that the County Town must be superior to

---

4   Hanc enim speciem libertatis esse, si omnibus, quod quis-quevellet, legibus experiri liceret. [Latin: 'For this would be a species of liberty, if all were allowed to try what they wanted by the laws.' —Ed.]

all others in point of beauty and extent, we were disappointed to find it a small place, consisting of about a hundred half-timbered houses forming a miserable street. It is situated on the declivity of a hill, and under the shadow of another: and, not excepting St. Asaph, is the smallest town in the kingdom. In the upper part of it stands the Guildhall, a handsome stone building, where the Sessions are held, in rotation with Poole and the other session towns in the justiciary of Chester. At the bottom stood a large mansion, called *Black-hall*, the seat of the Herberts, long since destroyed by fire: and a deep foss now marks the scite where once it stood. This town was built by Baldwin, Lieutenant of the Welch Marches, in the time of William the Conqueror, and called by the Welch Tre'Faldwyn, *i. e.* Baldwyn's Town. It took the name of *Montgomery* from Roger de Montgomery, Earl of Shrewsbury, who conquered it, whose inheritance it afterwards was, and by whom, according to Doomsday, the castle was built. It was made a free borough by charter from King Edward III. who also conferred upon it, among other privileges, that of sending one member to Parliament. But the privilege was not claimed till long after the grant; as the first Burgess summoned by the King's Writ was William Herbert, A. D. 1542. It is governed by a Bailiff and twelve capital Burgesses, in whom the right of electing the representative is vested. During the long contests between the Welch and English, this place was considered a most important station; was defended by a castle, walls with watch towers, and had four gates. It carries on a small trade in tanning, but is now so inconsiderable, as to put on the appearance of a deserted village.

Mr. Pennant was disposed to be facetious when he made the following observations:—

> Whether in old times this place abounded more than is usual with ladies of free lives and conversation, I do not pretend to say; but early the free Burgesses had the privilege of the Goging-stool, Cucking-stool, or Coke-stool, or what the Saxons call the Scealfing-stole. *Quia, says my authority, per objurgatrices et mere trices multa mala in villa oriuntur;*[5] and these were to have the judgment 'de la goging stoole:' and therein to be placed with naked feet and dishevelled hair, as an example to all beholders. Probably this was not found to answer the end intended, therefore immersion or ducking was in after-times added, as an improvement to effect a radical cure.[6]

Vid. Snowdonia, p. 370. Had the learned Antiquary told us what kind of instrument this was, the origin of the punishment, and the ceremony that took place on the occasion, we should have

---

5   Latin: 'Because, says my authority, many evils arise in the country through slanderers and mere trifles.' —Ed.

6   The custom, still in use in Scotland, of placing fornicators of both sexes upon what they call a repenting stool, in the church, and in full view of the congregation, was probably derived from this. Vid, Guthrie, Geog. p. 163.

been informed as well as entertained; but here he is silent: and why he should make this observation at Montgomery, in preference to any other part of the principality, it is difficult to conjecture; for this, so far from being a local, is not a provincial mode of correction: the custom was general to the whole island, and still remains as part of the Common Law of the Realm.

Blackstone observes in his *Commentaries*, B. iv. C. 13,

> A common scold, *communis rixatrix*, for our Common Law confines it to the feminine gender, is a public nuisance to her neighbourhood: for which offence she may be indicted, and if convicted, shall be sentenced to be placed in a certain engine of correction, called the tre-bucket, castigatory, or cucking stool;[7] though now it is frequently interpreted ducking stool, because the residue of the judgment is, that when she is to be placed therein, she shall be plunged into the water for her punishment.

---

7   It is called in Welch *Ystal Droch*, literally a stool of manifestation or exposition. Coke interprets cuck, or guck, a scold or brawl, taken from the word cuckow, or guckow, and ing in the Saxon language means water, because a scolding woman was, for her punishment, soused in the water. 3 Instit. 219. With all due deference to this high authority, such definitions corroborate the cynical remark upon etymology, that it is *eruditio ad libitum*. In the Teutonic language, to which the Saxon bears a very near affinity, gauch signifies *a fool*. The word gawky, evidently derived from this, used in many parts of the kingdom, means the same; gake is a cuckow, and figuratively a person despised: goking stool therefore must mean a stool of contempt and derision.

A commentator justly remarks,

> that it does not savour much of gallantry in
> our ancestors, that they supposed none but
> women could be guilty of this offence, as they
> did; for the technical words denoting the
> same, whilst the proceedings were in latin,
> were all of the feminine gender, as *rixatrix,
> calumniatrix, communis pugnatrix, commu-
> nis pacis perturbatrix*.[8]

The Castle of Montgomery, as before stated, was supposed to have been erected by the Earl of Shrewsbury; but it is more probable, that it was built by the founder Baldwyn; for in the year 1092, there is an account of Roger de Montgomery forcibly entering Powis land and taking Tre'Faldwyn, with its Castle. In two years after, 1094, the Welch, carrying devastation through this part of the country, took the Castle by storm, and put the garrison to the sword, while Rufus, and his discomfited army, were obliged to retreat precipitately into England. (*Vid. Bromton's Chron.*) The Earl of Shrewsbury rebuilt it, and the Welch soon after a second time destroyed it. From this period it probably remained long in a dismantled state; for history is silent till it mentions a *new* Castle, 1221, in the time of Henry III. By this Monarch it was granted to Hubert de Burgh with a considerable appointment. Under

---

8   Latin: 'a brawler, a slanderer, a common fighter, a disturber of the common peace.' —Ed.

Hubert it was besieged by the Welch, but opportunely relieved by the King.

It was for a long period the scene of much discomfiture and chagrin to the English, owing to the close and extensive forests in its vicinity; where the Welch, lying in ambush, were enabled by marauding parties to annoy the English, by cutting off the supplies for the garrison.

From this time, till it came to Roger Mortimer, 1354, it underwent a variety of changes. It was then included in the Hundred of Cherbury, and from that family it came to the Herberts. In the civil wars it was held for the King, but after a very feeble resistance, it submitted to the Parliament forces under Sir Thomas Middleton. On the appearance of the Royal Army under Lord Byron, Sir Thomas fled to Oswestry, leaving the garrison in a weak and unprovided condition. But before a regular siege could be commenced, Sir Thomas, being greatly reinforced, raised the siege, and the King's Army was obliged to retreat with terrible slaughter. It was soon after dismantled by order of the Parliament, and reduced to the melancholy heap of ruins, which now seem to mock the craggy steep on which it stands.

Near Montgomery is the famous mountain of Mynydd, or Cefn Digoll; celebrated for having been the spot where the liberty of the Welch gave its expiring groan. Here was fought the last contested battle between the hirelings of Oppression and the surviving Heroes of the fallen Principality.

Immediately on the death of Llewellin, Mad-owe, cousin to that Prince, assembled an army of the most determined partizans of independence, and having surrounded Edward in the Forest of Snowden, near Caernarvon, obliged the King to make an ignoble retreat; but, after defeating the King's Generals at Denbigh and Knockin, was himself here completely defeated, great part of his followers slain, and the rest put to flight, or taken prisoners. (*Vid. Warrington.*) It was again sacked and pillaged by Glyndwr, 1401, at the time he ravaged the borders of Poole, and destroyed the Abbey of Comhir. *Leland*, Vol. 5. p. 4.

Our next object was Tre'Newydd, or NEW-TOWN, pleasantly situated on the banks of the Severn, by which it is nearly surrounded. The houses being principally half-timbered, *i . e.* timber frames, with the intermediate spaces filled up with whattle and dab, or lathe and plaister, gives it an appearance of meanness, otherwise it is a neat, clean town.[9] It contains several streets, and is in a flourishing condition. An extensive manufactory of flannel is carried on in the town, and in the parts adjacent. This article is got up in a masterly manner, and employs the numerous poor of the town and neighbourhood.

Welch flannels have long preserved the ascendancy in the markets over those got up in other places, and probably will long continue

---

9   Newton, five miles from Montgomerike, is meatly well builded after the Walche fascion, Lel.

to do so. Two reasons may be adduced for this pre-eminence; 1st, the mountain sheep produce wool of a very fine, though short staple, peculiarly adapted for this useful article of female dress; and the proximity of New town to the hill country of Montgomery, Radnor, and Merionedd, gives an advantage to the manu facturer over his rivals in the market: 2d, the mode of bleaching occasions a still greater difference in the article, both in respect to softness and delicacy. These are all bleached by the atmospheric acid; being exposed, after immersion in an alkaline ley, upon bleaching grounds till thoroughly whitened; while those of Yorkshire, and other parts of England, are placed in close stoves, and subjected to the action of sulphuric acid, arising from the fumes of burning sulphur. After a little gentle friction between the fingers, the difference may easily be ascertained. All the flannels manufactured there are the effect of manual labour: machinery has not yet found its way into North Wales. The adoption of them by Messrs. Cooke and Mason into their large manufactory near Shrewsbury, will probably facilitate their introduction. There is certainly great room for improvement in several departments of this trade. Till very lately, the act of wool-stapling, or sorting, was unknown, or at least not practised. The fleece, at most, was broken into two parts, the neck wool and the rump. They are, however, in an improving state; and have learnt, that, notwithstanding a little additional expence in labour, it is great œconomy to attend to the staple of the commodity; and six or seven sorts are now frequently distinguished. This has effected a material change in the trade; instead of having but one strong useful sort, that used to sell from 8*d*. to 11*d*. per yard, they furnish flannels from 11*d*. to 4*s*. per yard. It has been observed, that in proportion as distinctions in the quality have increased, coarse goods have advanced in price, none being purchased under 11*d*. and 12*d*. per yard. This, perhaps, may be attributed to a more powerful cause; formerly, every manufacturer used to bring his own goods to market, but now a set of factors, or *middle-men*, as they are termed, go over the country, buy up all they can find, and attend at Poole, and even Shrewsbury market.

Their number increases, and consequently with it the price of flannels. This is considered as a ready-money article; the purchase money is deposited at the time of buying, and the carriage paid by the purchaser.

The exportation of flannels to America and the West-Indies, by the Merchants of London and Liverpool, is much more considerable than the home consumption. What is the quantity made in this district, it would be difficult to ascertain. Mr. Pennant says, there are brought annually to Welch Poole, between 700 and 800,000 yards of flannel; but he does not state the particulars upon which he formed his estimate. The number of people employed may be about 3000, 500 of which are weavers: allowing that every man weaves 30 yards per week, the aggregate quantity will be about 750,000 yards.

Adjoining the town is Newton Hall, an ancient family seat of the Prices. Hearing that the famous Roman Station of *Caer Sws* was at no great distance, we hastened towards it. The road crossing the old Roman way, from Chester to South Wales, called Sarn Swsan, soon brought us to Caer Sws, a place that lost, with its conquerors, its magnificence and importance. This now small hamlet, on the banks of the Severn, consisting of a few houses, was once of consequence, as the remains in the vicinity shew. The adjacent fields, by the inclosures intersecting each other at right angles, are said to represent the numerous streets it oncè consisted of; and the hollows, from their regularity, as evidently discover its ancient fosses, and shew that the fortifications were of considerable extent. On the North side are the remains of a rampart, called Gwyn Vynidd: Eastward, Rhos Ddiarberd, in the parish of Llanddinam, where, beside entrenchments, there is a large barrow; and at a place called Cefn Carnedd, on the West side, are similar remains. Above Llanddinam Church, on the top of the hill, is a remarkable Fortress, called Y Gaer Vychan, or the little Fortress, marked by several fosses, and, probably from the shape, a British Post. The Church of Llanddinam stands pleasantly on the abrupt rising, that juts out like a promontory into the vale.

Intending to follow the course of the river to its source, we took the lower way, by which we avoided the arduous and difficult passes of the Carno Mountains, and could proceed without the disagreeable appendage to the sentimental traveller, a guide. This tract of country is enriched by nature and population; it unites in a happy assemblage objects which please by their tranquil beauty, and those which surprise by their stupendous grandeur; woods, orchards, verdant pastures, and well-cultivated fields, are intermingled in rich profusion; neat farms; gentlemen's seats, and wooden bridges, of rustic workmanship, thrown in several places across the river, heighten the colouring of the landscape.

The road is highly picturesque; for the vale begins to contract, inclosed by steep lofty hills, whose bases in many places are fringed with close hanging woods. Among the most considerable are those of Berthlwyd, beneath which are the remains of an old mansion, belonging to the ancient family of the Llwyds. On the North side of these woods is a small lake, called Llyn y Afange, or *the Lake of Beavers*. From several places in Wales taking their name from this animal, there can be little doubt of its having been once an inhabitant of this country. That there are none found at present, cannot be an objection; since there is the greatest proof of the *Wolf* and the *Roebuck* having been very numerous, (*Vid. Rowl,*) and these have in the same manner given names to several places. The edict of Edgar[10] accounts for the extripation of the one, and the defalcation of the woods for the disappearance of the other.

An objection has been raised from the etymology of the word Afange, being an abbreviation of *Avonog, fluviatilis,* as *Llwynog,* a Fox, from *Llwyn, Sylvaticus,* and therefore might mean an *otter,* or any aquatic animal; but from the description given of it by the old poets, that it was an amphibious animal, having the fore feet like a dog, those behind like a goose, of a dark grey colour, with an oblong cartilaginous tail, with which in swimming it used to steer its course, there can be no doubt as to the identity of the animal. Gyraldus says, they abounded in his time; and in his *Iter* makes many remarks upon their superior instinct and subtlety.

The veracity of Gyraldus has been frequently questioned, yet if we consider that he wrote in an

---

10   The Princes of North Wales having, for a length of time, neglected to pay the tribute exacted by the King of London, Edgar appeared with an army to enforce it. By a measure, as wise as it was humane, he changed the pecuniary tribute into a requisition of 300 wolves annually; creatures that were very destructive both to the Welch and English on the borders. In the third year, it is said, there were none to be found; and the Princes of North Wales became exempt from acknowledgement to the King of England. Edgar seems in this instance to have been actuated by the same motives as Solon, who enacted, that whoever brought a he wolf was to receive five drachms, (the price of an ox;) and for a she wolf one, the price of a sheep. *Vid. Plutarch.*

age when nothing would please, that was not calculated to excite admiration (far less minuteness of observation, and accuracy of description,) allowances must be made; yet he will not shrink in comparison with his cotemporaries. If we allow some what for prejudice, and somewhat for the changes that must in several centuries have taken place, the Monk is far from being a despicable or unpleasant companion through the Principality, to this day. His account, in this instance, is unquestionably confirmed. The beaver was called Llost-lydan, or the broad-tailed animal, and the skin was esteemed a luxury, and formed the chief finery of dress in the time of the great Cambrian Legislator, Howel Dda; it was valued at 120 pence, while that of a martin was 24; an ermine, otter, wolf, or fox, was only 12 pence. *Vid. Leges Wall.* 260, 261.

Adjoining Berthlwyd is LLANIDLOS, a poor inconsiderable town, taking its name from the Saint (St. Idlos) to which its small neat church is dedicated. The roof is supported by six arches, the columns of which are surrounded with neat round pillars, enriched with capitals of palm leaves. The date in the roof, 1542, favours the account given by the people, that they were brought from Cwm Hir, in Radnorshire, at the dissolution of that monastry. This, though small, is the only town of consequence in this district; and from the regularity which appears in its plan, the streets crossing each other at right angles, with a good market-house in the centre, seems of Roman origin. It has a very old wooden bridge over the Severn, at present in a very decayed state,[11] and which is only used in times of flood; at others the river is fordable. It has a large market for woollen yarn, which is got up by spinsters in the country, and part unmanufactured is sent every fortnight to Poole.

At Glyn Avren the vale contracts so much, as to confine the waters within a very narrow bed; and the noble river, on whose bosom ride the wealthy fleets from the Western World, here dwindles into an inconsiderable stream. Salmon are known to force their way up to this remote spot for the purpose of depositing their spawn, and several sorts of fish, such as samlet, trout, pike, and grayling, are at times caught here. (*Vid. Pennant.*) Wearied with following the meanderings of the river, and meeting with few plants that are not found upon the banks of most streams, our anxiety increased to discover the appearance at the source, judging, from the ground we had already trod, we could not be far distant. Every human being we met was accosted with a volley of questions upon the distance from it, and the nature of the road; the result was, that we had yet twelve miles to pass, before we could obtain the object of this excursion. Our authority was of that dubious nature, as to render it impossible to

---

11   It was replaced in 1826, and the replacement widened in 1938. —Ed.

guess how many statute miles were included in
the number.

We had experienced so many disappoint-
ments from the variety of erroneous statements
and contradictory reports, respecting the distances of places, that we were little inclined to
place any degree of confidence in our informers.
However, when ignorant of the extent of country,
and the object of pursuit, it is natural to solicit
information; and though that information may
be far from accurate, yet coming from persons
supposed to know, we esteem it better than none.
The positive declarations of locality tend to cheer
the imagination under dreary prospects, and in-
cline the judgment to confide in the representa-
tions of hope. The vale was now shut in by lofty
mountains to the right and left, through the ap-
ertures of which several streams rolled down the
cwms to bring their tributary waters to the Severn. We pressed forward sometimes along the
trackless vale, sometimes ascending the steep
acclivities of the mountain barrier, to obtain a
sight of the surround ing country;[12] passing here
and there a miserable farm and cottage, destitute
of inhabitants. This is literally a land of sheep
walks, and of shepherds, though not of Arcadian
scenes. The numerous flocks are heard to bleat at
close of day, but no swains are heard to tune their
"Oaten reeds." The flocks, like those of Estram-

---

12   The extent between the Severn and the Wye is not two miles
      here.

adura, and other mountainous parts of Spain, are driven from distant places to these exposed pastures to feed the Summer herbage. The farms and cottages we had seen in the vale, are only Winter habitations, covered with the ancient British roofing Peithwydden, or Shingles, *i. e.* oak cut into lengths and split. The hills abound with slate of a coarse brownish kind, proper for this purpose; but to discover this, requires some portion of the art of mineralogy, and to bring it into use, past experience of its utility, or a disposition for new experiment.

Continuing our journey, with the Biga Mountains on our right, and those that separate the Vale of the Wye from the Vale of the Severn on our left, we met with little worthy of observation, save the Jassione Montana, and a few plants, the common inhabitants of boggy soils. Suddenly the Ardua Moles of Plynlimmon rose in sullen grandeur before us; the vale opening to the North and South discovered the mountain, appearing with less abruptness and elevation than we had been taught to expect. Its sides, as well as the adjacent hills, were totally destitute of wood, and naked hills furnish the chearless idea of solitary gloom. Nothing appeared interesting, but the consideration, that this, otherwise, dreary spot gives birth to four considerable rivers; two of which stand unrivalled in point of picturesque beauty, and the third, after Father Thames, in commercial importance: the Llyffnant, Rheidiol, Wye and Severn.

The Rheidiol flows from the Llyn Llygad Rheidiol, and taking a South-westerly course falls into
the sea at Aberystwith. On the South eastern side
issues from two large fountains the Wye, called
Wye, or the River, by way of eminence; which
taking a South-easterly direction, after watering
the counties of Radnor, Brecon, and Monmouth,
flows into the Severn below Chepstow this is instantly, so impatient of controul, as to rush with
great precipitation, and roll its impetuous torrents over a ledge of rocks, so as to form a bold
though barren cascade. The springs on the North
side unite in a considerable lake, called Glas Llyn,
whence flows the mountain river Llyffnant, which
joins the Dovey near Machynlleth. The ascent was
not difficult from the steepness, but troublesome
from the frequent bogs, that oblige the traveller
to change his course. Near the summit on the
North-eastern side, from a small pond, rises the
Severn; which running North-east to Shrewsbury,
turns suddenly to the South, and watering the
counties of Salop, Worcester, and Gloucester, an
extent of two hundred miles, empties itself into
the sea below Bristol.

You will, perhaps, expect some account of the
origin of its name; but consider how hazardous
even to conjecture, when the most able antiquaries have racked their brains in vain, and candidly
owned themselves at the most perfect loss respecting its derivation. *Vid. Camden, Lloyd, and
Pennant.*

Geoffry, of Monmouth, attributes it to Sabrina, the reputed daughter of Locrine, King of Britain, by Estrildis, one of the three captive virgins of match less charms, which he took from Humber, King of the Huns. Locrine had divorced his former Queen, Geondolen, in favour of Estrildis. On the death of Locrine, the slighted Queen assumed the government, pursued Estrildis and her daughter with unrelenting cruelty, and caused them to be drowned in this river; which, with a slight alteration, assumed the name of the innocent victim of female revenge:

———————In flumen præcipitur Abren
Nomen Abren fluvio de virgine nomen, eidem
Nomine corrupto, deinde Sabrina datur.

Milton alludes to the Story in describing it—

The Severn swift, guilty of Maiden's death: And the beautiful use he has made of the Story in his Masque of Comus, is familiar to most readers.

Camden ridicules the account of Geoffry, as a legendary tale; and frankly acknowledges, he could never learn whence the name was derived. That it had this name at a very early period is evident; Tacitus mentions it as well known in his time. Describing in his Annals the affairs of declining Rome in Britain, under the Proprætor, P. Ostorius, he observes, "*Ille gnarus, primis eventibus, metum aut fiduciam gigni, citas cohortes rapit; et cæsis qui restiterunt, disjectos consectatus, ne rursus*

*congloba rentur infensaque et infida pax non
duci, non militi, requiempermitteret: detra-
here arma suspectis, cinctosque castris An-
tonam[13] et Sabrinam fluvios cohibere parat.*

Lib. xii. e. 31.

Its English name is buried in equal obscurity.
It is by the inhabitants of the country named *Hafren* or *Havren*; and a small hamlet we passed,
is called Glyn Hafren, to distinguish it from another Glyn, three miles to the Northward. At
Llanidlos it is joined by a small river formed of
three mountain streams, and which, we were
informed, bears the name of Si or Se, so called
from the hissing sound of its waters. Here a double junction is formed of the names, as well as
the waters, of these cogenitors of the Severn. The
alteration is easy from Sehavren, or as we have it
in old maps Seavren, to Severn.[14]

The height of this mountain is not great, in
the scale of comparison with its neighbour Cader
Idris, yet the view from its summit is extensive-

---

13 Camden supposes the upper Wiltshire Avon, that joins the
Severn below Bristol to be the Antona of Tacitus; while Pol.
Virgil, with more reason, supposes it to be Wye. There is
room for conjecture, and I leave the point to the Society of
Antiquaries for settlement.

14 Here I cannot help paying a just tribute due to the merit of
Mr. Evans, of ———, for his great undertaking so justly executed, of furnishing the public with an excellent map of this,
before, badly surveyed country. In the course of this journey
I have had frequent opportunities of proving its faithfulness,
and admiring its accuracy.

ly grand; though part of it lies over the trackless sheep-downs of Montgomery, and the barren turbaries of Cardigan. On the North the Cader Chain appears enveloped with mists, stretching out towards the sea; on the East the Breidden and the Mountains of Radnor; on the West the romantic vale of the Rheidiol, the Estuary of the Dovey, and the beautiful Bay of Cardigan, diversified by a few sails of vessels at Aberystwith and Aberdovey; with the grand expanse of the ocean, uniting with the horizon in the distant prospect. This mountain is not only famous for being the father of rivers, but also as an important station held by the great Glyndwr in the first year of his insurrection. Unable to oppose the formidable force sent against him, he advantageously placed himself upon Plynlimmon, with a few chosen followers: a place admirably adapted for receiving succours from the North and South. And hence it was he so harassed the country, sacked Montgomery, burnt Poole, and destroyed the Abbey of Cwm Hir, in Radnorshire.

The land here is wholly maiden turf. The hand of cultivation has never yet approached the vicinity. The hilly pastures are covered with a mixture of stock; sheep, goats, black cattle, and numerous herds of diminutive horses.

Gyraldus informs us, that this country was famous in his day for the shape and stateliness of its horses, and the incomparable swiftness with which nature had indued them. Their appearance now, we must confess, was not flattering to the vanity of the country. It not unfrequently happens, that traditional fame, and the cause which gave rise to it, are like diverging rays, that become more distant according to the space they pass through; and that the name of excellence remains, when the superiority is no more. Mr. Pennant could not have read Gyraldus, when he supposed that this superiority arose from Queen Elizabeth's stud, kept at Carno; a set of Spanish horses made a present of to her Majesty by the Earl of Shrewsbury; by which the native breed was greatly improved. The learned author certainly borders upon the doctrine of equality, when he surmises such a familiarity to have subsisted between the royal manege and the merlins[15] of the mountains. Inclosed amongst these rude and barren scenes, and shut out from society, I began

---

15 These wild horses, for in no other light can they be considered, range at large over the uninclosed mountain pastures, where they promiscuously breed without the licence or knowledge of their owners. To ascertain whose property the successive generations are would be *opus et labor* indeed. To determine this, recourse is had to the only expedient practicable in the case. A day is appointed annually for driving up all they suppose belonging to each respective farmer; these they secure in an inclosure near the house, and the poor animals undergo the operation of the flesh mark; the initials of the possessors being burnt with a hot iron in the hide of the beasts. This is considered as a mark of unalienable appropriation, and a visible confirmation of a right that was of a very dubious nature, if it ever had an existence before. A Welch poney is seldom seen *that does not bear this stamp of property.*

to feel, that however the inquiring mind may be led to in vestigate nature, and feel a high degree of pleasure in discovering what was not known, or elucidating what was but badly described before; yet it is in the exercise of our social faculties we experience the most solid pleasure, and in the liberal communications of a mixed and polished society we are to expect the privileges of humanity. The stimulus of new scenes may rouze, and enlarged opportunities of inquiry may satisfy the mind, for a time; but it is by the reciprocity of collateral communication, and the mutual cordialities of friendship, that intelligent beings must look for the ingredients of happiness.

I remain yours, &c.

J. E.

Letter III

Dinas y Mowddwy

Dear Sir,

To a heart of disinterestedness and generosity, like yours, every narration that tends to correct the malicious or the erroneous statements of others, must be acceptable, as an offering at the shrine of verity. It is with reluctance, I assure you, that I shall have to appeal to that disinterestedness and generosity, more than once, in the course of my route, which falls within the compass of this Letter.

Retreading our steps to Newton, we took the old road to Llanvair, over the mountains, that we might be able to see the ruins of Dolferwyn, or the meadow of the Maiden Castle;[1] which stands on the summit of a cone-shaped hill of steep ascent, surrounded by a wooded dingle, whence rises a small stream that soon joins the Severn. It is built of the small shivered stone of the country, like Dinas plan. On the accessible sides of the hill deep trenches are cut through the solid rock. Evans in his *Diss. de Bardis* says, it was erected by Bleddyn ap Cynvyn, between the years 1065 and 1073: But Dugdale, on what authority I know not, dates it much lower down. In his *Mon.* II. 223, he says it was built by Dafydd ap Llewellyn, about the year 1242 and in his *Baron.* I. 142, that Roger Mortimer obtained a grant from Edward I. (A. D. 1278) to hold this castle with those of Sheri and Sheddwen for himself and heirs by the service of three Knights' fees.

At no great distance is the church of Bettws, dedicated to St. Beuno, and remarkable for a high steeple for these parts; built, as an inscription says, 1531, by its Vicar, John Meredyth, under the curious Latin title, of *Campanile*, for *Templi pyramis*. It formerly belonged to the Cistertian Nunnery of Llanlugan.

Passing a toilsome mountainous tract, we got into the road at Llanfair. We were now to bid adieu to our kind and obliging friends, from whose knowledge of the country we had obtained

---

1   Mr. Pennant supposes the name to allude to the story of Sabrina.

information that furnished a clue to our further inquiries; and from whose congeniality of mind we had experienced those exalted pleasures, known to those alone, who have tasted the delicacies of a refined friendship. We had fixed to leave Llanfair early the next morning. The evening was spent in expressing what we had felt since our first meeting, and forming schemes of seeing each other again: lamenting that the calls of duty should enforce so unwelcome a separation. The thought, that in a few hours more, we were to leave the hospitable and happy roof we had lately entered, hindered our sleeping too long, and at the dawn of day we rose. But our worthy friends had prevented us; and the servants were ready with an elegant breakfast. They were determined to give us the last greeting. No person can dislike the ceremony of a formal parting more than myself, yet, after all, there was something pleasing in an interview of a few moments with those we had so reluctantly bade adieu to the preceding evening.

The horses were waiting at the gate, impatient to be gone; and the grand luminary of heaven was just beginning to spread his spangled mantle on the mountains' top. The parting scene gave a sombre cast to the whole company, and rendered us to tally inattentive to the beauties of the surrounding country.

For miles I was wrapt in the most profound meditation.

"Alas!" said I, "how short is life; and yet how important the business of it! These people we have loved they were kindred souls—we would have pass'd the span of human life together: yet we have been obliged to part—and probably never—no never, to meet again! And this in the same little island, where from the distance a day or two would bring us together; yet perhaps their avocations will not be collocal nor commensurate with ours: Matrimonial alliances and the incumbent duties; a family and its relative interests; want of the means to defray the expences of travelling, even when inclination urges; loss of friends; of health; and a thousand things, that do not immediately occur, may preclude all opportunity of seeing each other more! Yet," said I, recollecting myself, "it is but a common emblem of that parting, which, barring all these preventive circumstances, even did we reside together, must ere long take place. Death levels his individual shafts, and life itself is but one continued state of *successive separations*. The present scene of things is so fleeting in its nature, that we have only just time to take a cursory view, and then rapidly pass from this theatre of existence. How strongly should this impress the mind with the vanity of fixing our affections on such transitory things; which cannot accompany us to the world to which we go, and which, if we could take with us, would from their nature soon perish; and only leave us possessed of the bitterness of disappointment. Not so we hope with rational friendship: though the objects may be separated and dispersed, amidst the confusion and disorder of the present mixed state of things; yet if founded in virtue and improved by religion, we may venially hope at least, that this will survive the dissolution of the body; and after the wreck of nature, and the conflagration of the world, will again revive, develope its fragrant flowers, mature its delicious fruit, and for ever flourish in the Paradise of God."

Hearing of good accommodations at the Inn of Cann or Canon Office, we intended that as our station for the night. The country here is but thinly inhabited, and less cultivated. A very small quantity is subject to the plough; the greater part being sheep down and cow pastures. Inquiring the price of land in the neighbourhood of Llanerfil, we found it from one shilling to three and sixpence per acre; and this, from the present mode of farming, might justly be considered too dear! It was near the close of evening when we arrived, and a thick rain seemed set in for the night.

The Inn of Cann takes its name from some religious house, which had probably been the seat of Jurisdiction for this part of the country, in the early times of the Britons, and some few druidical ruins in the vicinity favour this etymology. The house is white-washed, which gives it an appearance of neatness; but, "*Fronti nulla fides*,"[2] should be the motto on the sign: for the

---

2   Latin: 'No reliance can be placed on appearance.' —Ed.

filth within by no means corresponded with the cleanliness without. The landlord and his wife were from home, and the servants, left in charge, could not speak a word of English fortunately we made ourselves understood. But, so far from being able to obtain the comforts, we could scarcely procure the necessaries of life: a few old decayed potatoes and slices of fat bacon, with barley bread, was all this boasted inn could afford us for supper. Happy would it have been for us, if the lodgings had not corresponded with the larder.

The windows of the bed-room as well as the parlour, had in the course of time, met with many an unlucky accident; but the damages had been repaired, under the ingenious auspices of its proprietor, by filling up the vacancies with the refuse of the family wardrobe. The doors being neither furnished with locks nor bolts, I endeavoured to secure myself and party from any abrupt nocturnal visits, after my usual mode on similar occasions, by passing a couple of large screws through the door to the lintel. This, I soon found, was no more than a necessary precaution.

A country fair had been holden this day up in the mountains, and numbers of both sexes, whom the humours of the place or devotion to Bacchus had prevented returning in time to reach home, took up their residence here, waiting the light of morn to conduct them to their respective habitations. Separated only by a thin boarded partition, the hoarse garrulity of these too near neighbours did not fail to deprive us of sleep; and had it not been for the measure, above mentioned, we should have been farther disturbed by their obtrusive importunities. But we were fortunate in obtaining even these accommodations, and but for a sudden movement of some company, that arrived just before, we must have endeavoured to have lain down content with the motley groupe in the next room.

On our arrival here a gentleman with two ladies were just setting off in a whisky from the inn door: addressing himself to me, he inquired about the state of the road to Mallwyd; observing at the same time, he had heard it to be very good. I gave in answer, "that I was totally unacquainted with it, but that little dependance was to be placed on the accounts furnished by the inhabitants; that good and bad were relative terms, and men generally formed their opinion from the objects and circumstances around them; and that reasoning from similar reports compared with facts, I should not be inclined to take a journey of fourteen miles in such weather, and so late in the evening." When a man has resolved upon a plan, it is not easy to dissuade him from its execution; and he makes inquiries rather to fortify his resolution, than to influence his judge ment. Probably the ladies were disgusted with the interior of the inn, a view we had not been favoured with however, they set out on the perilous under taking, and we profited by their absence. Inspecting the road the next morning, we had no reason to regret having submitted to the miserable accommodations of Canon Office. It consisted of deep pitches and abrupt risings; and down a declivity, called the Bwlch of Edwyn, it required great exertions to keep the horses upon their legs, without their riders. It would have been inhuman not to have asked after the strangers, who had these difficulties to encounter in a dark and wet night. The whisky had been broken to pieces, the ladies much hurt, and obliged to take refuge in a miserable cottage, for the night, at the foot of the Bwlch; where one small room contained the hospitable inhabitants and their guests: while the horse was indebted for his lodging to the civility of a domestic swine. How little do we consider, while pride is murmuring at present objects, because they happen not to be exactly commensurate with our wishes, that they are the very best for us under existing circumstances; and that we owe to humility our safety, as we do our happiness to content.

Passing this abrupt and difficult descent, the road for several miles lay over a flat morass, abounding with the carnation and a few other kinds of grass; but all unfriendly for pasture. The Eriophorum polystachion was in great plenty, whose flowers had given way to the more striking appearance of its seed vessels; bursting with a downy substance like fine cotton this the natives gather and sell for stuffing beds, cushions,

&c. The Melica Cœrulea was abundant. In the Hebrides the fishermen make nets of this grass, and find that they are of much longer duration than those made of any other material: and the fair Andromeda Polyfolia appeared, shewing, at intervals, its elegant pink, solitary flowers.

The great extent of Rushy Moor and Heathy Bog, excited the idea of dreariness; and the meagre appearance of a few straggling sheep, and stunted black cattle, strongly reminded us of famine. The dress and manners of the inhabitants, (we were now in the wilds of Merioneth,) were calculated to furnish us with a sight of human nature in almost its rudest state. The covering of the females, males we saw none, was a coarse lindsey bed-gown, scarcely cut in any shape: at sight of us they fled to certain distances, where, considering themselves safe, they set up a kind of laughing noise, accompanied with ridiculous gestures; which brought to our recollection, the first reception of the Spaniards by the transatlantic Indians.

Consulting time, it appeared we had taken twice as much as was necessary, for the number of miles we had to go; and examining our compass, we found we had wandered several miles out of our way to the Northward. To inquire was useless; for many of these people have never heard of the places a few miles from them. Knowing that the station lay due West, we formed an angle for this point, and soon regaining the road, reached Mallwyd. This small village is placed between the salient angles of three abrupt mountains, Arran, Camlin, and Moel Dyfi, in a small vale, through which runs the river Dyfi or Dovey.

Surrounded by lofty mountains, with its neat small church, and a few straggling white-washed cottages, a more peaceful retreat cannot be imagined. Secluded from the world, it might be supposed almost deprived of the benefit of society; yet, even here, we found post chaises and respectable accommodations: a considerable posting business being done between this place and the towns of Dolgelly and Machynlleth. We met with the most pleasing behaviour from Lloyd and his wife, and two daughters of the most engaging manners were anxious which should be most forward in attention. The genteel address and polished manners of the lasses appeared remarkable in this sequestered situation. My curiosity was awake to inquiry. Lloyd committed the business of the inn to the female part of the family, while he occupied himself in a large farm a custom general with inn-keepers through Wales. He had, in his younger years, lived in England; and his daughters, agreeably to his wish, that they should adopt the manners of a country he so much admired, had received their education at Shrewsbury; which, though an English town, may properly be called the capital of North Wales: for there the inhabitants of the interior parts go to be supplied with those articles of convenience or necessity, they cannot otherwise procure, and thither the nymphs of the mountains are sent to finish their education. The church is an humble gothic structure, the floor covered with rushes,[3] and remarkable for having the Communion-table in the centre of the building. It is literally an altar-piece formed of stone, like a sacrificiary of the ancients. This, in former times, had been placed at the East end of the building; but during the noise of popish usages being introduced, and the Protestant religion in danger, in the time of Laud, Dr. Davis, the Rector of the Parish, and the learned author of the Welch and Latin Dictionary, in defiance of Archidiocesan injunction, had it removed from its supposed superstitious scite. This act, unworthy of so great a man, is a striking instance of the minutia of zeal that savours more of passionate warmth, than solidity of judgment; and discovers to us that the violence of opposition, so frequently manifested under professions of real or pretended reformation, did not always arise solely from a regard to the peculiar and pure doctrines of the gospel. But when we consider the imperfections of our present state, and that even a *Hooper* and a *Latimer* were not totally free from this littleness of contention; we

---

3   This is a practice almost universal through Wales. The floors are without pavement, and as straw is scarce, quantities of dried rushes are laid thick over the floor, for the sake of warmth and cleanliness.

must not be surprised, if the most perfect characters here are not without alloy for it is only in the unseen regions of purity, that we must look for the perfection of our nature, the fruition of peace, and the exercise of love.

In the church-yard are several large yews, whose branches furnish a canopy for the village politicians: one is more remarkable than the rest; it consists of six large arms issuing from the parent trunk, each of which might be deemed a noble tree, but thus united they are highly magnificent in appearance. The girth of the trunk, three feet from the ground, is twenty-two feet six inches, and the average radius of the branches thirty-nine feet; forming an extent of shade *two hundred and forty feet in circumference!* Various have been the conjectures of Antiquaries respecting this ancient and general custom of planting yews in these sacred places. The reason as signed by Trusler in his *Chronology*, as being planted for the use of *Archers*, as a place well known and fenced from cattle, is almost too idle for refutation. Are not *all valuable plantations* fenced from cattle? And why is there, for the most part, but *one* planted? *Horses and cows refuse it*—sheep and goats are not fond of it; and if driven by necessity they generally fall victims to its baleful properties. Add to this, nature has with no sparing hand scattered these trees over all the woods of North Wales. Thousands grow out of the fissures of rocks; and more are frequently seen together than the sum total of

all the church-yards in Wales.[4]
Mr. Pennant says,

> It was a custom in old times upon Palm Sun-
> day, to make this the substitute of the tree,
> from which that Sunday took its name, to
> bless on that day the boughs; also to burn
> some of them to ashes; and with these the
> priest, on the following Ash Wednesday,
> signed the people in the forehead, saying,
> *Memento, homo! quod pulvis es, in pul-*
> *verem reverteris!* And of the branches, so
> blessed, it was customary to stick some in
> the fields, in rogation week, or at the time of
> processions.

That this was a use sometimes made of these
trees, is very probable; but it does not satisfacto-
rily account for their being *planted here.*

Most of those in church-yards are the *male*
plant, which may easily be distinguished by the
deeper green of its foliage; an accurate idea of

---

4   The TAXUS BACCATA, of the class Diccia, (*i. e.* having only male
flowers on one tree and female on the other) has been generally supposed to be an exotic plant: but if those who have
doubted of its aboriginality, would visit the mountains of
Wales or Scotland, where it is seen growing in inaccessible
heights, which the hand of the planter never can have reached;
they must be convinced ofthe contrary. Added to this strong
indication of its being an indigenous plant, the fact authenti-
cated by M. de la Boyne, in the *Philosophical Transactions,*
dissipates every shadow of a doubt: "That yew trees with their
roots situated in the manner in which they had grown, have
been found in several parts of England beneath the surface of
the earth," *Motte's Abridgment,* Vol. II.p. 263

which is given by Parnel, in his mournful description of it:—

> ——————"Yon black and funeral Yew,
> That bathes the charnel house with dew!

See also White's *History of Selborne*, p. 324.

And probably for this darker appearance they were selected.

The use of emblems in funeral rites, borrowed from the Jews, was adopted by the different heathen nations. The Greeks and Romans carried branches of cypress before the corpse, which being once cut is said never to revive again as an emblematic representation of the miserable doctrine of *annihilation*. You know the elegant lines in the Idyllium of Bion, by Moschus; and while you admire the beautiful turn of the Poet, you will lament with me, that he who could so sweetly sing, should have had such darksome thoughts!

> 'Αι 'Αι ται μαλαχαι επαν κατα καπονόλωνται

> Alas! the meanest flowers the gardens yield,
> The vilest weeds, that flourish in the field,
> Which dead in wint'ry sepulchres appear,
> Revive in spring and bloom another year;
> But we, the great, the brave, the learn'd, the wise,
> Soon as the hand of death has clos'd our eyes,
> In tombs forgotten lie: no suns restore;
> We sleep! for ever sleep! to wake no more.
>
> FAWKES

In opposition to this, the Christians make use of rosemary, laurel, and ivy;[5] signifying, that though the body was cut down, yet, like these plants, it would revive again; and the soul was immortal, like these evergreens, on which the seasons make no change. Is it not therefore probable, that the planting of yew in church-yards is derived from this origin? Because from its perpetual verdure it is an apt and elegant emblem of the doctrine of immortality and placed *here* to shew the unlettered peasant, that although the body is committed to the earth, yet the soul still exists; and will exist forever? Whoever visits this secluded spot will certainly ramble as far as Pont Fallwyd, to the falls of the Dovey. The scenery, whichever way the eye turns, is prodigiously romantic. The mountains form a grand natural Amphitheatre, with sylvan sides; through which peeps here and there a white washed cottage; sufficient to remind us, that we were yet in an inhabited country. Camlin rising immediately with rude Majesty on our right, and the conical Arran lifting its resplendent head, with the different cwms were reflected in various tint and shade in the waters of the Dovey. Through the opening of the mountains, the ' minished scenery of the

---

5   Hedera quoque, vel laurus & hujusmodi, quæ semper servant virorem in sarcophago corpori substernentur, ad significandum, quod qui moriuntur in Christo, vivere nec desinunt; nam licet mundo moriuntur secundum corpus, tamen secundum animam, vi, yunt & reviviscunt Deo,

DURAND. Rit. Lib. VII. c. 35.

distant vale, appeared in camera-obscura before us. On the opposite view, the beautiful cascade formed by the Dovey was peculiarly fine. The river was swollen by the late rains, and impatient to rush through a narrow rocky channel, foaming against a high slate rock in the centre of the bed, it became irresistibly impetuous, and rushing into the pool beneath, hastened to meet the Estuary of the Dovey.

The pool below, fringed on its margin with brush wood, added to the brilliant appearance of its angry wave; while the mountain bridge of one extensive arch with a small chord, and its stones whitened with several species of lichen, formed a pleasing boundary to the lovely scene.

Returning to our inn, sensible of the pointed attention of Lloyd and his family to our comforts, we could not help paying our tribute of respect; and promising if ever Mallwyd should be in our route, we would endeavour to make a longer stay at the Cross Foxes.

Leaving Mallwyd, we passed a bridge of one arch over the Clwyedog, a small alpine stream that joins the Dovey near Mallwyd; whose waters, black as ink, pass sluggishly through a dark chasm of slate rock, rendered more gloomy by overhanging woods. Tradition says, it obtained the appellation of *Sickly*, from a bloody battle once fought on its banks; but more probably from the slow motion and unnatural appearance of its waters.

Whoever wishes to see the nature of a country, and become acquainted with the manners of its inhabitants, must not confine himself to the leading roads of it. He must frequently deviate from the beaten track, ascend the craggy steep, and traverse the secluded vale: he must enter the humble roof, and visit the habitations of the poor, who form the great mass of every society: where the customs of the peasantry have not amalgamated with those of their more polished neighbours.

Turning to the North, we made an excursion up the vale of the Mowddwy, on the banks of the Dovey. This valley, seven miles in length, is, in places, so narrow, as scarcely to admit a meadow between the river and the base of the mountains that form it. These rise here with such abruptness, as to appear to the eye almost perpendicular: others are verdant slopes, that furnish pasturage for numerous flocks. High up their sides the brown heath predominates, which affords shelter to quantities of the black and red grouse,[6] and ample amusement to the arduous sportsman:

---

6   But few of the black or moor game are now to be seen. The season for grouse shooting begins about six weeks before that of partridge shooting. The method is nearly the same. The grouse, which are very numerous on these peaty mountains, hide themselves under the heath or ling. Pointers, but more frequently setters and spaniels, are made use of, and the pursuers generally take a week's excursion; carrying provisions with them, and running the chance of a cottage or farm for their repose at night.

but their tops abound with bogs of greater consequence to the poor inhabitants of this wild country. Numerous turbaries furnish them with the fuel wanted; and equally curious and ingenious are the methods they use to bring the combustible treasure home. The mountains are so steep, that to use a cart or horses would be impossible; a sledge therefore is adopted, which is a machine formed of rail work similar to the bed of a cart; and holds from two to four hundred weight: this the owner carries up the hill upon his back, "*duris uterque labor,*" loads it with peat, then placing a cord over his breast, which is affixed to the sledge, he drags it to the verge of the summit; reversing his position he now exerts all his strength to stop the velocity of the sledge, going before it backwards, and guiding its various motions, till he arrives at the foot ofthe mountain; then reassuming his former position, draws the fuel home. When the turbaries are far distant, a small horse, which most of these cottagers possess, is brought up by a winding track, and employed to draw the peat to the edge of the declivity.

Such is the force of habit, that few accidents happen in this dangerous employment; although from the angle which the descent makes with the plane of the horizon, being little less than a right one, we could not unincumbered find footing and from the incumbent weight, a single false step would inevitably overwhelm the unfortunate peasant and he would be dashed to pieces!!

The only fuel of many parts of North Wales is turf and peat. The once extensive woods are nearly consumed, and coal is not yet discovered in any considerable quantities.[7] In appearance it is a mass of black earth. It has been stated by some chymists, that the earth of peat is of a bituminous quality. This was an easy way of accounting for its property of combustion but the light thrown upon the subject, by modern discoveries, has distinctly ascer tained its real nature.

Peat consists of mixt vegetable matter, principally formed of the remains of aquatic vegetables, or such as only thrive in moist situations. Their nourishment is afforded, and their growth promoted by the absorption of atmospheric air, the decomposition of water, and the calcarious matter generally held by it in solution. These substances, it has been proved, are sufficient to account for the production of aquatic vegetables; and the accumulation of such quantities of vegetable combustible matter, on the surface of the earth, that forms the numerous peat fens, and morasses. Trees of a considerable size have

---

7   Turfand peat differ in this, that the former contains the roots and stalks ofvegetables with a mixture of peat, clay, marle or sand; whereas the latter, when pure, contains no visible particles of any vegetable whatever. They are frequently found together; the turf lying uponthe surface, and the peat under, to six or seven feet deep. That which is found immediately beneath the turf, is esteemed the worst; and that at the greatest depth, the best . Sometimes in common life these names are indiscriminately applied to both sub stances.

been frequently found, buried many yards deep in some peat grounds. These probably were antediluvians; and left in the slime and sand, which must have accumulated in the upper vallies, at the retiring of the waters. Others have been found nearer the surface, with the appearance of having been cut down, or undergone the action of fire: In the *latter case*, the inference may be drawn, that peat bogs or moors did not give birth to such trees; but the destruction of forests, from natural or artificial causes, have given rise to the peat bogs and moors. The trees having been thrown down and impeding the waters in their passage to the sea, the alternate growth and decay of aquatic vegetables has, in the course of time, produced the accumulation of inert vegetable matter, known under the name of peat. *Vid. Lord Dundonald*, p. 32.

It is demonstrated, therefore, that decayed vegetables afford the combustible property, which once ignited, by heating the interposed earth to a redness, forms the burning mass. The heat, procured from this substance, is neither great nor lasting: it emits in burning a strong smell; and some kinds produce a very offensive one. It burns to yellow ashes, which contain a vegetable colouring matter, or small quantities of iron sometimes held in solution and found in the ashes. The quantity of ashes is not above one-nineteenth of the whole mass. This vegetable origin favours the tradition, that where peat

has been cut, *in a series of years it grows again.*
It is cut from the morass, or bog, with an angular
spade or scoop, which, at two motions, brings it
out in oblong pieces about ten inches long and
five thick; these are piled up in conical heaps to
dry, and in favourable weather are housed for
use in the mode above described.[8] While some
were thus engaged in preparing for that inclem-
ent season, which bids all nature rue; others were
equally busy gathering the scanty crops of grass;
and making a provision for their cattle. Men,
women, and children were employed, carefully
turning it by hand, and looking with anxious eyes
towards the heavens, which now darkly lowered,
and threatened confusion to their laborious toil.

Such is the unevenness of the ground, that
ploughs, as well as carts, are strangers to this
district. The accessible parts, deemed fit for
corn, are brought into culture by the spade; and
the manure, as in the arable tracts of the alps, is
brought on horses' backs. Yet these poor people
contrive to obtain a subsistence, which to many
would appear impossible but what nature has

---

8   It is generally, and with reason, supposed that tracts of peat
are injurious to vegetation in the vicinity. Peat is retentive
of moisture, holding it like a sponge; the solar rays produce
a great degree of evaporation and as heat is abstracted from
surrounding objects and cold generated, effects will arise
injurious to vegetation: and this not only to such plants, as
require a greater degree of heat and nourishment than such
soils will afford; but these effects will extend to the drier
lands, in the vicinity of such fens and morasses.

denied them they endeavour to supply by incessant toil,

In tenui labor, at tenuis non gloria.[9]

On the left the mountains finely opening, exhibited to us a grand view of the rugged and irregular summit of Aran Mowddwy, which rises statelily above the other mountains, that seem to crouch beneath his gigantic feet. A little farther up the vale is the small village of Llan y Mowddwy, famous only for having its church dedicated to an uncanonized saint, (Tydecho). Who this apocryphal devotee was, whom I have in vain sought for in the crowded *Panagion* of the Romish Church, it is not easy to learn: legendary tale, that makes him an Abbot of some convent in Armorica, who retired to this spot in the time of king Arthur, is extant in verse, by a bard of the noble house of Mathafarn in the reign of Henry VII. The cottages of this village and the neighbourhood are as rude as the face of the country: the walls are built of fragments of quartz and limestone, piled one upon the other in an irregular manner; with the interstices filled up with lumps of turf or peat. The roof is covered with broad coarse slates, and the chimney formed by a hole, surrounded for about two feet high with small sticks, kept in place by a rush or hay rope.

---

9   Latin: 'my toil is on a slender theme, but slender not is its glory.' —Ed.

Pursuing the course of the river, we arrived at the celebrated pass of Bwlch y Groes, the road of the Cross; so called from a cross that formerly stood on the summit of this pass, reckoned the most difficult and dangerous in North Wales: supposed to have been erected as a memento for thanksgiving, when the traveller had effected this part of his journey in safety. The face of the country puts on a terrific appearance, bidding defiance to the traveller and charging him to proceed no farther. A long range of very high mountains, running nearly East and West, and rising one above another in tremendous grandeur, divide the counties of Merioneth and Montgomery into two parts: a deep ravine through these forms the pass. It is a zigzag stair-case path of steep ascent, rendered still more dangerous by loose shivering slate stones, that slide beneath the feet. But this danger is nearly vanished: a noble road is making along the western side of the mountain, at a vast expence; and will, when finished, make the communication between the North and South, if not easy, less difficult and perfectly safe. The RUBUS IDÆUS and SAXIFRAGA NIVALIS flourish here.

On the northern side of this chain of mountains, on the banks of Llyn Tegid, in the parish of Han y Cil, lies the small town of BALA.

It is regular in its form, consisting of one principal street, the rest of the streets crossing it at right angles; and derives its name from its situation, *as a place where a river falls into a lake.*

Much of its consequence arises from its large fairs and markets, which, owing to its central situation, are numerously attended from distant parts of the country. It has a very considerable manufactory of knit woollen goods, such as stockings, gloves, &c. Knitting being the common employment of the neighbourhood, for both sexes and all ages: even the men frequently take up the needles and assist the females in the labour, whence the chief support of the family is derived. You see none idle, going out, or returning home; riding or walking they are occupied in this portable employment. During the long winter nights, from the dearness of candles and a social disposition, they form, what they call, Cymmortheu Gwau numbers assemble at each other's dwellings in rotation, and sitting round a turf fire, pursue their wonted task while tales of other times beguile the hours, or the village harper thrumbs his dulcet notes of harmony. The hills in the vicinity, particularly Tommen y Bala, are covered with these people in the summer months, spinning and knitting the woollen yarn: "Mean time the song goes round; and dance and sport, wisdom and friendly talk, progressive steal their hours away."

The wool is principally of one or at most *two piles*; and is chiefly bought at Llanrwst, except what is afforded by the neighbouring downs. The staple articles are woollen stockings, gloves, wigs, socks and other small knit articles. These are purchased by Welch hosiers, who travel through the adjoining English counties, whence they are distributed through the Island. The stockings are of all colours; white, red, blue, native black and greys of every variety of shade: price from six to nine shillings per dozen. No conjecture can be made of the quantity manufactured at Bala and its vicinity; it must be very considerable, when from *two to five hundred pounds worth* are sold every market day. *Vid.* Pennant.

This place is conjectured, to be coeval with the Roman government in Britain, if not of Roman origin: yet notwithstanding, no place has figured less upon the page of history: perhaps from its retired situation and the sterility of the adjacent country. The mount, on the South East side of the town, called Tommen y Bala, appears to have been artificial, and of Roman workmanship; it once had a castelet or citadel on its summit: on the opposite side of the lake is another, on which are the remains of walls, &c. Of both these the Welch took advantage in the times of invasion. Pennant supposes the latter to have been the scite of the castle, and to have been fortified by Llwelyn ap Jorwerth, A. D. 1202. *Vid.* Powel, p. 224.

After the Conquest, it was made dependent upon the castle of Harlech from the reign of Edward II. it was expressly committed to the custody of the constable of that castle. Subsequent to this period we scarcely hear of the place; and for centuries its inhabitants probably had to be grateful, that Bala did not exhibit a more prominent feature in the political history of the principality. Llyn Tegid, or Pimble Meer, is justly the pride and ornament of this sequestered spot: it is the largest lake in Wales; and is undoubtedly a beautiful extraordinary expanse of inland water. It lies in a direction from N. East to S. West, in length four miles; its greatest breadth little more than 1200 yards. It is many fathoms deep, and its greatest depth is near Bryn Goleu. Towards the S. West the depth diminishes, where the mountain torrents carry into the lake great quantities of loose earth and stones. The gradual accretions of these have formed small islands in this part of the lake. These, when the winds blow violently from the West, combine to form an encroachment on the North Eastern boundary. In stormy weather the billows run prodigiously high, and a heavy surf rolls over the gravelly banks; and it is not uncommon, on these occasions, for the waters to rise to the alarming height of *nine or ten feet*; so as to threaten the town with inundation: which it would certainly do, were it not for a great dyke or artificial mound of earth thrown up for its security. Before this, inundations were frequent; and many acres of excellent land were lost and even now, after heavy rains, when the superabundant waters descend from the mountains, if the wind is downward, the obstructed waters force a passage over the dyke, to the great injury of the otherwise rich pastures of the fair vale of Edeirnion. The quality of the waters is similar to that of most others in the lakes of North Wales, exceedingly pure, defying the most accurate chemical tests to detect the least quantity of earthy matter.

The lake abounds with a variety of excellent fish; salmon, pike, trout, perch, cels, and a fish peculiar to alpine lakes, called gwiniad: it is the *salmo lave retus* of Linnæus, and the same with the ferra in the lake of Geneva. It takes its British name, gwiniad, a whiting, from the peculiar whiteness of its scales: this is a gregarious fish, and some of the northern shores abound with them. They are very numerous in the lake: they spawn in December, increase prodigiously, and are esteemed by some very good eating; but they have a peculiar insipidity to me. They for the most part weigh about eight ounces, but have been caught as large as four pounds. They are seldom taken by angling, keep ing generally at the bottom of the lake; where they feed on small shell fish. Sometimes they approach the shallows to feed on the leaves of the Lobelia Dortmanna, when their flavour is esteemed peculiarly delicate.

The Fishery in the thirteenth century belonged to the abbey of Basingwerk: the whole property is now vested in Sir Watkin W. Wynne. It has been observed that the salmon are never found in the lake; nor the gwiniad in the river: hence the vulgar inference, that the waters of the river never intermingle with those of the lake, but the Dee flows through it unmixed, as the Rhone was fabled to do through the lake of Geneva; and the classic Alpheus through the waters of the Adriatic. This may generally be the case; "But by accident, (says D. Barrington) the gwiniad has been known to stray as far as Llandrillo, six miles down the river; and a salmon has now and then been found trespassing in the lake."

The boundaries of the lake consist of cultivated and wooded slopes, diversified by dark rocks; and now and then a crag presenting itself in conjunction with the expanse of water, forms an agreeable and striking landscape. The view to the South West is prodigiously fine: looking over the lake, a line of rich corn fields and verdant meadows is seen to bound its waters on the right: on the left the bridge through which they are discharged to the bed of the river, over which rises in picturesque beauty, a large rocky hill well clothed with wood: a range of crags thence leads the eye to the lofty Arrans with their summits Penllyn and Fowddy. On the North West are the cloudy tops of Arennigs, Vawr, and Vach; and, soaring high in the distant horizon, the triple head of the majestic Cader. At the North East corner issues out the river called *Dee*, which at its outset is a stream of respectable size and depth, even in dry seasons; in wet it is full, and rolls with great velocity in dark eddies through the arches of a rough stone bridge, thrown across it a few yards from the lake. No name perhaps has more exercised the prying eye of etymologists than this.

Some, considering the river to commence before it enters the lake, derive its name from that of the mountain torrent *Dwy*; others from Dduw, Divine; and a third part from Ddu[10] Black, from the dark appearance of its waters: as the matter is still *Lis sub judice*, I am strongly inclined to the first opinion: not because it flows from *two fountains*, for many rivers do this as well as the Dee; but taking into the account the generally received opinion, that this river flowed through the lake in a miraculous way, without the intermixture of its waters; and that the same quantity and quality flowed out as flowed in; it is reasonable to suppose it would bear the same name below as above the lake: and this very *interruption in the apparent bed of the river* might give rise to the appellation. If, however, with Mr. Pennant, you are determined to consider it of divine origin, I submit. *Divona* was a common name amongst the Romans, for any river they held sacred. Our original race, the Gauls, certainly deified lakes and rivers; and Deva's wizard stream was undoubtedly held in high veneration by the

---

10 Mr. Pennant in one place denies the dark appearance of its waters, yet in another he says, "I again crossed the Dee, at Pont Gylan, a bridge of two arches, over a deep and black water." But the general appearance of the upper part of the Dee, after great rains, is a deep *tan colour*: and this hue many of the Welch rivers assume, owing to the marshy peat soil, through which they flow: Rhaiadr Ddu is so called from the dark hue of its torrent; and whoever has followed the Dee through the lovely vale of Edeirnion, must have noticed the gloomy aspect of its waters there.

Druids.[11] Most nations had one more sacred than the rest: the Peneus was worshipped by the Thessalonians; and the Germans paid divine honour to the Tiber. The Rhine was famed for deciding legitimacy of birth; and the Ganges is still adored by the natives of Hindostan.

Gyraldus says the Dee was prophetic of good or ill to the Welch, by the shifting of its channel; and prior to great events, was frequently known miraculously to rage and swell, without the intervention of rains. *Vid.* Gyrald. C. XI.

This opinion was held long after the time of Gyraldus; and though it has ceased to be the boundary between England and Wales, and to witness contending armies on the margin of its flood, yet great or sudden alterations are still considered as the harbingers of extraordinary events.

Drayton in his *Polyolbion* beautifully alludes to this superstitious veneration for the Dee:

> ————Again Dee's holiness began
> By his contracted front and sterner waves to show,
> That he had things to speak, that profit them to know:
> Abrook, that was supposed much business to have seen;
> Which had an ancient bound 'twixt Wales and England been,
> And noted was, by both, to be an ominous flood,
> That changing of his fords, the future ill or good
> Of either country told; of either's war or peace;
> The sickness or the health; the dearth or the increase.

---

11   *Æres, terrestres, & alia minora Dæmonia, quæ in aquis fontium & Aluminum versari dicuntur.*
Vid. Procop. de Goth. Lib. II.

Recrossing the Bwlch and turning to the left, we crossed several small streams that issue from Craig Llyn, Dyfi, and other hills, which form the base of Arran Fowddwy; and soon forming a junction, receive the appellation of *Dovey*. Repassing the valley on the western side of the river, our attention was awakened by a sound of waters, proceeding from a considerable fall made by a small alpine stream, called Cowarch; that rises on the southern side of the Arran, and here bursting over a ledge of quartz, rock, contributes its mite to the Dovey: following the course of the stream we soon reached DINAS MOWDDU.

This village is pleasantly situated at the junction of three vales, formed by ranges of lofty mountains on the shelf of a rock beneath Craig y Dinas, on the banks of the Kerris, where it empties itself into the Dovey; the rapidity of whose streams must essentially contribute to the salubrity of the air. The houses, few in number, are principally mud cottages with rush-clad roofs; and, not being white washed, wear an aspect little inviting to the passing traveller.

From the wretched appearance of the place and its secluded situation, it might have been reasonably supposed, that it would ever escape the ebullitions of spleen and the animadversions of envy; but poverty and wretchedness are no protection against the malignant shafts of that cold philosophy which, like the blighting East wind on which it was borne, spreads alike its deleterious effects upon the humble trefoil and the majestic oak. That this was once a place of more consequence than its present state indicates, cannot be denied: indeed the annals of Wales (*Vid. Warrington*) notice it, as having been the seat of a chieftain; and its vicinity the scene of many a feat of valour and barbarity. But that it was ever a place endowed with all the privileges of a powerful corporation, bearing the ensigns of majesty, and exhibiting the pomp and paraphernalia of a proud commercial city, is an idea almost too extravagant to find admission in the regions of fancy. As well might the enthusiastic virtuoso, who finds a few cockle shells, or the traces of them in the strata of lime-stone and gravel on the summits of the mountains, conclude, that this must once have been the bottom of the ocean; and then, by a gentle stretch of the imagination, conjecture, that here must have been the harbour of some vast maritime power, where rode triumphant a victorious navy; and, from its eligible situation, have been the Emporium of the World! Supposing this had been the case, yet the man of sentiment and feeling would rather have lamented over its fallen grandeur; and the ill-fated circumstance of a dilapidated city and ruined corporation would have inspired sensations, far different from those of ridicule and triumph over its appearance of poverty and beggarly property. But the Antiquary of Birmingham could not let the *shadow* of a church or corporation pass without a discharge of venom at the established government.[12] The tour becomes a vehicle of aggression, and the cloven foot will appear upon the mountains of North Wales. For a time nothing was heard of this champion of equality: and it might have been conjectured, that, like the phoenix, he had perished in his self-kindled flames; but, like that fabulous being, he has the property of renovation; and the new-fledged bird appears in shape and instinct like the former, but with brighter plumage and redoubled strength.

It does not appear that *Dinas* strictly means a city. The Britons used to call *woods fenced with a vallum and ditch*, as a place where they might defend themselves as often as an enemy made an excursion, by this name: (*Vid. Cæsar. Com. Lib. V:*) and many places are distinguished by this appellation, that have not the least pretensions to be considered as cities, as Dinas Dinlle, Dinas Dinorwig, Dinas Cortin, Dinas Bran, all of which were fortified places; and several of them the seats of chieftains. The conclusion therefore from the name is, that it was so called from being a strong fortified palace of a prince; and as usual the district around was endowed with several privileges and exemptions, which continued

---

12   *Vid. Part of a Tour in Wales*, by W. Hutton, *F. A. S. Gentleman's Magazine*, Feb. 1798; where the gross attempts at wit, and the invidious inuendos at the church and constitution of the country, shew that the tour was undertaken more for an opportunity of sly attacks upon government, than with any view of giving a just description of the country.

under the general title of ancient usages, till restricted by the statutes of Henry VIII.; when the laws of England were generously extended to the conquered country.

This is the more probable, as this place, though not a parish, but included in that of Llan y Mowd dû, is the capital of an extensve lordship belonging to the Mytton family; which contains the whole parish, and seven out of the eight townships of Mall wyd.

Mr. Pennant says it is governed by a Mayor, Aldermen, Recorder, and several Burgesses: That the Mayor tries criminals; and the Recorder, in the absence of the Lord, matters of property not exceed ing forty shillings. That they still preserve the insignia of power: the mace, standard measure, stocks, whipping post, and the *vag-vawr*, or great fetter. But he does not say when, or by whom this charter was granted; nor how long its inhabitants have been thus enfranchised. (*Vid. Tour in Wales*, Vol. II.)

As it is a peculium under the government of its own lords, it is not improbable that this ostensible corporation is an appendage to the Baronial and Leet Courts; or rather a deputation from them, to rid the lord or his steward of the unprofitable part of its government. One of the houses still retains the name of the *Manor House*.

This district was famous, longer than any part of Britain, for retaining the barbarous custom, prevalent during the dark ages through all the northern nations of Europe, of commuting crimes, however flagitious, by a fine; called by the Saxons were-geld, and by the Welch *gwerth*. Nor was the insult upon humanity, of putting the life of man in competition with property, removed, till the 27th of King Henry the VIII. In this country the restitution was generally made in cattle. The fine for a Welchman's life, unless he was taxed as a vassal of the crown, was very low; seventy thrymses, (about ten pounds sterling;) the loss of a nose, or other principal member, six oxen and one hundred and twenty pence; of a finger, one cow and twenty pence; and other injuries in proportion. (*Vid. Leges Wal.* 278.)

The commutation, called *Gobr Merch* demonstrates, that the violation of chastity was considered as a very venial crime; and the recompence to a virgin, that had been seduced, was barbarously singular.

On complaint being made, that a damsel's lover had deserted her, the court adjudged her the opportunity of obtaining the *gobr merch*. A young three-year-old bull was to have his tail shaved and well greased; and this was to be introduced through a wicker door: if the injured female had sufficient strength to retain the bull by the tail, while two men were goading it, the beast was adjudged to her; if not, she was dismissed without further satisfaction!!!

Don't you, dear Sir, feel your indignation rise at the folly and cruelty of your ancestors, who could thus add insult to injury; and hold up to ridicule the misfortunes of the unprotected fair? I know you do. Yet how much more strongly does, what is ridiculous, unjust, or cruel in the Laws of other nations, or other times, strike us, than in those of our own? We consider ourselves as living in an age of great refinement; and then conclude it must, be an age of justice. Where is the mind of sensibility that would not shrink with horror at the base idea of his fair country-women being left unprotected by the laws of a constitution, the envy of the world? Yet can female virtue be considered as under the protection of the laws, when seduction and dereliction are deemed of so trifling a nature, and so unimportant to the welfare of the state, as not to be included in the list of crimes: and a small douceur to society even procures a privilege to commit the crime, while the injured party receives no compensation, save want and ignominy?[13] O! ye British Senators! read the history of your country, read the history of man; consult the code of reason, study the

---

13   The unfortunate female is liable to be imprisoned twelve months for incontinency; while the vile seducer is only bound to indemnify the parish for the maintenance of the child: which is generally commuted for the paltry sum of *ten or fifteen pounds*. In Switzerland the seducer is obliged to make reparation by marrying the party; but with us women seem of less value than the beasts of the field. If a man goes to his neighbour's fields and wilfully maims or wounds his cattle, it is felony without benefit of clergy; but he may seduce and debauch his daughter without any fear of legal punishment!!!

code of Divine Wisdom; and with prompt and animated hands tear, indignantly tear, these unjust and impious acts from the statute book of your country no longer suffer such a foul and disgraceful blot to deface the system of English Jurisprudence! Let equity be the standard of your legislative measures; and if any partiality must exist, let it exist in behalf of the weaker, and more amiable part of creation!—Hoping greater light will produce greater good, and that increasing wisdom will be accompanied with an extension of humanity,

I remain Yours,

J. E.

Letter IV

Dolgellau

Dear Sir,

eaving the *City*, (if city it must be called,) without a single wish to find pleasure in triumphing over fallen greatness, we took the road for Dolgellau. A grand pass through the openings of the Cader Chain, which comprehending the Arans and the Arenigs, forms nearly a right angle with the Ferwyn. It winds beautifully beside the rude mountain *Craig y Gwynt*, or the White Rock, which forms a lofty wall on the right; while the opposite one on the left consists of various slopes, with here and there a miserable looking cottage peeping in the different directions of the Cwms; the Kerris, widely flowing over a rocky bed in the vale, murmured beneath our feet, and the hills in softest whispers returned the melancholy tones. Near the top of *Craig y Gwynt* are some deserted lead mines. From great quantities of a bluish ochre being found, with which the shepherds mark the sheep, and other circumstances, it would appear, that the failure of success was rather owing to the want of skill and spirit of the undertakers, than shallowness of the vein or poverty of the ore.

On the left is Bwlch Oer Ddrws, noted for having been one of the three places, where, after the death of Glyndwr, the principal inhabitants of certain districts assembled, to form a compact for enforcing justice by the weight of their character, without the assistance of any legal sanction; which the confusion of the times, and the want of a due execution of the laws, had reduced to a state of debility. Various were the regulations made with respect to right and wrong; the mode of redress, and the measure of satisfaction. To these no sanction was annexed, except forfeiture of all benefits derivable from the compact. This appears to have been sufficient in those unsettled times, as it left the offending party unsupported, and in the hour of danger friendless. A general plan of associations of this kind for the encouragement of virtue and order would probably do more to discourage idleness and vice, and consequently prevent crimes, than all the severe penal statutes that ever were enacted.

Descending a very steep stony road for three miles we entered the town of DOLGELLAU.

We had been recommended to the sign of the Lion. The accommodations were not of the most striking sort, yet the attentive civilities of Williams and his wife would have made still more indifferent ones comfortable. We were detained here longer than intended, by the unfavourableness ofthe weather for Botanical pursuits; however we did not want for amusement. The morning was taken up in writing; the afternoon in listening to the enchanting Welch airs, and charming music of the harp, having enlisted an old harper in our service during our stay, and the evening was employed conversing with W. Williams, whom we found a man endued with a strong mind; and who, to solid observation had added a considerable fund of history and anecdote. The face of the country, its remarkable beauties or wonders, the state of agriculture and manufactures, the great families, and the changes that had taken place in them, their genealogy, instances of heroism, with many a tale of other times, furnished a savoury olla, and seldom failed to protract the length of the evening. A circumstance, which, had it not been for a declining day, and our horses inadequate to further exertion, would have been laughable, began to put on a serious aspect, and was very near depriving us of this feast of reason. From our arriving at this agitated time, and some suspicious traits in our appearance, we were taken for Irish, and it required much protestation and persuasion before we could obtain the promise of a bed, or the least refreshment. Mrs. W. insisted, that we were rebels fled from justice, while Williams recommended charity. The altercation became so violent, that we were apprehensive it would not terminate in *words*. At length Williams's choler was excited to that point, when indulgence gives way to pre-eminence of right, and loudly asserting his claim to submission, the good lady retired in dudgeon; and while we profited by the victory he had acquired, we could not refuse to admire the spirit that had obtained it.

Continual emigrations of Irish were daily arriving from their unhappy country, and dispersing over the secluded parts of the kingdom. And in some cases from want of principle, but in more, perhaps, from the distress that must necessarily attend such sudden departures, the debts they contracted at the inns were not always liquidated. But a few cases of this sort are not sufficient to account for the violent opposition, (not to say persecution,) experienced by these unfortunate people at the hands of the Welch.

In the earliest ages, when Wales and Ireland were peopled from the same Celtic stock,[1] family

---

1   A dispute has long divided the learned world, respecting the descent of the inhabitants of Cambria, or who were the im-

feuds had probably laid a foundation for a spirit of hatred. This was rekindled with redoubled fury by the barbarous and bloody excursions made by the former in the country of the latter; and, becoming inveterate by time, and strengthened by prejudice, seems now to defy all powers of conciliation. What ever conjecture may be hazarded as to its origin, the fact is too notorious, that a powerful and rancorous enmity possesses the bosoms of the Welch against the Irish; and is carried so far, even among the middling and better informed classes, as to induce them to refuse the duties of hospitality, and to deny civilities and accommodations in this country, which may be purchased in every other. Among the lower

---

mediate ancestors of the original Welch. *Leland, Sir John Price*, and others, in conformity to the printed and M. S. histories, derive their origin from a colony of Trojans, under their leader Brutus. The writers of the Camdenian School oppose this suggestion totis viribus, and have produced voluminous arguments to prove, that they could have been no other, than a swarm from the crowded hives of neighbouring Gaul. Sir John, in his *Defensio*, admits that Brutus and his Trojans remained some time in Gaul; but probably from not being very cordially received by the natives, made a further emigration to the western coasts of this kingdom. The learned Knight, with a spirit of humour well becoming the discussion of such an uncertain and unimportant subject, observes, "It is no great honour to have been descended from a vanquished people, who had deserted their country, and were now commencing vagrants as the Trojans were; yet facts should prevail, and the historian should lean where truth seems to reside." As it is one of these subjects, where conjecture is argument, and assertion proof, it still remains to the impartial reader an undecided question.

classes it rises from rudeness to insult. The spirit
and habits of loyalty among the Welch must necessarily clash with the ungovernable turbulence
too apparent in the other; and the relation of the
rebellious spirit lately manifested, and now broken out into actual outrage, against their legal
Sovereign, fanned the national hatred into a rag-
ing flame:[2] the least encouragement from their
superiors, would have brought thousands from
the mountains, with intentions of massacre, and
weapons of destruction.

Dolgellau, is so called from being situate in a
vale once abounding with wood; *Dôl* being of the
same import with *Dale* in English, and *Gelleu*, a
place where much hazle grows. Its antiquity has
not been noticed. Camden says, Roman coins of
Trojan and Hadrian were found in his time, near
a well called Fynnon-vawr. And a Parliament was
assembled here by Owen Glyndwr, A. D. 1404;
and though his affairs were in a prosperous state,
having formed an alliance with Charles, King of
France, yet to an impartial observer, Owen must
have appeared too premature in his declarations,
having assumed the style and claims of Royalty
before he had procured sufficient friends and
power to support them.[3]

---

2   Extemplo, turbati animi, concussaque fulgi
    Pectora, et arrectæ stimulis haud mollibus Iræ.

                                      Virg. Æn, 1. xi,

3   "Owinus, Dei gratia, princeps Walliæ," &c. is the stylein
    which he sent his Ambassadors to Charles; ending, "datum

This principal town of Merioneth, where the Summer Assizes are held, stands in a fertile vale near the river Onion; and though it is in a flourishing state, yet its appearance affords no striking evidence of the wealth of its inhabitants. The houses are chiefly quartz, or lime-stone, without mortar, smaller pieces of the same being forced into the interstices; few higher than two stories, with pent-houses in front upon poles, and the streets so narrow as not to admit two carriages passing each other. The Market-house is a low square building, and the Town-hall is scarcely distinguishable from the other houses.

Being here on a Sunday, gave us an opportunity of seeing most of the inhabitants: the poor were dressed in their holiday clothes, and made a respectable appearance. A large green meadow, (where, and abundantly in other places, grows ATHAMANTA MEUM) between the town and the river, forms a mall; and hundreds, after the evening service, were here enjoying the reanimating sun and refreshing breeze. We joined the perambulating party, and were pleased to see what an air of content and chearfulness pervaded every countenance. Inquiring the price of labour, and the general mode of living, we had to regret, that magnificent dwellings seldom administer to the real comfort of their owners; and that acquisitions of wealth, and elevation of rank,

---

apud Doleguelli, 10 die mensis Maii, M, CCCC. quarto, et principatûs nostri quarto."

are but rarely the paths which lead to the Elysium of Content.

The Church is a decent edifice of lime-stone, consisting of a handsome tower, and a large nave. The seats are forms, and the floor is paved with lime stone flags, a circumstance extraordinary for Wales. The desire of perpetuating the remembrance of departed friends is expressed in a whimsical way; the coffin plates, exhibiting the name, age, &c . of the deceased, are placed as *Memento mori*'s against the walls, and other conspicuous parts of the church.

The service is performed in Welch, three times every Sunday. We were sorry to observe, that the custom, which so much interested our feelings on entering Wales, did not prevail here; but the ancient custom (*Vid. Cicero, De leg.*) among the Heathens, of placing flat stones over the deceased. Lime stone slabs mark the graves of the wealthier people in the church-yard of Dolgellau; and it was impossible not to remark how pitiful and mean it appeared, in comparison with the refined one before described.

The town is improving in building and population; from the increasing trade in coarse cloth, it promises to become no inconsiderable place. That kind of woollen cloth called Gweu, or Webs, strong or high country cloth, occupies the inhabitants of the town and neighbourhood. Every little farmer makes webs; and scarcely a cottage is found without a loom. All kinds of wool are indiscriminately used; fleece, refuse from staplers, and even the skin yards. Some of the growers manufacture their own wool, and the produce from this is the best cloth. The webs run from six to seven quarters wide, and are two hundred yards long, divided into two pieces. In its rough state it may be purchased of the manufacturer from a shilling to three shillings per yard. The quality has varied, since the staple of wool has been better understood, and it has risen full 20 per cent within the last seven years. The webs used to be carried to Liverpool or Shrewsbury to market; but the Liverpool dealers have now persons in pay on the spot, to purchase of the makers; and to assist the poorer manufacturers with money to carry on their trade; as the Blackwell-hall factors do many of the smaller clothiers in the West of England. Here, as in that country, much is made by commission. Since this, the drapers of Shrewsbury are obliged to go up the country, and purchase the articles in small quantities at the farms and cottages. After undergoing the operation of scouring, bleaching, and milling, it is packed in large bales, and sent to Liverpool and London; and thence exported to Germany, Russia and the West Indies.[4] An attempt was made,

---

4   Formerly it used to be chiefly sold from the loom; but the
    people now embarked in the business, are sensible of the
    great advantage of exposing the article for sale, in a finished,
    rather than an unfinished state. The streams begin to re-
    sound with the fulling mills, and bleaching-racks are seen
    to extend along the sides of the hills. A few webs, for home

a few years since, to make Barmouth a general depôt for the woollen goods of North Wales, intended for exportation, but it proved abortive; nor can it be expected such an enterprize should prove successful, till the trade has more opulent manufacturers, and the port of Barmouth more wealthy and spirited merchants. It is impossible to ascetrain what quantity of cloth is got up, where almost every weaver is a master, and where no regular entries are kept. Mr. Pennant observes, that the amount of webs brought to Shrewsbury annually, is 700,000 yards; but this by no means amounts to the sum total made in North Wales.

We took an early opportunity of paying our respects to the pride and boast of this mountain ous country, and the principal object of our visit to Dolgellau, CADER IDRIS. The base consists of a long extent of dreary slope, formed by the secondary mountains of slate, over which the lofty Cader, the principal elevation of the chain, rises pre-eminent. The ascent is immediately over the town to the Southward, and so abrupt on this side as to deceive the eye, with regard to the conjectural height of the mountain. Its breadth is by no means proportionable to its length, the base

---

consumption, are dyed blue, drab, brown, &c.; these are sent at present to Shrewsbury to be dyed. They are getting into the finishing the articles, by rowing, double milling, napping, &c. and will, most probably, in a short time, add the improvement of colours, and facility of manufacturing by the introduction of machinery.

seldom exceeding eightmiles, and being in some
places not more than one. The higher parts are
composed chiefly of granite, porphyry, and hard
whin, intermixed with quartz, schorl, and feldspar. No minerals of any kind have as yet been
discovered in these parts. On the Southern side
it rises from the sea shore near Towyn, where an
Estuary is formed by the river Disanwy. The ascent Northwards, is regular for about three miles,
then taking an East, or North-easterly direction
for ten miles, it throws out a branch or protuber-
ance towards the summit, projecting for three
miles South-west.[5] The ascent, from the road to
Towyn, is perhaps the most eligible, though very
steep. On the right is Llyn y Gader, where a common horse path forms a communication between
this and the villages on the opposite side . Though
loaded horses pass this track, yet a person accustomed to a flat country will feel his nerves shake,
lest his feet should slip, and he should fall precipitately down over the rugged fragments of rock,
that lie on the sides of the mountain.

In the Lake of Llyn y Gader is found the LO-
BELIA DORTMANNA, NARTHECIUM OSSIFRAGUM,
the elegant NYMPHEA LUTEA, and aromatic
NYMPHEA ALBA, expanding their beautiful green
leaves and patulous blossoms upon the surface
of the water; the former yellow, the latter white.

---

5   The height of the highest summit is 2850 feet above the
     level of Dolgellau Green. As the tide rises 24 feet at Bar-
     mouth,perhaps 30 feet maybe added to the estimate.

These, with other aquatic plants, have the wonderful instinct, (shall I call it?) of rising to the surface of the water near the time of flowering. They expand their blossoms about seven o'clock in the morning, and closing again, repose upon the surface about four in the evening. This specious aquatic confirms the ingenious theory of the respiration of plants. The upper side of the leaf is the immediate organ of breathing, by which it emits azotic gas, and imbibes oxygen; and in which the sap, or blood of the plant, under a thin porous pellicle, is exposed to the action of the atmosphere.[6] Vid. M. Bonnet, *L'Usage des Feuilles*. Hence like insects, if the spiracula of the leaves are stopped by covering the upper surface with oil, death ensues; and hence, even to aquatic plants, submersion in their native element quickly becomes fatal.

On gaining the first ascent, much coarse grass and peat bogs are discoverable. The hollow of Cwm y Cay presents itself, out of which rises the most perpendicular rock of Craig y Cay, overshadowing Llyn y Cay, a lake whose waters are beautifully clear, and of great depth, which refutes the idea of this having been a volcanic crater. They are said, by Mr. Aikin, to have stood

---

6   The leaves only half expand, except in rainy seasons, forming a concavity, that, like the little nautilus, rides upon the wave, to avoid the injury that the agitation of the waters might otherwise do to the respiratory organs; hence they are vulgarly called can leaves.

the chymical test of pure water, and as he ingeniously observes, the lava and other volcanic productions supposed to have been seen here by some authors, might be no more than the quartz, whence feld spar having been decomposed, had been left in a porous state.[7] Here also grows the Narthecium ossifragum, and on the surrounding rocks, Rumex digynus, Rhodiola rosea, Thalictrum minus, Th. alpinum, Lycopodium selagonoides, and L. clavatum.

The waters of the lake cover an extent of fifty acres, abounding with trout and other fish; and a loud and distinct echo twice repeats the whispers of the speaker. Amidst the clefts and fissures of the rocks foxes find a safe retreat, and the favourite animal of the country, in its proper state of nature, leaps from craig to craig, browsing the mountain shrub, or alpine grass, in wild security.

The road from this shelf is still more perpendicular; the loose columnar stones, lying about in all directions, assume in many places so regular an appearance, that they might be taken for druidical remains; some of them stand erect, like Maen hirion, and one is dignified with the title of *Llêch Idris*. Nearer the summit numerous masses of irregular figures present themselves, and the disordered state of the strata becomes

---

7   The mineralogist will here seek in vain for "the rugged discoloured rocks, cemented by a semi-vitrified matter, which gives them a volcanic appearance, and quantities of pumice similar to the toad-stone of Denbyshire." *Vid. Pennant.*

more obvious. This mountain is *Cader Idris*, properly so called. Having gained this ascent, a small plain forms the base to the two eminences, or rocky heads, of nearly equal height, which constitute the bifurcated summit of Idris; called *Tyrrau Mawr* and *Pen y Gader*. The view from the latter is won derfully grand; the mountains we had looked up to with astonishment, now sunk into inconsiderable hills, while the lesser elevations appeared to vanish in the extensive plains. Lakes, rivers, towns, villages, castles, steeples, woods, and downs, intermixed with the numerous inclosures, and sheep, cattle, and men, in diminished perspective, formed a pleasing and varied map. Over these the eye ranged to the Wrekin, rising solitary on the plain of Salop, skirted by the winding Severn, the lake of Bala, with the Cader's rival, *Arran Ben Llyn*,[8] the Ferwyn, and the Breddin Chains. To the South, the Bay of Swansea, and the Channel peep through the openings of the mountains of Brecon. The Vale of Towyn, the fine curve of the Bay of Cardigan, with the immense expanse of the ocean dashing its foaming waves over the breakers, and against the rocky shores of Merioneth, add to the beauty of the scene; which is closed, at a vast distance, by the heights of Snowdon, and, dimly in the western horizon, appears like a faint cloud, the coast of Ireland.

---

8   Mr. Hughes says, that Arran Ben Llyn is only thirty yards lower than the summit of Cader.

The World, in elevations like these, seems beneath the traveller; and it is impossible not to feel, in such impressive scenes of grandeur, a principle of religion. The immensity of the ocean corresponding with the majestic height of the mountain, contrasted with the habitations and other laborious works of man, so diminutive in the scale, could not fail to excite ideas of wonder and delight. The sublime has a moral tendency, it elevates the soul by depressing it; it lifts it above every mean and groveling consideration. Here the mind is arrested with awe!—All points to *Him*, "who fixed the mountains on their base, established the earth on its immoveable pillars, and holds the immeasurable ocean in the hollow of his hand." Evident marks of Almighty power obtrude them selves on our observation, at every step, not only in the formation, but in the apparent changes that have taken place amid these stupendous scenes. What is vulgarly called great, appears little, and what we were accustomed to pronounce important, comparatively trifling. We might have been tempted to have indulged a degree of pride, at finding ourselves so superior, and the world so far beneath us, had not the rising thought been checked by the insignificant figure those edifices made, which we had been used to consider as the wonderful efforts of human art and human power. We blushed at our little imaginary self-exaltations, and wondered how we could ever consider ourselves as Beings of so much consequence. Surrounded by objects of such superior magnitude, the recollection removed us to our proper place in the scale of Being, and feeling a portion of self-abasement, which may be useful in less elevated scenes, we prepared to descend the mountain.

The plants towards the top of Cader, are AIRA CŒSPITOSA, FESTUCA OVINA, and the variety, called by Aikin F. VIVIPARA, he having probably only seen it in its viviparous state; and F. DURIUSCULA, POA ALPINA, &c. These plants have the wonderful property of a two-fold mode of increasing their species. When they grow in the plain or vale, where they experience the influence of the genial breeze and prolific sun to ripen their seeds, when committed to the earth to unfold the secret powers of the embryo, they increase in the usual manner; but in these alpine tracts, where the cold, even in the Summer months, is frequently severe, they change their mode, and become viviparous. The infant germ, developing itself, shoots into blade in the cap; and then falling, readily takes root, and becomes the parent of a numerous offspring. In other parts grow the SAXIFRAGA HYPNOIDES, S. STELLARIS, SPHAGNUM ALPINUM, RHODIOLA ROSEA, and VACCINIUM VITIS IDÆA abundant; GNAPHALIUM DIVICUM, PTERIS CRISPA, PINGUICULA VULGARIS, SEDUM TELEPHIUM, S. RUPESTRE, LYCOPODIUM SELAGO, CAMPANULA ROTUNDIFOLIA, C. VAR. ß, JUNGERMANNIA ALPINA, J. JULACEA, MNIUM JUGERMANNIA, LICHEN PASCHALIS, L. FRAGILIS, with a variety of other species, and the Arbutus alpina. This plant has often been confounded with A. uva ursa, arising from their trailing branches; but, not to mention the striking difference of the berries, (those of the former being black, and the latter red,) there is an infallible specific distinction. The leaves of A. alpina are wrinkled on the upper side, and reticulated on the the under, with their edges serrated; while those of the Uva ursa are *entire*. It differs from the Vaccinium vitis idæa, by its trailing branches, and its leaves not dotted underneath.

Taking a North-easterly direction in our descent, we passed by the side of a small lake, whose crystal waters discharged themselves down the sides of the mountain into the beautiful lake of Llyn Meingul, in the vale of Taly Llyn. This is very narrow, consisting of meadows and verdant slopes, covered with numerous flocks, with here and there a solitary shepherd lying by the side of a turf-built hut, at tended by his faithful dog; while in places the lake so far fills the valley, as only to leave a narrow path on one side; and the huge dark crags, near 1000 feet in height, tremendously overhanging the water, form a grand and majestic contrast. The termination of this little scene is highly picturesque. The lake gradually contracting, in the shape of a river, rushes through a good stone arch into a narrow bed below, having the church on one side, and cottages mixed with trees on the other.

Here we entered the Dolgellau road, but nature changed her face, and the relief which vegetation affords the eye was denied us. The mountains, uniting at their bases, support projecting rocks and impending crags, with large dark coloured columnar fragments, which have been disjointed from the strata, furnish ideas of horror. We were soon relieved from this scene, by passing near the side of Llyn y Tregraienyn, orthe Lake of the Three Grains; so called, says the voice of the vulgar, from the Giant Idris feeling some gravel hurt his foot and throwing it out into the lake, which became the three rocks now visible on the lake. These, and a thousand such stories you may hear, and he who likes may fill his budget. They are three vast rocky fragments, separated by some convulsion of nature from the adjacent mountains. This lake is esteemed bottomless, but the depth has been found at sixty fathoms.

These lakes, and several others, which receive their waters from the Cader, abound with trout, gwyniad, and other fish, peculiar to alpine lakes, which induce the amphibious otter to frequent them, who here makes his nocturnal and predatory perambulations. The cwms of the mountains are peculiarly fitted for his retreat, and the waters for his pastime and repast. This animal, which is seldom found in England, has soft brown hair, is about two feet in length, from the tip of the nose to the insertion of the tail; its head broad, nose blunt, and mouth flat, like a fish;

neck thick and short, tail broad at the insertion, and tapers off to a point; the eyes are remarkably small, and placed near the nose; the legs very short and strong, the articulations of the joints are so formed, that the animal can turn them quite back, and use them as temporary fins. Each foot is furnished with five toes, connected by a web or cartilaginous membrane, like the feet of aquatic fowl. He takes his general residence on the banks of the lake, hollowed by the waves; and here the female brings forth her young. The otter is not fond of rivers and running streams, but if driven by hunger, it swims against the stream in pursuit of prey. If this method of meeting the fish prove unsuccessful, endued with capacious lungs to take in a large portion of air at a time, he dives to the bottom, and as fish cannot see beneath, from the peculiar conformation of their eyes, he attacks them on the defenceless side, drags them to shore by the belly, and then leaves them for hours together to continue the pursuit. In lakes and ponds he varies his mode of attack. He generally drives them into some small creek or shallow, where they are infallibly taken. In this manner the otter, during the Summer months, obtains a supply more than adequate to his consumption, frequently with unpardonable cruelty inflicting death for amusement, and leaving the dead fish upon the strand, rather as trophies of his victory than necessity. He is so voracious as to kill more than he can eat, and, by this spirit of covetousness, he becomes so destructive to small fish ponds, as to destroy the whole in the space of a few nights. His wantonness, however, draws after it his own punishment: in winter he is obliged frequently to live upon weeds and grass, or the bark of trees; and, growing desperate from famine, he has the temerity to attack sheep, which brings down upon him the vengeance of man.[9] His mode of building is as curious as that of taking his prey. This ingenious free mason burrows under ground he begins by making an opening at some distance from the bank, frequently in a wood or covert place. He then works his way, by a circuitous route, to the lake or river; this done, he makes another, to communicate with the windings of this, at the side of the bank beneath the water. By the one, on the land side, he obtains admission for a supply of fresh air, and by the other he eludes the vigilance of his enemies, escaping by his aquatic passage.

It is difficult to take the old ones alive; if they cannot avoid the pursuers by diving, they retreat to their holes and escape; but if their retreat be unexpectedly cut off, they grow instantly desperate, attack the dogs with the most savage fierceness, and when once they bite, never quit their hold, so that few dogs care to face them. The young ones are taken with less difficulty. They are generally playing about the edge of the lake, but if the dam be present the task then becomes

---

9   Vid. Goldsmith and Pennant, *Brit. Zool.*

arduous. The old one teaches them immediately to plunge into the water, and escape among the rushes or weeds, that commonly fringe the margin. At this early period they swim with great velocity, and every part but the tip of the nose being submerged, they easily escape. Dogs are trained for this purpose, and this species of hunting furnishes great amusement. When the hunters come to the spot, the dogs discover by their barking that the otter is there, which instantly dives as related. If the female is absent, the young ones refuse to stir without parental protection, and fall an easy prey. Thus taken, they are fed upon fish and water; as they gain strength, this food is changed for bread, milk, &c. Then taught to fetch and carry like dogs, by training first with artificial, and then with dead fish, they become valuable animals, for such is their docility, they will even fish for their masters, as well as themselves, and obtain their own maintenance, and a supply for the family. This is one instance of a very savage animal being domesticated by human art, and furnishes a probability, that the terror of the thicket and the desart are not irreclaimable from their ferocious state; but instead of being the dread of man, might be made subordinate to his will, and subservient to his use.

When we reflect, that out of *twenty thousand animals*, not more than *a hundred* can at present be considered as his auxiliaries, what a majority remains to be subdued; and what a small portion of the divine grant he has yet possessed himself of. While his ambition is insatiably striving to lord it over his fellow-creatures, and to make his *compeers in being* the slaves of his pleasure, or his avarice, the extensive territories of the animal kingdom remain unsubjugated; he permits the strength of the stoutest animals, which in a domesticated state would essentially contribute to his resources, to be, as far as respects him, dissipated without advantage; and the animals themselves to range in absolute independency, mocking at his title of *Creation's Lord.* Wishing that the genius of war might for ever submit to the genius of peace, and mankind apply the powers of reason to sciences, to art, to economy, and humanity; we descended through Bwlch Coch, at the foot of which grows the POLYTRUCHUM ALPINUM, and P. URNIGERUM, and on loose stones the LICHEN CENTRIFUGUS, down a rough and rubbly road again to Dolgellau.

Yours,

J. E.

Letter V

he road for Barmouth is over a hand some stone bridge of several arches, thrown across the Onion; which here flows many hundred feet wide. On the right, about a mile from the town, on the bank of the river, are the ruins of Cymmer Abbey. Part of the church is still standing, exhibiting at the East end three lofty sharp-pointed arches; and over them three smaller ones mantled with ivy. The abbot's lodge and part of the abbey serve for a farm house. This was a Monastery of the Cistertian order, founded by Meredydd and Gryffydd, the sons of Conan ap Owen Gwynedd, A. D. 1198. In Llewelyn's charter the benefactions of the founder and the boundaries of the abbey lands are enumerated, and his own recorded, A. D. 1209: evidently proving, that it was founded prior to that period. The revenues at the Dissolution amounted to £.58 15s. 4d. *Vid. Speed.*[1] Two miles from Dogellen is Nanneau Park, the ancient seat of the family of that name, now of the Vaughans. The road is by a steep ascent, and the house stands on very high ground: it was but an old indifferent building. The present possesor, has erected a new and handsome mansion, which appears to great advantage from the elevated scite, and the rich woods that clothe the different parts of the park.[2]

---

1   Dugdale and Tanner confound this with the abbey of *Cwmhir* in Radnorshire, on the borders of Montgomery. To *that* must be referred what Mr. Warner says of *this abbey*, with respect to the fine its abbot paid to the English, to save it from conflagration; as well as the treachery of one of its monks, that led to the disaster. *Vid. Math. Par.* p. 311. *Powel*, 252. The foundations ofa castle are shewn near the abbey, built by Yetryd ap Edwin; and taken and demolished soon after A. D. 1116, by Euean ap Cadwyan and Meredydd ap Bleydden. *Vid. Powel*, p. 150.

2   But Mr. Pennant when he observed, "That this was the highest situation of any gentleman's house in Britain," *Vol.* II. p. 97; did not recollect that many parts of the kingdom, which form a much less angle with the plane of the horizon, are higher from the level of the sea, than those that form a greater. The land gradually rises as we proceed from the ocean; and it is probable, from this consideration, that the talle land called *Ridgeway* in *Warawickshire*, is the highest part of this kingdom.

In the upper part of the park is the remains of
a British post it is a high insolated rock, encircled
with a wall of stones, the common fortification
of our rude ancestors, called *Moel Orthrwm*, or
the Hill of Oppression. This park is celebrated
for the ancient deer of the country, remarkably
small but of exquisite flavour.

The traveller here cannot resist the invitation
to look at nature in her fantastic wildness, as exhibited in the celebrated falls of the Cayne and
the Mawddach. The weather for several days had
been prodigiously stormy, and consequently favourable for seeing them to the highest advantage. Who ever visits these scenes in the drought,
that frequently accompanies the most pleasing
time for travelling, will be totally disappointed;
for several of these falls will have vanished; and
the person, by whose description the traveller
has been allured to the spot, lie under the imputation of misrepresentation or of high colouring.

Proceeding northwards up the vale of the
Maw, at Doly Melynllin, six miles from Dolgellau, is a house inhabited by Counsellor Maddox;
here, turning to the left up a steep acclivity, the
eye meets the furious course of the Garfa, a wide
mountain torrent dashing its waters from rock
to rock through a thicket of various kinds of un-
derwood, meeting with short interruptions till it
arrives at a lofty precipice; down this it rushes in
separate channels fifty feet into the pool beneath,
shaded by lofty trees, that give the waters a dark

appearance, and the cataract its name, *Rhaiadr ddu*: here, struggling and foaming against the fragments of stone it has brought in its violent passage, in wild uproar, it is soon lost to the spectator in the thick woods below. A noble pendant birch of uncommon size overhangs the centre of the fall, and forms a high finish to this romantic scene.

A bridge is thrown across the river called *Pont ar garfa*, which conducts you to another cascade, formed by the junction of the Maw and Eden. A lofty angular wooded hill, corresponding with the glens through which these waters fall, forms the fork of the rivers; and is not unlike many of those scenes described by travellers in the wilds of America. But these were only introductions to other scenes of grandeur, with which nature has every where enriched this richly varied country.

Crossing a lofty slate mountain with numerous oaks on the right and left, called Tylyn Gwladws, with its opposite, Cwm Yssam, we descended into the deepened vale, through which the Mawddach flows. The mountains on both sides, dark with the umbrageous shade of beech and oak, which almost completely cover their declivities, except the brown crags sometimes making an appearance through the verdant clothing, formed a fine contrast with the naked country before us.

A difficult path, through wooded dingles, soon brought us to the river. Though precluded from the sight of the cataract, by the sylvan shades of

LETTER V

this fairy region, our ears were assailed by the noise of these troubled waters. The latent falls of the Cayne and the Mawddach were now distinctly heard, in angry roar, tumbling from ledge to ledge; while the sounds reverberated from the mountains' sides, like distant thunder, directed our steps to the *Pistil y Cayne*, (or the spout of the river Cayne.) This is no less than the whole river, in one uniform sheet, dashing down a perpendicular declivity of near two hundred feet, in full stream, into the deep rocky bason, or excavation formed by the violence of the water. But this magnificent object appears to the greatest advantage from below, by crossing a truly alpine bridge, formed of the trunk of an immense oak, laid from rock to rock over a narrow dark chasm; through which the torrent rushes from the Pool into the glen beneath.

From this situation the view is immensely grand. The prodigious height of the cataract to its first fall; the chasm over which the bridge is placed; its second descent through the rocky fissures; its mural front and sides, with trees here and there relieving the brown rock; the thick wooded glen, shaded by ancient oak and beech, with a profusion of under wood, through which the waters force their course, hoarse murmuring from rock to rock, till they mingle with Mawddach a few hundred yards below; combine to form a species of the picturesque, that may be equalled, but cannot be surpassed. Three hundred yards distant from this, is the fall of the Mawddach; which, though in the same enchanting style of romantic beauty, yet retains a peculiar character distinct from every other cataract we had seen. This is a remark that may be extended to the greater part of the scenery of Wales; which by new combinations of objects, and exhaustless variety of colouring, furnishes perpetual sources of novelty and entertainment to the Devotee of Nature.

This fall is more exposed to the day. A vista opens through woods to a bare mountain, enclosed by others, rising with salient angles for eight hundred feet high; over which, by three falls of about thirty feet descent each, with full stream the river rolls into a deep concavity: whence again issuing, it reassumes its violence, and rages over a congeries of craggy rocks, till joined by the impetuous Cayne, and is only heard in the distant woods. Though this was so materially different from the former, we were not less gratified: the Pystil is romantic, but that of the Mawddach is magnificently grand.

Mr. Pennant observes, what we should wish to see, "That in the nakedness of winter, there is an eminence, whence these two cataracts might be seen at once, exhibiting through the trees a piece of scenery as uncommon as it is grand."

Retiring from these lovely scenes, we regained the road at Llan Elltyd turnpike. At this place the tide flows to a considerable height; and a number of small craft, with a few large vessels, are built. A brig of about two hundred tons was now upon the stocks, and others of inferior size; but vessels of any considerable tonnage are obliged to be launched about the equinoxes, to take the advantage of the high vernal and autumnal tides, for floating over the bar of Barmouth.

From Llan Elltyd to Barmouth is ten miles of the best and most beautiful road in the kingdom. The road winds round the hill opposite to Dolgellau; and is formed with great labour, on a shelf of the rock, through the hanging woods, crossing a hand some stone bridge over the Mawddach, just where it joins the *Onion*. The expanse of water now becomes considerable, and at high tide occupies the whole of the vale; putting on the appearance of a large lake, enveloped with mountains. The waters of the Æstuary contract with the undulations of its rocky banks, which in some places are covered with brush wood to the water's edge; and in others foam in sullen grandeur against impending cliffs. A sprinkling of cultivation, and plantations of trees as a security from the spray of the ocean, mark the hand of industry. The openings of the surrounding woods display the opposite mountains, bowing with modest submission to the heights of Cader; which, with its bifid summit, now assumed the appearance of a volcano. The rolling clouds smoaked over the mountain, and the sudden bursts of light, occasioned bythe contending sun, had a grand and aweful effect.

The road follows the inequalities of the shore, till it occupies a narrow shelf of the perpendicular rock of Barmouth. Here we obtained a fine view of the waters of the river, discharging themselves into the beautiful bay of Cardigan.

The delight we felt during this pleasing ride, was nearly terminating in a disastrous conclusion. The road near Barmouth is on the shelf of the rocky mountain, on which part of the town is built; which, from the constant washings of the tide, had of late experienced considerable inroads. A spirit of necessary improvement induced the commissioners to devise means to widen it. The most eligible plan was deemed, blowing up the rock. This was now executing by means of gunpowder and the men were busily employed in the work.——We had scarcely passed the spot before our horses started at an explosion unexpected by the workmen themselves; and a portion of the rock gave way of many thousandtons weight, which completely blocked up the road: fortunately no lives were lost; but had we been a few seconds later, we must have been inevitably crushed to atoms.

To express gratitude for deliverance to *Him*, who permitteth not a sparrow to fall to the ground with out his paternal notice, may seem like enthusiasm to the eye of impiety; but to us, who consider the acknowledgment of our dependance upon the Deity, and his superintending Providence over our beings and concerns, as a reasonable service, this event has often on recollection been a source of pleasurable sensations; much more calculated to excite the envy, than the contempt of the votaries of irreligion:

> If smallest beings claim his guardian care,
> His noblest creature cannot fail to share.

Entering BARMOUTH, we met with good accommodations at the Corsy gedal Arms, the only inn in the place. This little town is seated close on the sea shore, at the mouth of the Maw; hence called *Aber Maw*. It is principally built upon a high rock; rows of houses standing upon the shelves one above another, like part of the city of Edinburgh and said to resemble the town of Gibraltar, A strect is formed by a few mariners' and fishermen's houses, built on the strand, which are completely overlooked by the buildings of their wiser neighbours, that are founded on the rock. The former are defended from stormy tides, by large hillocks of sand, which threaten to overwhelm them; and certainly would, were it not for the friendly assistance of two, other wise despised vegetables, the ARUNDO ARENARIA and ELYMUS ARENARIUS; which, by their long creeping roots intertwining together, stop the sand, and by causing it to aggregate, change it from a nuisance to a friendly barrier.

To those who conceive that a place of fashionable resort must be handsome in appearance,

Barmouth will occasion, disappointment. The *Coup d'œil* is by no means striking. The bathing is certainly as efficacious as any can be: the rough tides so frequent in St. George's Channel, and the rocky shores ofthe surrounding coast, must greatly tend to change and render salutary the waters of the bay.

The beach is a fine sand, extending from the Traeth Artro to the harbour. The accommodations for bathing, at present, are but indifferent: neither with horses, as at Weymouth and Brighton; nor with a winch and inclined plane, as at Cowes; but fixed on the sand at a certain distance within the reach of the tide, which renders it very inconvenient to the bathers: being confined for time.

The company, though not numerous, was genteel. Through the wetness of the season, few of the Shropshire and Hereford beauties had yet arrived; yet the place was expected soon to fill this being the resort of the indolent and afflicted from the midland part of the kingdom, as Weymouth is for the western part.

Adjoining to the inn is a large boarding-house, capable of containing a number of families. Here at one common table, which is well served, the company sit down to dinner and supper together, as at Matlock; an admirable harper is kept in pay. An assembly twice a week affords exercise and amusement for the evening; and the surrounding country furnishes objects for both, during the day.

From the friendly footing on which strangers meet here, they resemble one great family, united for the purpose of social intercourse and mutual pleasure. The lodgings are good and the expences very moderate; and, when the price of provisions is taken into the account, it would be extortion, were it otherwise. Mutton three-pence per pound; kid by the quarter the same; fowls ten -pence to one shilling per couple: most kinds of fish from one penny to two-pence per pound.

Every consideration is heightened, by the most pleasing attention from the hostess and her servants; so that he who cannot spend two or three months under the roof of Lowii Lewis, without experiencing *ennui*, must be possessed of a spirit not easily pleased; and has yet one of the most essential of all human sciences to learn.

The harbour is formed by a small island,[3] at the mouth of the river, that serves to secure a safe anchorage for the shipping. It formerly afforded pasturage for numerous flocks and herds; but, from a late inundation of the sea, it is the greater part laid under water; and the shifting sands threaten to destroy the harbour.

They are now busily employed in carrying stone to repair the damages; but without greater support, this work, essential to Barmouth as a port, must soon necessarily cease.

---

3   "At the mouth of Maw River lyeth a little islet, scant a bow shot over, without habitation. At ebbe it is fresh water, and at fludde salt." *Lel. V.* 42.

Some have been sanguine enough to suppose, that this might be made a place of extensiye trade; but a bar of sand, over which the tide rises only a few feet, prevents vessels getting out and in, except at high spring tides; and forms an insurmountable obstacle to Barmouth ever becoming a port of great consequence in the commercial world. In conjunction with this, another obstacle presents itself; a long range of sand and gravel runs out in this part of the bay of Cardigan for more than twenty miles, called *Sarn Bardrig*, or the Ship-breaking Causeway; from the number of vessels that have been wrecked upon its horrible breakers; which mark its course when the tide flows; and at low spring ebb the shoal is dry.

Tradition says, that all this part ofthe sea was once an habitable spot, under the name of Cantiêr Gwalod,[4] or the Lowe Land Hundred; and that in the time of Gwyddno Goronhîr, A. D. 500, it was wholly inundated by the sea.

From the observation of Taliesin, that it was occasioned by those who kept the floodgates, the sea might have been kept out by dykes, like those of Holland.

A similar event happened a few years ago to the Low Marshes near Liverpool. At Abergeleu

---

4   Wher now the wilde Se is, at the mouth of Deuy and further into the Se, were ons 2 commotes of good, plentiful, but low grounde, caullid Cantre Gwaylode: *i.e. terra demissa, vel subsidens planitie; now cleene eatin away. Vid. Lel. Iter*, Vol. V. p. 45.

an inundation of this sort is recorded by the natives: and there are evident proofs of greater part of the bay of Swansea in Glamorganshire, having been once a forest. I have frequently, at low water, seen more than a mile out, the roots of large oaks; some of them in the state of perfect peat, and others still exhibiting the marks of fibrous texture.

These and many more facts, which might be adduced, are demonstrative proofs, that many of the present friths and bays were once part of the land; and that the ocean for centuries has been making encroachments upon the western and southern coasts of the kingdom.

In spite of all these obstacles, however, the spirit and industry of the inhabitants contrived, prior to the war, to carry on a considerable trade in the coasting line, and to Portugal and Ireland; which gave a degree of life to this little port. But war, baleful war! has cast a paralysing damp upon the industry of the inhabitants, and almost extinguished the spirit of adventure.

To the man, whose eye has been used to sparkle, and his heart to glow at the sight of Commerce spreading her sails to the propitious gale, it could not but be a subject of regret, to see numerous vessels lying heeled upon their sides, or moored in the mud, their sails laid up; and their owners out of employment, or earning a scanty pittance for their families, by the precarious profits of an uncertain fishery.

This coast and the adjacent country furnishes a variety of objects to the naturalist: of birds here are Geese, Gulls, black and white Sea Crows, Penguins, Puffins, Ring Owzles, Cormorants, Wheat Ears, and many smaller birds.

On the sands we added to our collection of plants, GLAUX MARITIMA, ANTIRRHINUM ORONTIUM, EUPHORBIA PELIS, CINERARIA PALUSTRIS, ARENARIA MARITIMA, A. PEPLOIDES, and A. RUBRA VAR. ß; the CHEIRANTHUS SINUATUS perfumed the air with its delicate odour. On the rocks, PLANTAGO MARITIMA, CRITHMUM MARITIMUM, SALICORNIA ERITH MOIDES, and a single rock near the harbour was almost purpled over with flowers of the ARMERIA STATICE.

But you will want to learn something of the inhabitants. I will introduce some to your notice, from "The plain and simple annals of the poor:" and while the rich and gay are feasting upon delicious kid, and drinking seasoned port; dipping in the salubrious wave, or climbing the steep ascent for appetite, you will not refuse to hear of the secluded peasant; shut from the common eye of observation, eating his scanty meal, and struggling with disease in the habitation of penury.

In one of my morning walks I took up a little bye path, rendered less inviting by the stench of an adjoining pigs' cote. The weather was hot, and I had not yet dined. Had it not therefore been for an obastinate and headstrong curiosity, that leads me to investigate and see if possible the end of every thing, and to study nature in her reclusest haunts, I should have made this an excuse for not proceed ing farther. The cry of an infant at no great distance attracted my attention and hastened my steps. As I farther ascended the hill, a hut, little better than the cote I had left, forbade my approach. At the entrance, for door there was none, stood a tall female figure, which from her tattered dress and sallow countenance, you would scarcely have supposed to have been human; with a distorted figure at her breast. I spoke, but she, not understanding my language, and little supposing I would enter such a dwelling, still kept her post. I then took the child by the hand and pointed for admittance. The hut consisted of one room upon the ground floor; divided by a partition of lath and reeds. The floor was the *native soil*, rendered very hard and uneven from long and unequal pressure. At the farther end was a fire of turf, laid upon a few stones; near which stood a three-legged stool, a small cast iron pot, some branches of broom tied up for a besom, and a few bundles of rushes thrown down for a bed. These constituted the principal furniture! At the other end was a lank meagre figure sitting in a loom, weaving coarse linen; the father of the family.

At this employment, after fourteen hours' toil, he could earn eight-pence. But a chronic illness,, occasioned by low debilitating diet, prevented his following it so close as constantly to earn this.

A similar cause prevented the wife from properly looking after four sickly children. The eldest was stinted in its growth; the second lame; the third blind; and the youngest, though two years old, still at the breast, and wasting away with the tabes dorsalis.

Entering farther into their history, I learnt that the linen trade had been much better and provisions cheaper; when they might, if Fortune had smiled, have done something: but owing to a very severe illness, in consequence of a bad lying in, the wife had been incapacitated for taking an active part in the business, as she used to do; and consequently they were unable to put any thing by for a day of adversity. The same cause precluded them the benefit of medical advice. Even when a transient appetite returned, they were destitute of the means to procure more than a coarse and scanty morsel, hardly sufficient to satisfy the immediate cravings of hunger. The world had no value in their estimation; their hearts were grown callous to its concerns. In such a truly deplorable state, life itself appeared to have no charms; and death was looked upon as a welcome messenger that would bring them consolation. They talked of it with chearfulness, and seemed reanimated when I mentioned that state of retribution, where the sincere, though humble, Christian, Shall have all tears wiped away; and sorrow and sighing should flee away.

It is in scenes like these, my friend, that the precious, though neglected jewel, *Religion*, rises in our estimation—it is here its power is seen, and its efficacy demonstrated. This last resource of misery appears in all its unrivalled charms; opens to the despairing mind new paths of consolation and delight; changes the parched desart into refreshing springs, and the barren wilderness into a blooming Paradise. But for this the condition of these people would have been intolerable: their case would have been a case of desperation.

You will readily suppose I could not hear this distressing history without manifesting symptoms that my feelings were interested. My hand had involuntarily slid into my pocket; and I was about to offer a mite of charity before I had scarcely heard the tale to excite it. A thousand ideas you would have read in my countenance at this time: one moment I felt sympathy for the objects around me—regret for not feeling more; and that I had not more ability to relieve their varied distresses: then indignation at my species, to think that they could spend months and months in plenty, if not in luxury, without attempting to rescue their fellow-creatures from such complicated misery.

Ah! little think the gay licentious proud,
Whom pleasure, power, and affluence surround;
They, who their thoughtless hours in giddy mirth,
And wanton, often cruel, riot waste;

Ah! little think they, while they dance along,
How many feel, this very moment, death
And all the sad variety of pain!
———————How many drink the cup
Of baleful grief, or eat the bitter bread
Of misery.—Sore pierc'd by wint'ry winds,
How many sink into the sordid hut
Of cheerless poverty.

Thomson.

Unable longer to witness distress which I could not effectually relieve, I blessed them with a feeble accent; promised I would see them again, and on returning to my inn, found I had beguiled the hour of dinner. I congratulated myself, however, that though unable effectually to relieve them, I had given them some comfort; and that a disposition of benevolence had again been excited, which tends to soften and ameliorate the heart; while it awakened sensations of gratitude for the numerous and undeserved blessings with which Providence had made my cup to overflow.

It is a doctrine of your own, that a proper comparison of ourselves with others, is generally productive of beneficial effects. It tends to give us just ideas of our relative situations—of the necessary divisions, and consequent distinction of rank in society, calculated for due subordination and order: and the varied duties arising from them, essential to its existence and welfare: it removes the veil, which pride is too apt to cast over our true nature and real condition; and leads us back to that orderly state of reverence and submission, so justly becoming such frail and dependant creatures: induces us to acknowledge ourselves dependant upon that August Power from whom we derive our being; and that all we possess and all we see, is the free and unmerited gift of *Him*, from whom man receives life and breath, and all things. To his undeserved bounty it is I owe my superiority to the poor weaver at Barmouth; and the recollection of his wretched case, while I feel the blessing of contrast, compels me to confess it.

These sentiments, conformable to those virtues, which form a striking feature in your character, cannot fail to afford you satisfaction: and feeling a disposition to admire the example, I strongly wish for the power of imitation.

——————————dextræ se parvus Iulus
Implicuit, sequiterque patrem, non passibus Æquis.

Your's,

J. E.

Letter VI

We directed our course towards Harlech. The road lies along the flat undulating shore of the Bay of Cardigan. On our right was the western termination of the Upper Merionethshire Chain, ending in abrupt crags and rude precipices, down to the strand. On our left, the ocean foaming with maddened rage over the irregular sands, and against the rocky shores of the Peninsula of Penmorfa, that lay stretched before us, forming the northern Horn of the Bay of Cardigan. Here the road strikes off from the shore, and the space exhibits a few small inclosed farms in a tolerable state of cultivation. We ascended from the coast to visit the environs of Corsy Gedol, the ancient seat of the Vaughans. There is nothing worth notice about the mansion; the woods are noble, and abound with large timber, but so affected by the West winds from the ocean, as to wear the appearance of being shorn at top, like the famous wood of Margam, in Glamorganshire, the property of Mr. Talbot.

The vicinity of Corsy Gedol abounds in British antiquities; and to the antiquary affords ample room for speculatiou and conjecture.

Craig y Dinas is a conical hill, whose summit is surrounded with a vast heap of rough stones, used as ramparts, and supposed to have been a British post during the invasion of the Romans. It has an oblique entrance with stone facings, and near it are two other ramparts of stone; the whole is upon the steep extremity of a mountain, adjoining a narrow pass into the interior of the country. Northwest of this, on the top of another hill, is *Castell dinas Cortin*, entrenched round with an advanced work in front; at a small distance in the plain, between these posts, are a variety of druidical remains; cromlechs,[1] carnedds, stone circles, maenhirion, and kist vaen. The

---

1   The cromlechs here differ from those of Anglesea, and other parts, bylying near the ground, and in an horizontal position; one, called Brym y boel, is surrounded by a circle of small stones, and is of an extraordinary size.

above fortifications were supposed to have been raised for the protection of these sacred monuments of British superstition . Near are the small lakes of Llyn Bodlyn, and Llyn Irddim; the former famous for its Char, and the latter for a species of trout, with a long toad-shaped head, mentioned by Gyraldus.

Declining the arduous pass of Bwlch drws Ardudwy, we returned into the road, and soon reached HARLECH. We were surprised to find the *county town of Merioneth* a few miserable cottages on the top of a bare rock. From its situation the name is derived. It was originally styled *Twr Bronwen*, and afterwards Caer Kolhwyn, from Kolhwyn ap Tagno, who resided there in the time of Prince Anarawyd, A. D. 877. However probable this derivation, from Roman coins being dug up, and a golden torques, mentioned by Camden, as well as their usual mode of prefixing *Caer* to a station they fortified, there is reason to suppose it of much higher antiquity.[2] By whom the castle was originally founded, it is not easy to learn; Powel thinks probably by Bronwan, sister to Bronwan Llyr, King of Britain. History records

---

2   Edward the First erected it into a free borough, and conferred upon it grants of land, and other privileges; yet in its present state it is the most wretched looking place I ever saw. Though it is the county town, there is no vestige of a public building, unless four roofless walls, like a barn, that has undergone the ordeal of fire, can be termed one. This however is the county guild, and here, at the last election, Sir Robert Vaughan was chaired as Knight of the Shire.

one built here by Mael Gwyn, Prince of North Wales, A. D. 552, (*Vid. J. Rossi. Antiq. Warw. Langhorne.*) A. D. 877, it was in a very respectable condition; (*Vid. Row. Mona Antiqua*;) so that the present fortress, said to be built by Edward the First, was probably no more than the former building repaired, and put in a better state of defence; and indeed this is evident from the ancient walls and remains upon which the building stands; and it is even probable, as this differs greatly from the other castles of this Monarch, that the original plan was preserved. It is a noble square edifice, the shell of which is very entire, furnished with four heavy round towers, one at each corner, with turrets issuing from each. The gateway is formed by two large circular bastions, and was defended by three port-cullises, beside the gate. It was completed A. D. 1283, as appears by the salary granted to Hugh de Blakiston, as chief constable, of 100*l.* per annum .

A garrison of twenty soldiers was allowed, with 140*l.* per annum, for the maintenance of them and their Captain. The present constable, or governor, is Sir Robert Vaughan, of Nanneu, with an appoint ment of 50*l.* per annum. The scite was admirably adapted for defence; built upon an elevated rock, just above high water mark, the face of which forms an angle with the horizon, of about 39 degrees, and washed by the sea, on the North and West, it was so far impregnable; and on the other it was defended by a prodigious foss, cut with great labour out of the solid rock on which it stands; through which flows a cascade, that gives an additional effect to this bold scenery.

This, like other fortresses, has witnessed many tempestuous scenes, and been frequently subject to a variety of masters. During the civil wars, between the Houses of York and Lancaster, Dafydd ap Jenkin ap Einion, a British nobleman siding with the House of Lancaster, defended his castle nobly against Edward the Fourth, till William Herbert, Earl of Pembroke, forcing his way through the Alps of Snowdon, (a passage deemed impracticable,)[3] at length invested a place before considered as impregnable. Pembroke committed the siege to his brother Sir Richard, who sent a menacing summons to the British Commandant. Dafydd returned an answer becoming a man of such distinguished merit: "He had kept a castle so long in France, that he had made all the old women in France talk of him and he was determined to keep this so long, that all the old women in England should talk of him." He was however obliged by famine to surrender: but upon terms as honourable, as his defence was obstinate. Richard stipulated to save his life, by

---

3   The difficulties he and his men encountered were incredible; sometimes up the steep acclivities obliged to go upon all fours, and in their descent to throw themselves down from craig to craig; the road to this day retains the name of *Le Herbert.*

interceding with the King; but Edward indignantly refused when Pembroke stepping up, told him plainly, that he might take his life instead of the brave commander's, or he would assuredly replace Dafydd in his Castle, and his Majesty might send whom he pleased to take him out again. (*Vid. Life of Lord Herbert.*)

A. D. 1460, Margaret of Anjou here found a secure asylum; and hence was enabled to take vengeance on the Duke of York, at Wakefield. During the civil wars of Charles, it more than once changed masters. It was well defended by Major Hugh Pennant, till basely deserted by his cowardly men. While Owen was Governor, it finally surrendered to General Mytton, A. D. 1647; its garrison, consisting of twenty-eight men, obtained favourable terms; and this Castle had the honour of being the last in North Wales, that Loyalty held for the rightful Sovereign. Near the Castle grows the JUNCUS ACUTUS, BRASSICA OLERACEA, and within, CIRCEA LUTETIANA.[4]Near this place is a curious antique monument, called *Cœton Arthur*. It is a large flat stone, lying horizontally, supported by three others; the incumbent stone is nearly of an oval shape, about eleven feet in length, of unequal breadth from five to eight feet, and in some places two feet thick;

---

4   This plant called Enchanters Night Shade, was, in ages of ignorance, celebrated in the mysteries of witchcraft, and for raising the Devil, that *chef d'œuvre* of Necromancy, whence its English neme.

the three supporters (originally perhaps four) are about twenty inches square. The two at the thickest end eight feet high; the fourth may probably have sunk into the ground, so that the upper stone lics in an inclined position, like the roof of a barn. Several stones of this kind are found in Anglesea, and other parts of Wales.

We inquired into a very extraordinary phenomenon related by Camden, said to have happened here, A.D. 1624. It is still strong in the traditional recollection of the people. It was a mephitic vapour that rose from the sea, commencing from the shore of Morfa Vychan, near Criceith. It extended itself in every direction for several miles, carrying devastation and dismay wherever it came. It set fire to numerous hay ricks, appeared like a blue lambent flame, but did not injure persons exposed to it. It so infected the herbage in many places, that numbers of the cattle died, and the mischief attendant upon it constantly happened in the night: it continued its depredations for eight months. It was observed in stormy, as well as calm nights; in all weathers; and any great noise, as the sounding of horns, or the firing of guns, would disperse and extinguish the flame. (*Vid. Philosoph. Transactions.*)

It has been seriously thought, that eclipses of the sun in Aries have been fatal to this neighbourhood; (for in the years 1542 and 1567, it suffered exceedingly by fire, and after the latter eclipse the fire spread so far, that 200 houses of the suburbs of Caernarvon were also consumed.) To those who believe that the motions and conjunctions of the planets are intimately connected with human affairs, and the efficient causes of human events, this information must prove a valuable *morceau*. But the philosopher will look for the cause of such a wonderful phenomenon as the vapour already mentioned, in some source more upon a level with common understandings.

It was conjectured, at the time, that it might be occasioned by a quantity of locusts, drowned in the sea, and cast on the shore; and instances of their appearance and death, causing pestilential vapours in many places, have been adduced, particularly on the coast of France, 1374, attended with a dreadful mortality of men and cattle.[5]

Without calling in question this account, or doubting the property of creatures, while living, mentioned by Pliny, L. xi. c. 29, "*Multa contactu adurunt;*" from the infrequency of these visitants it is more probable, that it proceeded from large shoals of herrings, driven by whales on the

---

5   Mouffet gives an account of a plague in Lombardy, about the year 591, which arose from the fall of a cloud of locusts, that corrupted the air to such a degree, that upwards of 80,000 men and cattle died; and Otho Frisingensis mentions a pestilence in France, A. D. 1374, occasioned by locusts drowned in the Channel, and cast upon the coasts. *Vid. Theatre des Insects.*

I have known great quantities of common cock-chafers thrown upon the coast of Somersetshire, near Burnham, emitting such a putrid effluvia, as to render it very dissagreeable to walk upon the beach for several days together.

strand, and there permitted to putrify. An event of this kind, often puts on a serious aspect on the coasts of the Isle of Man and Scotland, and is not unfrequently followed by deleterious effects.

Animal bodies, in a state of decomposition, emit lage quantities of hydrogynous gas; this is pernicious to animal life, and mixed with a small quantity of oxygen, becomes highly inflammable: and when it meets with electric matter, with which the atmosphere abounds, will instantly explode. A continuance of the cause would for the time produce a continuance of the effect. The period of the duration was probably much shorter than stated by the people. It is in the nature of fear, for consternation to remain long after the objects of it are removed.

It was now near evening, and prudence invited us to make this cheerless spot our residence for the night; but the inn offered no bed, nor any thing better than a dirt floor, strewed with a few rushes. The chilling idea determined us to proceed to encounter difficulties, which could we have foreseen, would have thrown an air of comfort over these unusally miserable accommodations. It was our intention to have passed the Traeth Mawr, but the sands have of late become so shifting, as to make it highly dangerous to attempt the passage when the tide is out, so we altered our course for Tany Bwlch. A circumstance in this interval occurred fortunate for us, and which, as it may be useful to future visitors to Harlech, it may be proper to mention. While inquiring for a guide, we observed a decent looking man at a cottage door, directly opposite. From his physiognomy, and his eyes being fixed upon us, I was induced to address him: he ingenuously owned the guide was absent, but as he understood every inch of ground, he would, if we pleased, conduct us safe to our destination. An air of frankness visible in his countenance, and a fluency in speaking English, (very unusal here) prejudiced us in his favour, and we instantly closed with his proposal: and to his credit, let it be recorded, we found in him a faithful and intelligent guide; and had not to regret, as some have done before us, that after employing a guide, they were obliged to give him information of the way.

To you, my Friend, fond of a retired life, and whom I have often heard express more satisfaction at the detail of actions performed in humble life, than the proud memorials of more exalted characters, as coming more within the reach, and appealing more forcibly to the bosom of mankind, a simple biographical sketch of this very civil and attentive guide, will not appear unworthy of your notice.

John Richards, was the son of industrious parents, natives of this place; his father had acquired a little property in the exercise of the united trades of skinner, brecches-maker, and glover. In the exercise of these trades our guide was brought up, and in this line he continued a few years, till business declining, hard necessity and the cravings of a numerous family, obliged him to turn his attention to something else. Nothing more natural than the wool trade, as he must have acquired some information, in a smaller way, in the sale of refuse wool from the skin yard. His father-in-law dying about this time, gave life and spirit to his scheme, by a bequest of a few hundred pounds. He formed connections in London, purchased a good deal by commission, and as far as his little capital would command, on his own account. A trade wherein judgment was a principal point, (of which Richards possessed a considerable share in which many who had the article. to dispose of were deficient,) and in the vicinity of mountainous pastures covered with millions of sheep, promised a profitable field for speculation. For some time the annual returns were beyond his most sanguine expectations: every day added to his little stock, and every day produced in creasing demands, and opened new sources of acquiring wealth. While providing decently for his family, he was considered as the leading man within the precincts of Harlech. Flushed with his plenteous harvest, and wrapping himself in golden dreams, he hoped soon to purchase an estate near his native spot, and to live in some portion of that independence, of which his ancestors had experienced a very large share, and which his genealogy entitled him to expect. For a few years Richards was the envy of the neighbourhood.

He had discovered a way of realizing money unknown before to this unlettered spot: but, from the transient nature of riches themselves, as well as the precatious tenure by which all earthly possessions are held, it is seldom a very distant period before Envy is gratified, by being deprived of the object of its malevolence.[6] Richards to a sound understanding, and an accurate judgment in the trade, had neglected to add the *sine qua non* in business, a knowledge of the world. Far less was he in possession of the arts and finesse, the general concomitants of trade in the present day; and destitute of which, a man stands upon disadvantageous ground with his neighbours. Honest himself, he had no idea that others were devoid of the principle; or if such a surmise arose, a noble indignation spurned it from his bosom. Induced by a desire of arriving sooner at the acme of his wishes, he changed his connections in town for others that appeared more advantageous, from their making larger allowances in the trade. For some time the remittances were regular; but at length, after very extensive orders, which Richards strained every nerve of credit he possessed to fulfil, he was informed by the Firm, that the failure of a large house on the Continent had occasioned a little embarrassment

---

6   "How soon can Fortune shift the scene,
     "And all our earthly bliss destroy:
     "Care hovers round, and Grief's fell train
     "Still treads upon the heels of joy."

in their affairs, which a short time would effectually relieve them from; begging him not to be
alarmed at any little temporary inconvenience
the delay of payment might produce. Richards,
unacquainted with this finesse, which is the usual cloak made use of by a set of harpies, who prey
upon the vitals of the honest and industrious
trades man, sate down with patient submission,
till his creditors became clamorous and importunate. Pressing for a decisive answer, he was informed the house had stopped, and that as soon
as matters were properly arranged, he would be
entitled to a dividend with the rest of the creditors! This was a death-blow to Richards's sanguine hopes of independence. In a moment all
his fairy scenes were vanished, and what was still
worse, the only prospect before him was a dreary
habitation in a gaol for life, without any other
support but the starving pittance, called debt-
ors' allowance. The stroke had like to have been
too much for him; but the din of so many needy
farmers, accusing him of having defrauded them,
roused him from the depression. He laid before
them his correspondence and concerns; and for
the credit of that generous and humane spirit,
which pervades the people of North Wales, let it
be told, that instead of having him hurried away
from his family to a prison, they entered into his
interest, and finding that his case was unfortunate, and not arising from any dishonesty on his
part, but the knavery of others, they unanimous-

ly forgave their respective debts, permitted him to keep his little furniture, and stock of leather, (for he still *gloved* a little,) and promised to deal with him for the support of his wife and family.

In this state we found him; as before observed, the trade had been long on the decline, and was almost dwindled to nothing. Formerly a number of hands were employed in this, and other towns of North Wales, in the manufacturing of strong tan leather gloves, sent to England; but of late years, the English glovers have bought up all the skins, and from a superior art in dressing them, are able to send a much neater article, at a lower price, into Wales. Richards was therefore reduced to the precarious emolument arising from the few journies he took in the summer months as mountain guide, and the low profits upon a few strong country gloves, made during winter, to support a sick wife and five children.

A short time before our acquaintance, he became candidate for the place of Deputy Captain of the Castle, which, had he obtained, might have produced him about 20*l*. per annum. But having neither skill nor influence in the trade of election, his petition lay unopened, upon the table. And were it not for his very superior knowledge as a guide to that of the present Deputy, he would be precluded from the advantage accruing from this laborious employment.

I need not tell the friend of my younger years, that I felt deeply interested for this unfortunate

man, and considered myself absolutely bound
to do some thing to alleviate the hardships of his
condition. I observed that in England a person
of his abilities and information might obtain a
decent livelihood. I proposed several schemes
to him, in which I promised to assist him; and
which, for their eligibility, perfectly met his
approbation. But a most unfortunate and insurmountable barrier was placed in the way
of his advancement. Richards's wife had never breathed in any other place, and partly from
prejudice, and partly from the strength of habit,
she was possessed of an invincible "*Soli nata-
lis amor*:" so much so, that a spare meal once a
day, and a bed of rushes, appeared preferable in
sight of the castle, to plenty and comfort out of
it. Richards had an affection for his wife, and as
the money he had lost in the wool trade chiefly
came by her, he had accustomed himself to humour her caprice, and submit to her requests,
more than was consistent with a spirit of prompt
and determined resolution, necessary for emigration and adventure. She fancied, if removed
from this beloved spot, she should instantly die;
and poor Richards, however reluctantly, gave up
to her weakness. "Thus (to use his own words)
am I chained down to this wretched spot, without the least opportunity of bettering my condition, or the most distant hope of deliverance
from this forlorn state; but what is suggested by
the prospect of the death of one I sincerely love;

while my children, destitute of employment, are growing up under my roof in want and idleness. And I have little else to do but to behold, without the power of remedying it, and to brood over the probable consequent evils." This brief sketch, drawn up from his own artless tale, will, I trust, induce the future visitor of Harlech to inquire for this able and honest guide; and finding him essentially useful, as we have done, bestow a small mite to cheer the gloom of his unhappy lot.

With Richards in our van, we engaged in the arduous undertaking of reaching Tany Bwlch that night. We ascended a difficult stair-case path, up the steep side of a craggy mountain, and took a North-easterly direction over the trackless plain, known to our guide by several upright stones, called Maen hirion, and concentric circles of stones, many of them pebbles, said to have been formed for religious purposes in the ages of Druidism. A tumulus and Carnedd, larger than the rest, is distinguished by the title of *King Ingo's Tomb*. But as no name of that kind is found in History, except within the period when the Principality was christian, it is improbable his remains should be pointed out by an emblem of Heathen superstition. As the place is called Bontleff Hir, or the loud Shout to Battle, it was probably the scene of some bloody contest, and a Pagan chieftain who fell in the conflict, might have been here interred. One conjecture I will hazard, from the appearance of these and other similar

works, that though some of the Cromlechs, &c.
may have been remnants of druidical altars, and
some of the Carnedds, &c. monuments of the
mighty fallen in battle, yet it is more than probable that the greater number of them have been
the work of shepherds, as an amusement to fill
up their leisure hours while tending their flocks,
or to clear the pasture for the sake of grass.[7] As
this conjecture will probably bring down the ire
of the whole Camdensian School upon my head,
I will shield myself under an observation of the
author, (*Mr. Windham,*) of *A Gentleman's Tour
through Monmouthshire and Wales.*

> I suspect that many of, our Druid antiquar-
> ies are by far too sanguine in their favourite
> pursuit, and that they attribute to religious
> uses, what was originally intended only for
> private advantage. A profusion of learning
> has been expended upon the Carnedds of
> Wales, when I am convinced that many of
> those heaps of stones were put together for
> no other reason than that the rest of the field
> might afford a clearer pasture.
>
> In the melancholy waste between Pont Aber
> Glasllyn and Llynywenwn, I observed many
> modern carnedds, which had been thrown
> up in large piles by the industrious inhabit-
> ants, for that profitable purpose. I pass no
> reflection on the single monuments, or on
> the circular upright stones, which abound in

---

7   It is a general custom in Merioneth and Carnarvon, to make
     walls for no other purpose but to clear the ground from the
     large stones, that every where hinder the use of the plough.

most parts of this country. These may, perhaps, deserve notice, but a stranger would
scarcely make them the principal object of his
Tour; as they will not bear a comparison with
Stone Henge or Aberz, either in magnitude of
stones, or regularity of design.

P. 142.

We passed the small lake named Llyn Tegwyn
isa, near which is the small village and church of
Llan Tegwyn: a little farther, environed with lofty
mountains, is the fine lake of Llyn Tegwyn ucha;
which, from the transparency of its waters, as
well as the diversity of the surrounding scenery,
merits its name of *Fair and Lovely*. The moon
was now rising, and her silver beams, reflected
from the waters of the lake, heightened the beauty of this recluse but enchanting scene. The road
is a narrow and dangerous path along the shelf of
a perpendicular rock, on the left side of the lake,
which is composed of shale or shivering slate,
and many impending projections over-hang the
traveller's head, and threaten him with destruction. We appeared shut in by the mountain barrier, with nothing but craggy walls of rock on each
side, and before us the dismal gloom of an im-
penetrable forest, which the pale beams of Cyn-
thia represented in all the grotesque shapes, calculated to increase the appearance of horror, and
fill the imagination with ideas of terror. Every
moment we appeared to be precipitating into the
lake, by the deception of nocturnal vision; while

the frequent cautions of our guide, who himself was not destitute of fear, served to strengthen our apprehensions of danger. We descended into a deep glen or ravine, so thick with forest trees and under wood, as scarcely to admit a ray of light, though the night was clear, and the moon at full. We passed over a black and dismal stream, called *Velyn Rhyd*, or the yellow Ford, and soon got into the turnpike road, near the village of Maen Twrwg; crossing a bridge of three arches over the Dwyryd, our guide, with accents of joy, pronounced *the inn of Tany Bwlch!* It was now about two hours past midnight, and the people had been long retired to sleep; but the landlord, when he had heard our story, with great alacrity arose, and furnished every comfort the house afforded. Time had made changes here: the lady who kept this inn a short time ago, so celebrated for her attention to travellers, was dead; yet it is but justice to say, that we found the accommodations equally good, and *Cartwright* not behind his predecessor in point of attention and civility. This inn has been recently fitted up, in a peculiar style of neatness, by Mr. Oakly, and forming the central house between the plain and mountainous country, is a great accommodation to travellers. The village of Maentwrog, with its whitewashed cottages, is truly picturesque. It takes its name from a large upright stone, called the Stone of St. Twrog, standing in the centre of the vale. The hills are moderately high, and thrown about in pleasing variety; the sides in general are well wooded, especially to the North, being defended from the violence of the West winds. In one of these native hanging groves, stands Tany Bwlch Hall, the elegant seat of Mr. Oakly; who, at a great expence, has taken advantage ofthe munificence of nature, by cutting walks and vistas through the woods for a considerable extent. The house just peeps through the trees, and the majestic oak, and spreading beech, wave their branches in the wind over the sylvan mansion; while the meandering river widening into the estuary, called the Traeth Vychan, or Little Tide, in opposition to the Traeth Mawr, into which it opens to the South, gives a view of the ocean, and the peninsula forms a pleasing termination to the view.

This gentleman unites the refinement of English manners, with the hospitality of the country in which he has fixed his residence. Instead of being a dead weight upon society, and a drawback upon the exertions of less opulent neighbours, his spirit is a blessing to all around him. He invents methods of improvement, and sets the example. A long tract of marshy soil, rendered useless by the overflowing of the tide, Mr. Oakly has regained from the sea,[8] by an ingen-

---

8   This design, now in part executed, was conceived by Sir John Wynne, of Gwedir, in the year 1625. He consulted his illustrious countryman, Sir Hugh Middleton, the great projector of the new river; but the scheme was never carried into execution, owing to want of money and encouragement for so vast an undertaking at that period.

ious method of embankment. The banks are ornamented with white rails, and form pleasing
walks to visit these *regenerated meadows.* By
means of the grand discovery in agriculture,
Underdraining, this land before useless, is become worth 3*l.* per acre per annum. The Traeth
abounds with NYMPHEA ALBA, and in the tide
ditches the rare and extraordinary plant, the
RUPPIA MARITIMA, displays its truly wonderful
properties. This blossomless plant consists of
several linear hair-like leaves, proceeding from
a tuberous root, formed below in the mud, with
little umbels of oval seeds pendant upon single
foot-stalks, which distinguish it from the POTO-
MOGETON, to which in its habit it is closely allied.
These foot-stalks consist of elastic spiral lines,
having the power of elongating or contracting
themselves; and thus adapting themselves to
the varying heights of the water, for the preservation of their seeds. Swimming, like the little
Nautilus, upon the bosom of the wave, appeared
the CONFERVA VAGABUNDA. This plant, destitute
of a root, is composed of jointed threads, of a
pale green colour, about two inches long, greatly branched and waved in various directions,
the branches being divided and sub-divided into
many capillary segments, appearing like wool.
As this plant swims along upon the ocean, it
may be called an *itinerant* vegetable, and from
being wafted from one shore to another, a *Plant
of Passage.* This, and others of the Order Algæ,

must confound those positive people, who pronounce decisively upon things, and prescribe bounds to nature, making locomotion the test between the animal and vegetable kingdom.

Here are two neighbouring plants, the one endued with the power of depressing or raising itself at pleasure, and the other of moving from place to place. And if these are not sufficient to demonstrate, that plants possess a power of volition, let the doubting naturalist watch the different motions of the HEDYSAURUM GYRANS, and the tacking and veering of the vegetable Mariner, the CONFERVA ÆGAGROPILA. The proximate links which form the grand chain of nature, though of such different shapes and sizes, yet are so similar, as to defy the skill of man to say, where a division should take place. It was long contested, whether Funguses should be arranged in the animal or vegetable department. Their animal smell, when burnt, and taste in cookery, with a tendency to putrefaction, and many of them growing without light, shew they approach towards animals. They certainly form an isthmus between the two great continents of animal and vegetable nature.

Nothing can exceed the beauty of this little vale of Maentwrog; it may, as Mr. Pennant observes, be justly called the *Tempe of Wales*. We pursued the course of the stream by which it is divided. It is a tract about four miles in length, composed of rich meadows, whose sides are edged with thick groves, and barren rugged precipices close the enchanting scene. The little river, which beautifully meanders through it, is named Dwy'ryd, or the two Fords, from the Cynfael and another stream, whose name we could not learn, uniting their waters just above.

The Cynfael tumbles through a deep rocky chasm, covered with large trees, whose collateral branches meet and form a dark shade, and thence by three falls descends foaming into a deep pool, encircled with bold impending rocks. In the midst of the torrent rises a columnar rock, termed Pulpit Hugh Llwyd Cynfael. Hugh lived in the time of James the First, was esteemed a magician of the highest magnitude, and is said invariably from this station to have delivered his incantations.

Near the village of Festiniog, is a portion of a Roman road, Fford or Sarn Helen. It is a high military way, thrown up with stones about eight yards wide, for the convenience of the Roman army across this almost impassable tract. There is every reason to suppose, that there were several roads of this kind, communicating through the whole Principality. A similar one is discoverable at Craig Ferwyn, in Merioneth; at Y Gym Wynas, in Caernarvon; and Llanbeder, in Cardigan; and the road. from Neath to Brecon is distinguished by a similar appellation from which Camden conjectures, it was one of the many public works performed during the reign of Helena, mother of Constantine the Great. *Brit. Vol. II. p.* 791.

Near Rhyd Halen[9] is the celebrated hill of Micknant, on which are the monumental remains of the Men of Ardudwy, called Beddeu gwy Ardudwy. They are almost six feet in length, with a small stone at the head, and another at the feet: they are about. thirty in number, from two to three feet high, and twelve inches broad: there were probably many more. Near them are still remaining a Carnedd and several circles of stones, the largest fifty feet in diameter. A circular wall of stones once encompassed the whole, which is no longer complete; the stones having been carried away for the purposes of building. That these are monumental remains of men slain in battle, at a very early period, there is no room to doubt; but on what occasion it is not easy to develope: Tradition attributes their cause to a battle fought between the Men of Dyffryn Ardwdwy, and the Men of Denbighshire, on an affair of gallantry. The former wishing to increase the population of their country, as a means of becoming better able in future to cope with their more powerful neighbours, made a speculative inroad into Dyffryn Clwyd; and laying hands upon a number of the beautiful damsels, for which the vale was famed, proceeded with their fair booty towards their own country; and had arrived thus far in safety. Here the ravishers were overtaken by the Men of Denbigh; when a desperate conflict ensued, in which most of the Men of Ardwdwy were slain; and the

---

9   Here grows Lefidium petræum and Cardamine petræa.

prey rescued out of their hands. The story adds, that the ravishers had so far won the hearts of the fair, that, on their defeat, they refused the offered protection, and rather than return home, unanimously rushed into an adjoining lake, thence denominated Llyn y Morwynion. I need not observe, that in this story, you will readily recognise *the Rape of the Sabines*.

Yours, &c.

J. E.

Letter VII

Caernarvon

Dear Sir,

eaving the fairy vale, we had eight miles of the worst road in the Principality[1] to encounter; from Tany bwlch almost to Bedd Kelert. It is the only communication between the wild mountains of Merioneth, and the alpine

---

[1] A subscription was now going forward for making a new road round the foot of the mountain, which, though longer, will be a great accommodation to the traveller: and a letter from a friend informs me that a number of hands are already employed in the work; and that it is likely to be completed the ensuing summer.

heights of Caernarvon: *Ergo nil desperandum sed omnia tentanda.*[2] Accompanied by our intelligent guide, and having given the horses a day's rest, we ascended the steep hill that overlooks Mr. Oakly's house.

Mountain now rose above mountain to the clouds; so that the difficulties we had past seemed lost in comparison with the unwelcome prospect. The retrospect was highly pleasing: the opposite verdant hills and luxuriant woods; the church and comfortable village of Maentwrog, the diminishing vale, with its fertile meads and winding stream, formed a striking contrast to the rude and terrific scenes before us.

The mountains, almost bare, consist of huge projecting rocks; fragments lying in undigested heaps, with crumbling strata; and the whole surface destitute of any thing like vegetation, save the LICHEN CALCAREUM,[3] here and there changing the colour of the rock, exhibited the wildest confusion. Perhaps nothing can exceed the dreary aspect and awful desolation of the first five miles of this road. No vestige of a dwelling; no mark of human foot step, nor the least trace of its being

---

2   Latin: 'Therefore there is nothing to despair of, but everything to be attempted.' —Ed.

3   This plant is the first that vegetates on naked rocks; covering them with a kind of tapestry: drawing its nourishment principally from the air. After it perishes, sufficient earth is left for different mosses to take root; and thus in the course of time soil enough is produced for the support of more succulent vegetables.

inhabited. It appeared like a country shaken by internal convulsions, from which vegetable, as well as animated nature, had affrighted fled. It seemed matter incapable of form or usefulness; left in its elemental state; dismissed by nature from her care, and disinherited of her favours: and forcibly reminded us of Burnet's observation on Caernarvonshire, "That it was the fragment of a demolished world."

Ascending for a mile, we attained a mountainous plain, with a scanty sprinkling of half-starved sheep, almost equally barren and rude in its appearance. The country here afforded very little variety; what was not naked rock, was covered with heath and ling, giving shelter to the black and red grouse; with now and then a stream gushing from the fissured rock. Justly is it observed, the eye accustomed to view the fertile parts of nature, to roam over golden harvests and flowery pastures, must be astonished and repelled at this extensive tract of hopeless sterility.

Ascending still higher, we gained the summit of Moel Wyn yr Hŷdd; leaving the more lofty one of Moel wyn Gwyn on our right. Here the lengthened gloom was relieved by the surrounding views; and the eye was diverted by the distant scenery. Before us the dark naked rocks of Snowdon; be hind us its rival Cader; to the West the Dwyryd, opening in the Traeth Mawr to the bay; the Irish Sea, Barmouth, Harlech Castle, and the extensive peninsula of Penmorfa, stretching out to sea visible to its point of Aberdaron.

However difficult we found the acclivities, the trouble of descending the Cwms, into the vales, was still more so. Both ourselves and beasts, sometimes up and sometimes down, were glad of every shelf in the rock as a place of halting. Hitherto we had borne up with tolerable temper, full of the idea, that *Pont aber glas Lyn*, would more than compensate for any temporary inconvenience; but we were now to encounter a scene that beggars all attempts at description, *an alpine storm*.

The morning was lowering, and as we gained the different ascents, the peak of Snowdon, Moel y Wyddfa, capt with clouds, became invisible. The darkness began to gather round, as we proceeded; and we perceived driving clouds passing rapidly beneath our feet, round some of the hills we had just ascended. The sheep were filing down the declivities for shelter, as though apprehensive of danger.

From these appearances our guide prognosticated an approaching storm: we halted and deliberated what was best to be done: but being rather more than halfway towards Bedd Kelert, deliberation only served to remind us of our unpleasant situation. To retread our steps would have been attended with equal inconvenience as proceeding. The country afforded no shelter; no vestige of a hut; nor was it to be expected in a country devoid of vegetation.

The darkness momentarily increased, the misty clouds left their towering heights, and gaining strength by approximating towards the heavier ones beneath, soon became formidable from coalition. The winds became clamorous from the West, and North; and, meeting with currents from the mountain vistas, soon blew an hurricane. All foreboded a dismal issue. The guide forgot his usual gaiety and loquacity, and began to shake and mutter a few inarticulate sounds. Despairing of making our escape, we relaxed in our exertions, and became less quick and firm in our steps: the very beasts shook their heads and snorted, as though sensible of the perilous situation.

A general torpor at length seised the whole party; and visibly panic-struck we patiently waited the as sailing elements; like mariners, who after every effort to save the vessel proves abortive, give up their toil in despair, and patiently look for the coming destruction.

A general gloom, like that, of a total eclipse, pervaded the whole atmosphere: the diversified mountain scenery we had before admired, had entirely vanished. Heaven and earth seemed blended together the crumbling strata and shivering rock beneath our feet, afforded us the only vestiges of the latter; while in the former cloud dashed against cloud in angry conflict. To this war of elements, succeeded the fiercest torrents of rain that the imagination can conceive: to say it *poured*, would be to trifle with language: no words are adequate to a description of the storm. To those who have seen a water-spout at sea, the conception may be easy; but to those who have not, we can only say, that we appeared in the situation of persons placed under one of those mountain cataracts before described, with its waters rushing down upon our heads. To those who never have visited alpine countries, no adequate description can be given; and to those who are familiar with them, this colouring will appear extremely faint.

Impelled by imperious necessity to adopt every method for self-preservation, after being frequently beaten down, we had recourse to crossing arms and joining shoulders; closing like wrestlers for support. This from the violence of the wind, at length failed; and had it not been from a circumstance, otherwise too trifling to mention, it is probable we should have been materially injured, had we escaped with life. A boy, about fifteen, had followed us several miles, to open the gates, in the walls that separate the different lordships, whom we had just before dismissed with a small gratuity. To our surprise he was not gone; but setting up a plaintive cry, he ran towards the south; and instinct induced us to follow. We were not able to keep pace with him, but found him safe lodged behind a vast, rock, which raised its head above the other fragments. On a shelf of this, to the leeward, by an habit he had probably learnt of the sheep, he lay rolled up like a sleeping tortoise. Behind the covert of the same rock, we obtained shelter till the violence of the storm was past. In about an hour we were able to proceed through what, in England, would be called *heavy rain*.[4]

On a boggy plain we found the beautiful OS-MUNDA REGALIS, and the air was highly perfumed with the odoriferous buds of the MYRICA GALE. It is a little extraordinary that this plant, certainly

---

4   It is an observation that has frequently been made by those who have travelled over mountainous countries, that when on the summits they often experienced heavy rains, thick fogs, snows, &c. but, descending into the vallies, they enjoyed a serene and pleasant sky.

It is generally supposed that mountains have a péculiar power of attracting clouds and meteors; this we leave to those skilled in the doctrine of occult causes. The air in vallies, it is well known, is much heavier than flying vapours; and therefore better fit to support the light air that floats on the tops of mountains. When vapours are put into a violent agitation, and partially condensed by winds, or other external causes, they collect into clouds and mists; and by their own specific gravity fall till they meet with such air as is able to support them; with this they mix and swim about, being every way dispersed, and the sky becomes serene and clear: but if they meet not with such air on the tops of hills, then they are condensed into drops, and fall in rain to the ground. *Vid. Varen. Geog. Edit. Sir I. Newton.*

There is another cause of the prodigious condensation of moisture; the dashing of moving clouds against the mountains. In misty days this may be seen in plains; where an eminent tree, by obstructing the mist in its course, will have a much greater quantity of moisture drop from its leaves than falls to the ground at the same time in its vicinity. *Vid.* White's *History of Selborne.*

possessed of powerful qualities, should find no admission into our *Materia Medica*. The poor inhabitants are not in attentive to its virtues; they term it Bwrli, or the emetic plant, and use it for this purpose. An infusion of the leaves as tea, and an external application of them to the abdomen, are considered as a certain and efficacious vermifuge. It is made a substitute for hops in brewing: a decoction is used in the *morbus pedicularis*, and in the vulgar species of herpes. It furnishes a yellow dye for woollen cloth; and by its powerful odour is fatal to moths and bugs.

Linnæus suggests that camphor might be procured from it. The cones boiled in water yield a scum similar to bees-wax, capable of being made into candles, like those made in America from another species, Myrica cerifera.

Descending a gullied road, formed by the action of water, we came on a sudden upon

Pont aber Glas Lyn

The first view, having recently passed so much of the wonderful, was not particularly striking. It presented only a narrow bridge of one arch, thrown over an alpine stream. But entering on the bridge, the surprising scenery began to be developed. The arch is sprung across a deep rocky chasm, through which a rapid river rolls its waters down the steep declivities of the mountains, in angry roar, over huge fragments of rocks, which intercepting and arresting its course, add to its maddened rage and irresistible impetuosity. Just above the bridge, a semicircular ledge of rock lifts itself about fifteen feet above the water; forming a small, but beautiful fall, and an admirable *Salmon Leap.*

In the season,[5] shoals of salmon, crowding from the sea, pass up the river to the shallows; when they come to this obstruction, with an instinctive resolution not to be dismayed, they throw themselves up with surprising agility over the bar into the pool above, which they perform by bending their tails to their mouths, thus making a circular spring.[6] Sometimes, that they may leap with greater force, they seize hold of their tail with their teeth, and by disengaging it with violence, cast themselves up from the water several yards high; to the great amusement of the spectators. Ausonius has recorded this admirable property:

---

5   At the latter end of the year, sometimes as early as the begin ning of October, the salmon begin to press up the rivers as far as they can reach, to deposit their milt and spawn: having effected this, and left it in security on the shallows, they return to the sea or deeper parts of the rivers: consequently we had not the pleasure of seeing them perform these feats of agility.

6   Mr. Pennant contradicts this, as a vulgar error; and says, "those he saw sprung up quite straight, and with a strong tremulous motion." *Brit. Zool.* Vol. III. p. 287.

It is possible, as many of them make several attempts, that when one mode fails, they instinctively adopt the other.

Necte puniceo rutilantem viscere, salmo,
Transierim, latæ cujus vaga verbera caudæ
Gurgite de medio summas referuntur in undas,
Occultus placido cum proditur æquore pulsus.
MOSELLA.

Near is a salmon fishery, and the quantities taken formerly must have been much greater than at present; as it was once honoured with regal observation. In the time of Henry IV. this was deemed a *royal wear*, and rented of the crown by Robert ap Meredydd. It probably was in royal favour prior to that period; for the salmon was in high esteem among the Welch, was considered as game, and the only species, Mr. Pennant observes, that was protected by law.

The salmon are taken by strong cord nets; and many by spearing; at which, as I have before hinted, the Welch are very expert: this may be a less refined, but it is certainly a more noble mode of capture, than that of alluring them by some fascinating bait to the fatal, though concealed hook. The former is like the manly blow of an open enemy; the latter the insidious thrust of the treacherous assassin.

This celebrated bridge, thrown across the united torrents of the Colwyn and Glas Lyn, connects two craggy precipices, one in Caernarvonshire and the other in Merioneth, by a semicircular arch of stone, the span of which is thirty feet, the crown about fifty feet above the water level.

Passing the bridge the scenery is the most magnificent that can be imagined; the eye becomes fixed, and the mind wrapt in emotions of silent wonder. Below the bridge the torrent still flows over ledges of rock towards the sea; encompassed with sloping rocks, diversified by a few forest trees and brush wood on the margin of the waters. Above, the perpendicular dark cliffs rise one beyond the other, as far as the eye can reach, ascending in the greatest irregularity a thousand feet high; and their summits terminating in the most grotesque and fanciful shapes with dark excavations, and lateral fissures, whence issue tributary torrents that roar in distant murmurs, to the very bowels of the mountains; the opposite projecting crags threaten to overwhelm the road; which is a narrow shelf cut out of the solid rock at a considerable expence. In a word, every thing contributes in a high degree to render this a scene of sublimity, arising from the combination of gloom and grandeur. The mountains exhibit on both sides similar strata; they run in a serpentine form nearly parallel, and so close as barely to leave room for the waters, that descend from the lakes, to pass between them. Above the bridge there is scarcely a symptom of vegetation, save a few solitary yews; and here and there a tuft of grass, sufficient to tempt the famished goat to its destruction. The poor animal will sometimes leap down to these verdant spots; and, without a possibility of return, is left to perish, after it has finished the dear bought repast.

Winding round the mountain, on the margin of the flood, we passed an adit of a copper mine, belonging to Sir W. W. Wynne. From one of its levels issues a stream of water, strongly impregnated with sulphat of copper, which in time must prove injurious to the fishery: the work is in a thriving state, and the ore very superior in its quality to that of Paris mountain. Every step we proceeded unfolded new scenery; the strata of this immense chasm, not only assume all shapes, but all colours; every shade from the lightest grey to the darkest brown and black; while the sun emerging from behind a cloud, tinged the variegated tops with all the brilliant tints of light and gold.

In contemplating this wonderful pass, we had forgotten our difficulties in approaching it; nor did we think of our wet condition, till cold shiverings reminded us of our uncomfortable situation. We now hastened our steps, and soon obtained sight of the threefold vale, in which stands the village of BEDD-KELERT, near the conflux of the Colwyn and Glas Lyn. It consists of a few straggling houses, little inviting either in appearance or situation, and the inn is only distinguishable from the rest, by a rude board over the door, "*The Guide to Snowdon lives here.*"

Thoroughly drenched, and having no change but what was in the same condition, we judged it prudent to retire to bed, while our cloaths we presented to the fire. In this laughable dinner position, the host quickly brought us a dish of fried eggs and bacon, and excellent cwrw. With an appetite suitable to the food, we made an excellent meal.

Much of our pleasure, and that of the highest kind, arises from reflections of an heterogeneous nature. Miserable as these accommodations would have been considered on other occasions, on this they were productive of comforts scarcely to be expressed. We contrasted the ruthless situation we had just been in, to the snug warm birth between the blankets; and every morsel and drop tasted sweeter on the reflection. The quiet of our little cottage seemed fairy land to the region of winds we had left; and was delightful, because it afforded us a welcome refuge from the merciless storms, with which we had been recently persecuted.

You would have smiled to have seen us reclined on our respective couches, and fed like so many invalids in the clinical wards of an hospital. And it is not improbable, from the surly appearance of our host, that he might augur from this beginning, that he should have his apartments occupied by Valetudinarians, for some weeks; and was casting about in his mind, (for our dirty appearance wast against us) how he was likely to be paid for his food and attendance.

However the precaution was founded in wisdom; and we have to attribute to this prudential measure, our escaping a severe indisposition, and being able to pursue our route in health and spirits. The origin of this village is so singular, that it would be unpardonable not to give it you. The story is handed down by tradition, and there is nothing upon the face of it to induce me to doubt of its authenticity.

At an early period, when wolves were formidable by their numbers in Wales, a prince (Llewelyn the Great) came to reside for the hunting season at this spot, with his wife and children. While the family was one day absent, a wolf entered the house and attempted to kill an infant that was left asleep in a cradle. The prince's faithful dog named Kill-Hart, that was watching by the side, seized the rapacious animal, and killed it. In the struggle the cradle was overturned, and lay upon the wolf and child. On the prince's return, missing the child, and observing the dog's mouth stained with blood, he immediately concluded Kill-Hart had murdered the infant; and in a paroxysm of rage, drew his sword and ran the animal through the heart. But how great was his surprise, when on replacing the cradle, he found the wolf dead and his child alive! and what was his mortification, when the faithful dog that had preserved the infant, lay dead at his feet a victim to his too hasty resentment! He caused the creature to be honourably interred, erected a monument to his memory, and built a church, and dedicated it to St. Mary, as a grateful offering for the preservation of his child.

It is situated by the side of the river, and though small, is said to be the highest in Snowdonia. It consists of an aisle and one nave, with marks of another. A chapel on one side is supported by pointed arches, and two neat pillars. It was conventual, and formerly belonged to a priory of Augustine Monks, of that class called *Gilbertines*.

As you may not have heard of this singular order of Recluses, I will introduce them to your acquaintance.

A. D. 1148, contrary to the constitutions of Justinian, one *Gilbert*, Lord of Sempringham, in Lincolnshire, judging it unnatural that beings whom God had formed to be a mutual blessing to each other, should be separated; contrived a plan that should further the spirit of devotion, while it offered no violence to the social principle: that of *double monasteries*.

Having studied in France, on his return, he instructed in the liberal arts a number of youth of both sexes. Out of these he selected a certain number of each; and gave them a rule to observe, partially extracted from those of the orders of St. Augustin and St. Benedict. This order appeared so reasonable, that it was immediately confirmed by Pope Eugene III. It quickly excited public attention, became fashion able, and so increased, even in Gilbert's time, that he had lived to see thirteen houses founded; in which were seven hundred brethren and thirteen hundred sisters, associated under the name of *Gilbertines.*

It appears from the regulations of St. Bridget, there were to be a double number of nuns; that both sexes were to meet daily at chapel; but the men to keep below and the women above. One of the monks to be confessor under the title of Prior, who was to have the regulations of religious matters; and one of the sisters to have the regulations of the household, as *Lady Abbess.* But I must not omit, that to avoid all suspicion of scandal, at ordinary times they were to keep their respective apartments. To which a cotemporary wag humourously thus alludes:—

> The Monks sing the mass, the Nuns sing the other;
> Thus sister and sister take part with the brother;
> Bodies, not voices, a wall doth dissever;
> So, devoid of devotion, they sing both together, &c. &c.

But I refer you to *Nigel Wireker*, in *Speculo Stultorum*, for further information.

Here formerly was an abbey, probably erected at the same time as the church. Tanner attributes it to the last Llewelyn. But this is evidently an error, as Rymer records a charter for certain lands bestowed upon it by *Llewelyn the Great.* It was taken under the protection of Edward I. and bestowed on the abbey at Chertsey, by Henry VIII. At the Dissolution the revenues, according to Dugdale, amounted to £.70 3s. 8d. There are not the smallest remains of this once celebrated abbey; nor is the spot positively known where it stood. A place called Dôl y Lleian, or the Meadow of the Nun, is shown for it: If so, it confirms Mr. Pennant's idea of its having been a house for *Religious of both sexes*.

Entering the pleasing vale of Colwyn, we came to the source of the river Llyn y Cader. On our left was Llyn y Dywarchen, or the Lake of the Sod; celebrated by Gyraldus for its *Insula erratica*, or wandering island. He says, "it is set in motion by the winds towards the shore, and sometimes rejoins its native banks that cattle have been surprized on it by a contrary gale, and carried a short voyage from the shore." Gyraldus has been considered as an unfaithful topographer; and this, amidst a variety of others, has been one of the errors set in array against him. It is with pleasure I assert, that the fact corroborates the statement of his always lively, and often accurate pen. It is a piece of land, which consists of turf and peat, torn off bysome convulsion, and kept compact by the thick entangling roots that abound in this species of soil. It is of an irregular shape, about 30 feet long.

To those who are inclined to smile, at so diminutive a sod being termed an island, the recording it may appear trifling; but if a small portion may become sufficiently buoyant, to bear the weight of cattle and float upon the water, a larger may also; and thus the fact be established, that an author may describe *a floating island*, without deserving the imputation of *an hyperbolical writer.*

On our right we passed another ascent to Snowdon, where the base extending to a considerable breadth, presented a track less steep than some others. The Sons of Snowdon Moel, Elian, and Castell Cedwm, arose to the right; while the beautiful Lake of Cawellyn expanded its waters on our left; which is near two miles in length and half a one in breadth. The road lies close in its margin on the eastern side, which is flat; when the wind is high the waters overflow the road. At the back of the lake, on the opposite side, rises perpendicular of a semicircular shape, Moel Mynydd Mawr; the dark appearance of whose fissured rocks, forms a fine contrast to the beautiful transparency of its waters. The different shades of its precipices, reflected from the surface, appeared variegated in stripes of the richest colours, like lutestring; and the passing clouds increased the moving diversity. This delightful effect was heightened by the golden rays of a bright declining sun; who, before he retired to the ocean, was beaming his departing smiles on the objects around us.

This lake is noted for a species of Charr, (*Salmo alpinus, Lin.*) called Torgoch, or Red Belly,[7]

---

7   This is the Welch generic name for both the red and gilt charr. Mr. Pennant thinks them both one species, but the difference observable in the formation of the jaws, as well as the time of spawn ing, is sufficient to establish distinct

found formerly in Llyn Peris, and in some of the lakes of Switzerland and whoever has travelled through the Grisons, would, from the great similarity of the scenery, conceive he had been wafted by magic to that alpine country. The road we had passed, was not unlike that from Grenoble to Susan.

The Charr are taken in nets during the first winter months;[8] and after the season retire to inaccessible depths.

Alittle farther is a fine cascade formed by the

Fai, or Gwyrfai issa, running from the lake, and rushing into the vale; which now begins to expand, consists of fine meadows, the hills retiring to a distance, in which is the small village of Bettws Garmon, its church being dedicated to St. Germain.

Quitting the vale, we ascended an extensive plain, strewed with a number of cottages, that gave an idea of considerable population. The cottages of Caernarvon appeared worse than those of Merioneth; and this was generally the case, as we proceeded in a westerly or north-westerly direction, towards the sea. Here turf or clay with chopped rushes, supplies the place of stone. The form is generally oblong, the length very considerable, compared with the breadth and height. The walls are about six feet high, over which are raised

---

species.

8   The season commences in November, and continues about five or six weeks.

maiden poles, not even stripped of their bark for rafters, and pegged at top and bottom; afew smaller ones interwoven serve the place of laths; over these is placed heath or rushes, kept down by ropes of the latter, extending netwise over them, as a security against the turbulent winds, by which in this exposed country, even these humble dwellings are liable to be assailed. Some of them have lattices for the admission of light, formed by interwoven sticks; but for the most part the light is admitted through the entrance way, for door there is none: but this deficiency is supplied by a hurdle, formed of a few watlings and rushes, which in bad weather is raised perpendicular to stop the gap. An aperture in the roof serves for a chimney. This is not made directly over the fire, lest the rain should extinguish it; but a little distance from the perpendicular line. The smoke, therefore, as may be expected, fills the place before it is able to obtain vent; but this inconvenience habit has rendered tolerable.[9]

Such are the dwellings in which part of the inhabitants of the most opulent and powerful nation upon earth at present live, and in which the Genius of Virtue and Content seems to delight to dwell.

---

9   The houses of the farmers are in a superior style, generally having one or two bed-rooms *above stairs*; as well as one separated from the kitchen: but even here, pigs; asses; and other domestic animals, take up their abode and form part of the family.

Curiosity tempted me to enter one of them; the dark mud wall, rocky floor, and a few brown rushes, the family bed, suggested the idea of a den; the parents and their numerous progeny, were assembled round a small fire of peat, which the father had just brought home from the adjoining moor; this the wife was economically placing upon the stones, to produce a commodious heat, while the ragged off-spring were lisping, in language hoarse, their dad's return. A large stone jug of liquor, called *diodgriafel*,[10] which the good woman had been sedulously preparing against the husband's arrival, stood near, and was now, with the supper of potatoes, about to be quaffed; the success of the past day's exertion, and the hopes of still better to-morrow, were the subjects of conversation; and the day conclded with the setting sun.

To those habituated to magnificent dwellings, and the luxuries of polished life, it might appear

---

10   This is made of the berries of the SORBUS AUCUPARIA, (Roan Tree) abundant in most parts of Wales; by pouring water over them, and setting the infusion by to ferment. When kept for some time, this is by no means an unpleasant liquor; but necessity obliges these children of penury to use it, without waiting for the fermentative process. In Scotland a spirituous liquor is obtained by distillation; and Gmelin informs us, the same use is made of them by the natives of Kamschatca. This tree is held in high veneration by the superstitious: a small part of it is carried about as a defence against inchantment; and a branch of the Roan is considered infallible in protecting cattle from the injury of witchcraft.

impossible, that any thing, but discontent and despair could be the associates of such apparent want and wretchedness. But discovering, as I did, much cheerfulness and satisfaction, I was led to assent to the assertion, that "Man wants but little, nor that little long" and to say with the Poet—

> Yet still, e'en here, Content can spread a charm,
> Redress the clime, and all its rage disarm.
> Tho' poor the peasant's hut, his feasts tho' small,
> He sees his little lot, the lot of all;
> Sees no contiguous palace rear its head,
> To shame the meanness of his humble shed;
> No costly lord the sumptuous banquet deal,
> To make him loath the vegetable meal;
> But calm, and bred in ignorance and toil,
> Each wish contracting, fits him for the soil.
> Cheerful as morn, he wakes from short repose,
> Breathes the keen air, and carols as he goes;
> At night returning, every labour sped,
> He sits him down, the monarch of a shed;
> Smiles by his cheerful fire, and round surveys
> His children's looks, that brighten in the blaze;
> While his lov'd partner, boastful of her hoard,
> Displays her cleanly platter on the board.
> Thus every good, his native wilds impart,
> Imprints the patriot passion on his heart.
> GOLDSMITH.

We crossed the Rhythell, which here assumes the name of Seiont, over a stone bridge of no striking appearance, either as to its plan or execution. It contains a tablet, informing the traveller, it was built by the modern Inigo, Harry Parry.

This had the appearance of egregious vanity, but, on inquiry, we found, that H. P. could claim this title, without the least arrogance of pretension; since he had thrown bridges across alpine rivers, that had baffled the skill of more celebrated architects, several of which, after having resisted the violence of floods, were still remaining, and likely to remain, as monuments to perpetuate the fame of this humble mason.

Passing the church of Llan Beblic, we soon arrived at CAERNARVON.

This was the ancient *Segontium,* mentioned by Antoninus; was a Roman station in the time of Constantine; and Matthew Paris says the body of Constantinus, the father of that Emperor, was found buried here, A. D. 1283. The scite of the old city is about a mile from Caernarvon, by the road, to which from Pwllheli it is intersected. The remains of a Roman road are still visible from this place to Dinorwig. It lays on the eastern banks of the Seiont. Some remains of the walls are still to be seen, the cement of which appears harder than the stone itself. A single stone remains here, with these letters S. V. C.; probably for *Segontium Urbs Constantini;* Helen or her husband Constantine having built it. It was defended by a fort, erected on the steep western bank of the Seiont, where it forms a curve, about four hundred yards from the present town, which is almost entire. The walls are about twelve feet high, and about eight yards square, with circular parallel holes running the whole length.—Where the facings are dilapidated, the peculiarity of Roman masonry is easily discoverable. The church of Trer' Beblic is very ancient, and apparently of Roman origin, dedicated to St. Publicius, son of Maxen Wledic, and of Helen, daughter of Eudda, Duke of Cornwall, who retired from the World and took a religious habit. (*Vid. Mona Antiqua.*)

Richard II. gave this church, and its dependent Chapel of Caernarvon, to the Nuns of St. Mary in Chester, in consideration of their great poverty. On the Dissolution, they were annexed to the See of Chester, and at present form part of the patronage of that bishopric.

This city, after the departure of the Romans from the island, was occupied by the Britons; and by them denominated Caer ar fôn, *i. e.* a strong hold opposite Mona; which with the insertion of an *euphoniæ gratiâ*, made Caernarfon. Gyraldus mentions it as a considerable place 1138; and a charter dated 1221, issued by Llewelyn the Great, proves that it did not receive this name from King Edward. This at a very early period was a seat of the British Princes. Roderic resided here A. D. 750; (*Vid. Mon. Antiq.*) and the royal residence by a posterior Roderic was removed from hence to Aberfraw, in Anglesea.

Out of the ruins of this city arose the present town, justly the boast of North Wales for its situation, buildings, harbour, &c. but above all for the grandeur of its castle. It was by a charter of King Edward, made a free borough. It is governed by a Mayor, who is *pro tempore* Deputy-Governor of the Castle, one Alderman, and two Bailiffs; there are also a Town Clerk and two Serjeants at Mace. The town sends one Member to Parliament, who is returned by the joint suffrage of Conway, Pwllheli, Nefyn and Crickaeth; and the right of voting extends to every person resident in these places. One extraordinary privilege was, that no Burgess of Caernarvon could be convicted of any crime, committed between the Conwy and the Dovey, but by a jury of his towns men.

The town was originally contained within its present walls; but the suburbs are become of greater extent than the town; the streets are at right angles, corresponding with the four gates; and what was formerly a chapel to the garrison, serves now as the parish church. The streets are clean, and the houses well built, and it is become a place of fashionable resort, during the Summer season; and when the elegant hot and cold baths, erecting by the Earl of Uxbridge, are completed, it will probably be inferior to no place in this respect. Here are assemblies during the Winter months, and a company of comedians from Chester were performing, three times a week, at the theatre for the season.

An inducement for many genteel families to reside here and in the neighbourhood, is the cheapness of provisions, as well as the pleasantness ofthe situation. Fish is in such plenty, that salmon may be bought for 2*d*. per lb. a pair of fine soals for 6*d*., and other sorts much lower.

A circumstance that daily happens here will obviously strike a stranger. The beverage of the generality of the people is butter-milk. Persons collect it from farm houses, and bring it in pots on horses, and with a cry not unlike that of the London milk-maids, retail this useful article at *one penny per quart*. The demand is frequently so urgent, that if any obstruction happens to the supply, it occasions temporary feuds. On my observing to a genteel woman, I wondered there should be any contention about an article, that in England was considered of little value, and wishing to be informed, if they substituted this for beer at meals, I received a reply in a key bordering on indignation, *Aye, sure! and cood enough, Cod knows!* I perceived I had inadvertently touched upon a tender string, and with a submissive bow I retired; remarking to myself, that a traveller should he very cautious how he intermeddles with the customs or the prejudices of any country in which he sojourns,

The entrance to the port of Caernarvone is rather dangerous, from the extensive sand banks near, but the harbour is capacious, and vessels of six or seven hundred tons ride in security; and the quay is peculiarly convenient, as large vessels can ride close to it, and deliver and take in their cargoes.

The trade has of late years been increasing, though it at present consists more of exports than imports, slate, &c. to Liverpool, Bristol, and London; copper ore from Llanberis and Paris Mountain to Swansea; flannels, webs, stockings, and an ochre found in Anglesea, to America and the West Indies. Its imports consist chiefly of Irish cloth, fine wool, hides, tallow, and grocery goods, for the use of the interior.

There is nothing but capital wanting to make Caernarvon a considerable place. The County Assizes are occasionally held here, and the room over the eastern gateway, formerly used as a Custom-house, is converted into the Sessions-house. This was done, as an inscription in front informs us, by the munificence of Sir W. Wynne, and his nephew, Thomas Wynne, Esq. A. D. 1767. A new Custom-house is erected within the walls on the Menai, much more convenient for the commerce of the port. I am indebted to the Comptroller of the port, for the annexed accurate list of vessels that have cleared out, and entered inwards, from the port of Caernarvon, for the last ten years inclusive.

Cleared out				Entered inwards			
Years	Foreign	Coasters	Total	Years	Foreign	Coasters	Total
1790	105	180	285	1790	15	217	232
1	116	162	278	1	15	232	247
2	105	181	286	2	17	243	262

Cleared out				Entered inwards			
Years	Foreign	Coasters	Total	Years	Foreign	Coasters	Total
3	110	168	278	3	9	234	243
4	96	282	378	4	14	218	232
5	96	301	397	5	17	284	251
6	129	228	357	6	23	229	252
7	74	137	211	7	29	198	227
8	64	145	209	8	11	190	201
9	108	130	238	9	18	201	219
	1003	1914	2917		168	2198	2366

This port is subject in its customs to the Comptroller of Beaumaris.

We added to our Botanical list of Plants, in a salt marsh opposite Caernarvon Castle, PLANTAGO MARITIMA, P. CORONOPUS, TRIGLOCHIN GLOCHIN MARITIMUM, SAMOLUS VALERANDI, GLAUX MARITIMA, EUPHORBIA PORTLANDICA, &c. On the shore near Llan Vaglan, GERANIUM MARITIMUM, CHENOPODIUM MARITIMUM, and SILENE MARITIMA.

The Castle of Caernarvon is certainly the most magnificent fortress in North Wales. It is well situated for natural strength, one side bounded by the Menai, another by the Estuary of Seiont, a third by a Creek of the Menai, and the fourth isolated by art. The scite was admirably calculated for a strong post, and could not fail to strike a Prince of military talents, like Edward, as a proper place to erect a curb for his newly conquered, and consequently dissatisfied, subjects. It is supposed by some to have been of more ancient date; (*Vid. Welch Chron.*) but the architecture is that of the tenth century. As the conqueror of the country there is great reason for supposing, that Monarch to be the founder of the present edifice, (perhaps upon the ruins of one more ancient) to check the spirit of insurrection, that might arise in Snowdonia, as he did on the Denbighshire side, by the Castles of Conway and Rhuddlan.

The style of architecture is far from simple; and the observation of Mr. Barrington seems well found ed, that the plans of the Welch Castles, erected by Edward I. were borrowed from the Asiatic fortresses which that Prince had seen in the Holy Land, because they appear precisely similar to many copied, and inserted in the valuable tracts of Le Brun.

After the conquest was nearly compleated, in 1282, the Castle was begun, and in little more than a year, this immense building was finished. For still further to subdue the haughty people, already mortified by a foreign yoke, he imposed the hateful task of forging chains for their country, and putting the last fatal hand to its independence. The peasantry were compelled to perform the required labour, and their chieftains to defray the expence in curred. It is built of a mixture of lime and grit stone; some of the materials were furnished by the ruins of the old town, and some were brought from Vaenol. It forms a bold and striking object, and the shell is nearly entire.

The walls with which the new town was originally inclosed, were defended by a number of round towers, but are much injured in the battlements. It had two entrances, that to the South facing the mountains, and that to the North the Menai.

The entrance into the Castle is grand, by a massy tower; in front of which, over the gateway, is placed a statue of the royal Founder, with a dagger in his hand, in a menacing posture. This was defended by four portcullises. The form of the Castle, inclosing an area of about three acres, is oblong: the towers are elegant, some pentagonal, some hexagonal, and others octagonal; two of these stand pre-eminent: and of these the eagle tower, so called from a figure of that bird placed at the top, is peculiarly beautiful, three small angular turrets issuing from it. A magnificent apartment is shewn in this tower, where Queen Eleanor was delivered of that unfortunate Monarch, Edward II. Mr. Pennant says, he was born in a little dark room adjoining, the area of which does not exceed twelve feet by eight; and adds, so little did a royal consort in those days consult either pomp or conveniency. But it is of so little moment, which was the spot, where so weak and degenerate a Prince first saw the light, that I feel no inclination to attempt a decision of the point at issue. Let the day of his birth be blotted out of the calendar, and the place of it erased from the records of antiquity.[11]

The view we obtained from the summit over the Menai, the cultivated fields and valleys of Anglesea, the high mountains wrapt in clouds, the harbour opening into the bay and the ocean, was far more interesting to us.

The walls of the eagle tower are ten feet thick, and those of the fortress in general eight . A gallery runs all round, with frequent openings, for the discharge of arrows on the besiegers.

---

11   In his 16th year, this pusillanimous Prince attended at Chester, invested with royal dignity, to receive the homage of *his duped subjects*, according to a convention of his father. The King finding all methods prove abortive, to win the affections of the Welch, had recourse to a politic, though dangerous experiment. His Queen being far gone in a state of pregnancy, though the season was severe, being the depth of Winter, he ordered her to repair to the Castle of Caernarvon. Supposing the time of her delivery to be near, he assembled the principal men at Ruddlan to consult about the *public good*. Informed while here, that the Queen was delivered of a son, he addressed the Welch nobility, observing they had often intreated him to appoint them a Prince. As he had occasion to leave the country at this time, he would comply with their request, on condition they would swear allegiance to the person he should nominate. With this proposition the Welch acquiesced, with the single reserve, that he should appoint *one of their own nation*. The King gave them his assurance, that he would nominate "*one born in Wales, who could not speak a word ofEnglish, and whose life and conversation would bear the strictest inquiry.*" This person the Welch agreed to own and obey; but what was the astonishment of these deluded men, when the King named his own son, just born in Caernarvon Castle! *Vid. Powel, p.* 301.

Its establishment was a Constable with a salary of 40*l*.; and the Captain of the town 12*l*. 3*s*. 4*d*. Twenty-four soldiers were allowed for the defence of the place at 4*d. per diem* each. This probably was onlythe peace establishment. *Vid. Doddridge.*

A short period after its erection, the strength and importance of it was to be tried. A general insurrection was excited in different parts of Wales, under three different leaders. Madoc, an illegitimate son of the unfortunate Llewelyn, styling himself Prince, put himself at the head of the insurgents of North Wales. This was occasioned by a subsidy for the French war, directed to be levied on the new subjects. Madoc seized upon Sir Roger de Puleston, Grand Comptroller, first hanged him, and then ignominiously severed his head from his body. The fate of the leader befell all his associates. Madoc then proceeded to Caernarvon, which was crouded with people, attending an annual fair. The unarmed people were barbarously slaughtered, the town reduced to ashes, and the castle taken. *Vid. War. V. II.* p. 334.

In 1644, the town was taken by Captain Swanley, a Parlimentarian, who pillaged it of the stores, arms, and ammunition, making four hundred prisoners. The royalists afterwards dispossessed him. While Lord Byron was Governor, it was besieged by General Mytton, 1646, and surrendered upon an honourable capitulation.

In 1648, General Mytton and Colonel Mason were besieged in the town by Sir John Owen, who hearing that Colonels Carter and Twisleton were advancing to relieve it, raised the seize and marched to oppose them. The parties met at Llandegai; Sir John was defeated and made prisoner, and North Wales soon after submitted to the Parliament. *Vid. Whitelock.*

This Castle, like its rival in strength and grandeur, is going fast to decay; and the dilapidating hand of Time promises soon to deprive the country of one of its principal ornamental objects.

In ruminating on scenes like these, contemplation takes a retrospective turn; the changes they have undergone forcibly obtrude themselves; the mind is involuntarily hurried away to the periods of their decline and grandeur; and their prosperous and disastrous days pass in solemn review before us.

I reflected on the events, that led to its erection; the military prowess and courage of the Princes, and the invincible spirit that characterised their followers. The violent efforts and obstinate struggles that Liberty here made, for centuries, before power and despotism could awe it into submission. Hordes of these simple mountaineers appeared, descending from their fastnesses in the hills, giving battle to more numerous and well-appointed troops; and with an ardour and enthusiasm, inspired by the desire of living free, easily overcoming them, and with tumultuous clamour marching to victory and to triumph.

Again these indignant, because outraged Britons, appeared, with their councils divided by internal cabals, and foreign bribery, in their turn discomfited; driven from their strong fortresses, and forced to defend their native birth-right, in want and nakedness, amidst the deep ravines of their barren mountains.

After these portentous and devastating scenes, the horizon has again cleared up, the atmosphere become serene, and the most perfect calm ensued. These plains of carnage have again become the habitations of innocence and peace. These fortresses (the natives' best hope) whose noble defenders had been reduced to famine, despair, and death, have echoed to the festive noise of banquetting and hospitality. The liberal board has smoaked with the richest viands, and the horn gone round with the choicest mead. The hills have resounded with the melodious harp, and the nimble feet tripped lightly to the song of victory and of freedom. Period after period arose, distinguished by artifice on the one hand, and determined bravery on the other; till intrigue got the better of courage, and perseverance overcame a divided spirit; and Cambrian Independence and Cambrian Liberty gave the expiring groan together, under the walls of Caernarvon.

Proud Pile! thy tempest-beaten towers, still rear
Their heads sublime, and to the angry storm
Bid bold defiance; though their aged brows
Bear visible the marks of stern decay,
While Superstition, with a frensied eye,
And wildering fear, that horrid forms surveys,
Affright the lonely wanderer from thy walls.
Far hence thou busy world, nor here intrude
Thy sounds of uproar, arguing much of fear
And impotent alarms. Behold, fond man,
This feeble monument of mortal pride,
Where time and desolation reign supreme
With mildest havock; o'er the solemn scene
In silence pause; and mark this pictur'd truth;
That not alone, the proudest works of man
Must perish, but, as this tow'ring fabric,
That lifts its forehead to the storm, till time
And the wild winds shall sweep it from its base,
Pass but a few short hours; the dream of life
Is fled; and sinks to the cold grave man's faded form.

The vision that passed before me, led me to
contemplate the temporary nature of earthly
power, and the instability of all human things.
This nation, for centuries unconquerable, we see
yielding with the most suppliant submission to
that very power it hated; receiving with a cordial welcome, those laws and constitutions it despised; and permitting its manners and its language to bow before that of its detested victors.

Thus, my Friend, that for which Princes fight
and Heroes die, is no more than a phantom in
the in the passing wind; and they themselves are
like the insects of a day, that flutter in the sun to

display their colours, and shew their short lived consequence in its beams; which the breeze of evening wafts from the theatre of life, and hurries to the next stage of existence.

Yours,

J. E.

Letter VIII

Caernarvon

Dear Sir,

I t is surprising, with how much greater facility some travellers obtain the objects of their desire than others. To them the most elevated mountains become accessible on all sides, and in all weathers; and a journey to the peak of Snowdon is as easily performed, as that from Caernarvon to Bangor. Almost every person that has made the Tour of North Wales, has obtained the enviable prospect from the elevated summit of Snowdon. I was not so fortunate, having waited a fortnight in vain, for an opportunity to make the ascent. Though it was now the season, when favourable weather might have been expected, yet almost incessant rains, and cloudy skies, baffled every attempt. A gentleman we met at the hotel, had been waiting six weeks prior to our arrival; and, after several attempts proving abortive, strongly disappointed, relinquished the design.

Mr. Pennant observes,

> It is seldom the traveller can get a proper day to ascend the mountain, even when it appears clear; by the attraction of clouds, the summits become enveloped with clouds, when they have appeared, a few minutes before, at a very great distance. They are frequently observed to lower suddenly half their height, and, even while appearing to separate to right and left, they suddenly wheel round, and combine to envelope the mountain in one common obscurity.

It was with regret I witnessed the truth of this observation; as I had promised myself the pleasure of examining those plants styled ÆTHEREÆ, but many of which are inhabitants of Snowdon, principally confined to the highest part of the mountain.[1]

Determined, however, to obtain what was practicable, we made an excursion into Snow-

---

1   Though the seeds of these plants must frequently be wafted to the lower parts, yet they are scarcely ever found to vegetate below, disliking perhaps the denser atmosphere, and milder breeze, the concomitants of the vale.

donia, visiting some of the lower mountains in quest of plants.

Taking the vale of the Seiont, where is found the ORCHIS CONOPSEA and SATYRIUM ALBIDUM, and passing Llanrûg, or properly Llan Michael (the church being dedicated to St. Michael) we entered Nant Peris, at Cwm y Glô, the northern extremity of the lower lake of Llyn Padern, whence issues the Ryddol, which soon after assumes the name of Seiont.

Llyn Padern is about three miles in length, half a mile in breadth, widening to the South, where it is separated from the upper lake by a projecting rocky eminence, on which are the ruins of *Dolbadern Castle*.[2] A round tower, thirty feet in diameter, with a dungeon below, and a few fragments around constitute the remains of this British post.

By whom it was erected is not said: the intent was evidently to secure this narrow defile into Snowdonia. It is constructed of the schistose stone of the country, and mortar made of marine shells. From the form of the building, as well as the commanding situation, it must have been of great importance. Owen Goch, who instigated David into rebellion against their brother Llewelyn, languished twenty years within its walls.

In the last struggle for Cambrian independence, this fortress was at times in possession

---

2   So called from a meadow named Dôl Badern, or the field of St. Paterninus near it

of Henry and Glyndwr, and by both considered ofthe greatest consequence, as the grand keyto this part of the country. Near it grow PHALARIS ARUNDINACEA and BRYUM ALPINUM.

Nothing can exceed the beauty of this ruin as it appears from the lake; the promontory on which it stands; its image reflected from the crystal waters, the lofty mountains on each side; the upper lake stretching to the church of Llanperis, with Snowdon in the back ground; while the waters rushing from the upper into the lower lake, form a fine natural canal.

Llyn Peris, though not of such large dimensions, is not less beautiful. It is of prodigious depth, a line of seventy fathoms in places not finding the bottom. It formerly abounded with the red and golden Charr; but these have long left it: the streams from the copper levels, and other works, having impregnated the waters with that poisonous metal. It however furnishes the Botanist with SUBULARIA AQUATICA, NYMPHEA ALBA, ALISMA NATANS, ISOETIS LACUSTRIS, SPARGANIUM SIMPLEX, and SP. NATANS.

At the upper end of this lake, a few scattered miserable cottages form the village of Llanberis, with the little church dedicated to St. Peris;[3] (said to have been a cardinal:) another of those reli-

---

3   Peris was a Monk, who lived in retirement in the beginning of the thirteenth century. Leland says in his time, the narrow pass leading to the church was called Nant y Monach, *the Monks' Valley.*

gious,[4] with which the church of Rome swarmed, that had more fame than merit. But where fame has established a character, it is useless to reason. The Saint could perform miracles, and bestowed a blessing upon the place of his residence, by endowing a spring, from which he drank daily, with sanative powers. It is at present inclosed with a wall, under the name of St. Peris's Well; and is still famed for the cure of rachitis, and other cases of debility: and the traditional history of the neighbourhood abounds with extraordinary cures performed by its waters. The sibyl of the place divines your fortune, by the appearance or non-appearance of two small fish, that lurk in the holes of the rock; if they come out, good is foreboded, if not, ill is to be dreaded.[5]

There are many others famous in the vicinity for healing; *i. e.* Ffynnon Kegin Arthur, and Ffynnon Moel Rhiwen, which will (says report) spout its waters in the face of malefactors; and Ffynnon Pen i gaer; but you will wish to hear no more of them, when I tell you, that they contain very pure cold water, devoid of any mineral or

---

4   The principal Welch Saints are David, Daniel, Beuro, Elian, Padern, Cybi, Seinol, Twrog, Peris, and Teilian. To these the churches through the Principality are dedicated . An account of these, an and enlarged list, is contained in that truly learned work, the *Mona Antiqua*.

5   Those are two small dark looking trout. Those who visit the well, generally procure food and lay opposite their holes, to entice them out. Inthis case they seldom disappoint the traveller, except they have been satiated by recent visitors.

earthy property, a thing so common in this country as to diminish the value of the blessing.

The visitor of this rude country meets with a great difficulty, and a drawback upon his pleasure, for want of a house of accommodation, at or near Llanberis. Would Mr. Smith take it into consideration, and have the public spirit to build an inn, on this part of his extensive property, he would perform an act worthy of his own character, and serve the cause of science and humanity.

The plants furnished by the immediate neighbourhood of Llanberis, are PAPAVER CAMBRICUM, COCHLEARIA GREENLANDICA, CAMPANULA HEDERACEA, SCUTELLARIA MINOR, FESTUCA CAMBRICA, TRICHOMANES TUNBRIDGENSE, PTERIS CRISPA, POLYPODIUM PREOPTERIS, GENTIANA CAMPESTRIS, SILENE ACAULIS, ASPLENIUM NIGRUM, ASPLENIUM RUTA MURARIA, ARENARIA LARICIFOLIA, TREMELLA VERRUCOSA, T. UTRICULATA, POLYPODIUM LONCHITIS, HIERACIUM MURORUM, GALIUM BOREALE, FONTINALIS SQUAMOSA, CUCUBALUS ACAULIS, COTYLEDON UMBILICUS VENERIS, CAREX ATRACA, ARENARIA VERNA, CHELIDONIUM GLACIUM, with different species of MUSCIR and ALGÆ in great profusion. In Ffynnon vrech, ISOETIS LACUSTRIS, SUBULARIA AQUATICA, and LOBELIA DORTMANNA.

Mr. Pennant gives an account of an heroine by the name of Margaret Uch (properly *Verch*) Evans, a celebrated huntress, who resided at Pen Llyn, near the end of the lakes. She is said to have killed two hundred foxes, besides a vast number

of other noxious animals, and destructive ver-
min. She was a robust masculine woman, and so
strong, that no man cared to try a fall with her:
she died about seven years ago, unmarried, at the
age of ninety-four.

Asimilar instance of a person endued with
prodigious strength, occurred at the same time,
in the same parish; though he has not had a Mr.
Pennant for a biographer, he claims attention; as
the circumstance tends to prove that the inhabitants of this alpine tract are a very hardy race, and
though not in general above the middle stature,
are possess ed of uncommon bodily strength.

Foulke Jones, who lived at Tydu, was noted for his prodigious strength.[6] The esteemed
Champion of Wales for boxing, wrestling, &c.
came to see him from Denbighshire, for the sole
purpose of trying their relative strength. When
the stranger arrived, Foulke was mowing hay in
the field, near to his house. The stranger went
up to him, and inquired, if he knew one Foulke,
not supposing from his size and appearance this
could be the person he sought. Foulke answered,
that his master was in the house, or not far distant, at the same time begged to know what his
business was? I have heard, the stranger replied,
that he is accounted the strongest man in the

---

6   This extraordinary portion is generally confined to par-
     ticular families. Foulke has left several sons, some of them
     inheriting a considerable share; and his ancestors were fa-
     mous before him.

Principality, and am come to try our strength together. If that be all, Foulke observed, I can soon inform you, whether it will be worth your while to see my master, for I am a tolerably strong man myself, but *nothing* in his hands; as I have often experienced to my cost, when I have had the temerity to contend with him; therefore I would have you try, what you can do with me first. They immediately engaged, when Foulke, by his superior strength, flung his antagonist over a high wall into the road. Fully satisfied, he exclaimed, if this be the *man*, what must the master be! and mounting his horse rode home, fully convinced of his superiority.

Another anecdote is told, that evinced his peaceable disposition, as well as his uncommon strength. A troublesome fellow at Caernarvon, wished to irritate Foulke to fight; who begged he would cease, as he had no desire to quarrel, far less to fight with any man. At length he grew so impertinent and grossly insulting, that he struck Foulke in the face; his ire thus justly roused, he took him by the neck, and lifted him over the battlements of the bridge on which they stood, suspending him over the water, crying most loudly for mercy. Having held him in this unpleasant situation for some time, he lifted him back again, and dismissed him with an ignominious kick on the seat of honour.

Many are the feats of strength he performed; such as taking a cow upon his back, and bearing it home; carrying a tree he had felled, which seven other men were unable to perform, &c. &c.

From every account he seems to have been a more extraordinary person than Margaret Evans; but while she has been noticed by several writers, Foulke has only been celebrated in the tradition of his neighbourhood. He died about seven years ago, at the age of seventy-five. The inhabitants of this country are remarkable for longevity. The registers contain many ages of a hundred years and upwards; and it is common to find persons alive at a period little short of it.[7]

At a small distance fromthe village, on the western side of the lake, are mines of copper, the property of Asheton Smith, Esq. of Vae nol; and by him are leased to Messrs. Roe, Hudson, Smith, and Mills, under the firm of the Macclesfield Company; who are also concerned in the Cronebane copper works in Ireland.

---

7   This may arise, not only from the sharpness and salubrity of the air, but also from the regular mode of living, and the undebilitating food on which necessity obliges these mountaineers to exist.

> The mountayne men live longer many a yèere,
> Than those in vale, in playne or moorish soyle;
> Alustie hart, a clean complexion cleere,
> They have on hill, that for hard living toyle.
> With ewe and lambe, with goates and kids they play;
> In greatest toyles to rub out wearie day;
> And when to house and home good fellows drawe,
> The lads can laugh, at turning of a strawe.
> CHURCHYARD.

There are seven levels driven into Snowdon. The rock consists of hard whin, and schistose hornblende. The ore is chiefly formed in a matrix of *quartz*. It is a rich yellow ore, containing copper in union with iron and sulphur. The copper *Pyrites*, or first family of Kirwan *Min. Vol.* II.

Though there are seven levels, two only are worked. The one called the new level is a hundred and eighty yards in length. The shafts are numerous, as they are the communications from the one level to the other. A person therefore may enter at the first level, and by the different shafts pass through the intermediate ones, and emerge into day-light again at the seventh level.

The mode of draining the work does not reflect great credit upon the spirit, or ingenuity of the undertaking. A shaft is sunk, about forty-five yards below the depth of the new level. Into this the superfluous water runs from the work; and as it collects, is raised into the level by means of a winch and barrels; and hence it is carried down into the lake. These mines were discovered about fifty years ago, by John Jones Roberts, who, by a simple process, obtained ore enough in six months, to sell for 300*l*. After this they lay neglected, till they were taken up by the Company, who at present work them.

The number of Miners are about eighty, who work by the square yard in blasting the rock; their earnings consequently are very uncertain, depending upon the nature of the matrix that contains the ore. They work by candle-light, clad only in a shirt and small cloathes; and they observe, that it is warmer under ground in Winter than in Summer: which corroborates the doctrine of the mean temperature of the earth being about forty-eight degrees. This, compared with the height at which the thermometer stands in Winter and Summer, in the open air, will account for this paradoxical sensation, without having recourse to *subterraneous fires*. The ore contains a quantity of sand, or superfluous earth, from which it is cleared by means of breaking, stamping, decanting, &c.

Women and children are employed with hammers, to break the large pieces of ore, and then to wash and sort it into three different kinds of diverse qualities; some containing one-tenth, and some one fifth copper. It is then taken to the stamping mill, where it undergoes the further process ofpulverisation. The stamping mill is formed of six large oaken beams, shod at the end with steel, placed vertically over a large trough; by means of a crook, these are alternately raised by the power of a water wheel, and let fall upon the ore contained in the trough. When pounded sufficiently small, it is carried into a reservoir by a stream of water, where it is again purified by decantation, &c. It is then removed in boats down the lakes, whence it is conveyed by cart to Caernarvon Quay, and shipped for the Company's smelting works near Swansea.

SNOWDON

We were now in the midst of Snowdonia, a range of mountains extending from Conway to the sea at Aberdaron, in a direction nearly from Northeast to North-west; and unlike other mountains, they are one pile upon another, consisting of groups of cliffs rising above cliffs, as they gradually ascend from each extremity to the center.

Snowdon, the common escarpement, or declivity, fronts the Menai; and ranges in a parallel line with it. The escarpement of particular mountains generally depends upon the inclination of the strata. The principal are Carnedd David, Carnedd Llewelyn, Trevaen, Moel Siabod, the two Glyders, the two Llyders, Moel Llyfni, and Moel Mynydd mawr; all emulous to support their superior and Father Snowdon: yet his proud Peaks of Crib ydistil, and y Wydd Fa, appear scarcely to outrival some of the summits that surround them.

The height of mountains, as they affect the eye, must be considered from the spot where the ascent begins to make a considerable angle with the plain. But, philosophically considered, they are computed from the surface of the ocean. Mr. Caswell, who was employed by Flamstead to measure it in 1682, with instruments adjusted by that able philosopher, made the height ofthe highest point, 1240 yards (3720 feet) *above the level of Caernarvon Quay*. But later, and

probably more accurate experiments have somewhat reduced its height; and the estimate now
stands 3560 feet above the quay; which, taking
the height and the quay, will make it about 3600
feet above the level of the sea. Carnedd Llewelyn
ranges next, and Moel Siabod third, in the scale
of eminence. The rocks that compose the higher
part of the chain, are principally Porphyry, Granite, and Granitel of Kirwan; the secondary rocks
are chiefly Horneblende, Schiller Spar, Toad-
stone, Rowley rag, Whin Stone, Schistose Mica,
Schistose Clay, mixtures of Quartz, Feld Spar,
and Mica, and Argillaceous Schistus in all its varieties.

On the western side are a number of basaltic
columns, on a bed of hornstone, or chertz; and
large coarse crystals, cubic pyrites, and various
mineral bodies, are frequently found in the fissures. In the Schistose rocks are several slate
quarries; very considerable ones near Dolbadern; some in Llanddeiniolen; some in Llanberis;
a few in Llan Michael; and very large ones at
Kilgwyr; the products of all which are brought
to Caernarvon, and hence shipped for market.
Those of Lord Penhryn are at Dolawen; and there
is a large quarry of the *Novaculite* of Kirwan, varieties of second and third of that species, near
Cwm Idwal; where great quantities of *Hones* are
cut, and annually sent to London and Dublin.

The name of *Snowdon* was formerly given to
the whole of Caernarvonshire, under the appel-

lation of *Cregery*; (*Vid. Leland*;) which was covered with immense forests in the glens, and on the sides of the mountains. It was considered as a Royal Demesne; and two grants are upon record, the one in the time of Elizabeth, and the other in the time of Mary, for killing deer in the *Royal Forest of Snowdon.* Leland says, they abounded so much in his time, as to destroy the little corn the farmers attempted to SOW. But the history of Gwedir informs us, they were extirpated before the year 1626. It was called *Snowdonia* and *Arvonia*; and was the country to which the Welch were the last and longest attached; the inhabitants of which refused submission long after they were conquered; and proved that a country may be possessed without being subdued, by an invading enemy.

The traditional opinion of the country is strong in favour of the British name of *Creigiau r Eryri*; (*i. e.*) Eagle Rocks; from these birds having been used to frequent the summits in great quantities.[8] They do not constantly however now frequent them; and when they do it is in small numbers.

Mr. Pennant, following Camden, inclines to its being written *Creigian r Eiri*, (*i. e.*) Snowy

---

8   These carnivorous birds of prey in many places formed a for midable banditti; seizing upon the poultry, sheep, and even young children. A custom is still prevalent in the Orkneys, *that whoever kills an eagle may lay claim to a hen out of every house in the parish where the bird was killed.*

Mountains; and reason is certainly in favour of this etymology. For the English name of Snow dôn, (dôn signifying a hill or high pastures for sheep) will be a literal translation of the British name, Snowy Mountains; from the circumstance of snow being seen to remain on its tops many months in the year, like the Niphates in Armenia, and the Imaus in Scythia.

The story, that snow remains here *for years* with out melting is fabulous. Between April and September there is seldom any to be seen, though some years it has been seen in *July*; for it sometimes happens that snow falls late in June, and has been several feet deep; that which was rain in the vallies being snow, from the intense cold, on the tops of these mountains. Mr. Aikin observed on the morning of July 5, 1795, just after sunrise, the thermometer at 84; and in the afternoon it stood at 48; while at seven in the morning, at Bedd Kelert, it stood at 62. *Vid.* p. 99.

Though we were not able to ascend this prince of mountains, yet it may amuse you to give the route laid down by a friend, as the most eligible of the three, generally taken by the guides to the top of Snowdon.

> 1. Ride to Cwn y Glô, in the parish of Llanrûg; take boat up the lake of Llyn Padern; land in the little Isthmus, between this and Llyn Peris, near Dolbadern castle; there take your guide and ascend by Conaunt Mawr, or the great Chasm. Here is a fine water-fall. Climb

up along the South side of the ridge, that separates Cwm Peris from Cwm Brwynog; thence ascend in sight of Llyn du yr Arddu, which you must leave on your right.

The steep rock over this lake called Clogwyn du yr Arddu, (*i. e.*) the black rock above the Arddu, is celebrated for a great variety of rare plants.

Ascending a steep and difficult pass, called Llech wedd y Re, you arrive at a cold spring, called Llyn coch, which is within a mile of the highest summit called y Wydd fa, or the *Conspicuous*. The steep and almost inaccessible crags on the North side of this peak, are termed Clogwyn y Garnedd; and known to Lloyd and Ray for the habitats of alpine plants. The traversing of them is very hazardous, and often dangerous, being at all times slippery; and after rains fragments of rocks give way, and roll down with a thundering noise to the small deep lakes of Ffynnon Las, and Llyn Llydaw, that lie beneath. The distance from the castle to the sum mit is four miles.

2. The usual ascent is now from Llyn Cawllyn: but this route is wet and boggy in places, and very rocky and stony in others: the distance much the same.

3. Another begins about three miles on the Caernarvon side of Bedd Kelert. But this is extremely steep and dangerous; as the ridge called Clawdd coch, which you must ascend, is not more than two yards wide for a considerable way: whence you may drop a stone from each hand, and before they stop they will be at the distance of two miles from each other; one would roll a mile to the West, and the other a mile to the East.

This gentleman, who, to a variety of other accomplishments, has added a knowledge of Botany, also favoured us with a list of rare plants, growing about the different parts ofthe mountain.

On Clogwyn y garnedd—ANTHERICUM SEROTINUM, SERRATULA ALPINA, CERASTIUM ALPINUM, C. LATIFOLIUM, SAXIFRAGA STELLARIS, and S. RIVALIS, LYCHNIS ALPINA, POLYPODIUM ILVENSE, P. ALPINUM, ACROSTICUM SEPTENTRIONALE, OSMUNDA CRISPA, PAPAVER CAMBRICUM, RANUNCULUS ACRIS, PHASCUM MONTANUM, VIOLA ALPINA, GEUM RIVALE, DRYAS OCTOPELA, SAXIFRAGA AZOIDES, JUNIPERNUS COMMUNIS, & VAR. ß.

On Clogwyn du yr Arddu, CARDAMINE PETRÆA, and RUBUS SAXATILIS. Near Cwm Brwynog, in a boggy flat, JUNCUS SQUARROSUS, SCIRPUS CESPITOSUS, SCHOENUS NIGRICANS, AGROSTIS CAPILLARIS, POA ALPINA, and HIERACIUM ALPINUM.

Leaving the two Llyders, that form the eastern boundary of Nant Peris, the road lies through a dingle, called *Conaunt yr Esgar*, up a considerable ascent of loose stones, that render the footing extremely difficult; yet this is the easiest and most eligible pass to the sons of Snowdon.

Here is the small lake of Llyn y Cwm, famous, according to Gyraldus, for a remarkable phenomenon—"The lake," he says, "abounded with trout, perch, and eel, and all *monocular*." At present there are no documents to disprove his relation; all the fish in this lake having been destroyed about forty years ago by an earthquake, which happened during a violent thunder storm; by which a fissure was made communicating, probably, with some of the mineral strata of the mountains; as arsenical and cupreous particles are abundantly diffused in its waters. This may be a disappointment to those fond of the marvellous, but the botanist will feast his eyes instead with the SUBULARIA AQUATICA, ISOETES LACUSTRIS, and LOBELIA DORTMANNA; and near it, RUUS SAXATILIS, JUNCUS TRIGLUMIS, HIERACIUM ERACIUM, SOLIDAGO CAMBRICA, and PLANTAGO MARITIMA.

Passing by Rhiw, the celebrated Glyder Vawr presents itself. The prospect is singularly fine from the top of the Glyder: Snowdon, with his biforked head, is seen from thence to advantage. The varied vales of Nant Peris and Nant Frankou; the Menai, and the island of Anglesea, are all in full view. Upon a small plain on its summit, huge fragments of stone, in grotesque shapes, lie in all directions; some of them of many tons weight. They are weather beaten, and by time become cellular, and of a grey colour. Part of this mountain the people call Carnedd y Gwynt, the residence of tempests.

The vicinity of the Glyder, between Llyn y Cwm and Llyn Idwal, abounds with a variety of rare and curious plants; and is styled the Botanical Garden of Snowdon. Amidst a numerous assemblage are the following, growing upon Hysva Bengam and Trygyvylchi rocks:—GEUM RIVALE,

JUNIPERUS COMMUNIS, (VAR. ß.) SOLIDAGO CAM-
BRICA, THALICTRUM MINUS, TH. ALPINUM, ARE-
NARIA JUNIPERINA, RHODIOLA ROSEA, in great
plenty. ASPLENIUM SCOLOPENDRIUM, STATICE AR-
MERIA, SEDUM RUPESTRE, SPHAGNUM ALPINUM,
LICHEN CRASSUS, SWERTIANA PERENNIS, THLASPI
HIRTUM, MYRICA GALE, ANTHERICUM SEROTINUM,
CERASTIUM ALPINUM, DRABA INCANA,[9] and VE-
RONICA HYBRIDA.

The immortal Linnæus laid it down, as one of
his essential data, that a certain number of species of plants were created at first, capable of producing the like; and that these will remain to the
end of time. Numbers of his scholars have tried
to sap this important doctrine, by discovering a
variety of mules in the vegetable kingdom; (*i. e.*)
plants produced by the farina of one species fecundating the pistilla of others, and producing
hybrid plants. Thus the URTICA ALIENATA is supposed to be between the URTICA and PARIETARIA;
and the VERONICA HYBRIDA is said to be a mule
from the VERONICA OFFICIALIS & V. SPICATA.

Much has been said in the *Amcem. Acad.*[10] and
other works, and the parallel has been so far run
with the animal kingdom by some, as to assert,

9   It is peculiarly worthy of note in this diminutive plant, that
to its beautiful head of white blossoms succeed pods on
short hairy peduncles, twisted in a spiral direction, and contrary to the diurnal motion of the sun.

10 Though Linnæus himself may be said to have countenanced
the doctrine, yet what he did was with a view to expose its
fallacy, and establish the data of his own system.

that the *Fructification* in mules resembles the female, and the *external habit* the male plant. Others, taking advantage ofthis concession of the Linnæan School, have asserted, that vegetable mules are *capable of increase*; and hence new species and endless varieties adorn, and will continue to adorn, the theatre of vegetation. Thus are we hurried, without knowing it, to continual generation and reproduction: the floodgates of doubtful definition are let open; and confusion again spreads darkness over the regions of Botany. It is laughable to see to what lengths a spirit of conjecture, when trammeled by no restraints of truth, will carry the bold fabricators of theory.

M. Bonnet observes, that the antheræ of aquatic plants do not emit farina like other plants; but a *fecundating liquor*, which, at the time, may be seen like a little cloud in the water and then asks, *who knows but the powder of the stamina of certain plants may not make some impression on certain germs of the animal kingdom? Lett. à Spallanz. 43.*

Risum teneatis, Amici?[11] The ingenious French man did not recollect the *Vegeto-animal*, POLYDIUM BAROMETZ, vulgarly called the Tartarian Lamb, from its supposed resemblance to it; or his triumph would have been complete.

It should be remembered that Bonnet tried to do in the vegetable kingdom what his master, Buffon, tried long in vain to accomplish in the

---

11   Latin: 'Can you hold your smile, friends?' —Ed.

animal: after a whole life spent in torturing the Royal Ménagerie at Paris, he was not able to produce a single new species!

I would ask has any person witnessed the in crease of these mules? No, it is *conjectured so!* Have they been known to produce a similar off spring? It is *probable* they have.

Why, says Ray, if plants may thus combine and interchange their properties, and form *a tertium quid*, &c. may they not, *ad libitum*, or by accident, change their *magnitude?* Why do not trees grow up to the skies, or extend their branches horizontally miles over the earth? Because there is a *maximum quod sic*, says this learned Botanist, appointed by *Him*, who at the Creation issued the fiat:—"Let there be every herb and tree yielding seed after its kind."

Every part of nature, if we reason from fact or analogy, has its respective bounds, which mark the hand of Order; but, in many instances, the transitions are so minute, as to demonstrate *that hand to be divine.* The advocates for the doctrine perhaps are not aware they are inadvertently strengthening the hands of Infidelity.

From the most minute investigation of the VERONICA in question, it appears to be the V. SPICATA, with no greater alteration than what commonly occurs in plants growing in a rocky and exposed situation: however, if botanists will have mules, let them rank in their proper places as *Varieties*, not as *Species*.

Another part of this mountain forms a dreadful looking precipice, under the title of Clogwyn dwymheu y Glyder, awfully impending its dark crags over the baleful waters of Llyn Idwal, or the *Avernus of the Britons*. The shepherds believe it to be the haunt of demons; and say it is fatal to any of the feathered tribes who venture to stretch their wings across it.

A little farther on the left is a horrid fissure in the rock, called Twll du, or the *Black Cavern*. It is an open gap in a huge dark precipice; in depth about three hundred feet, and six wide; extending in length for a considerable way. Through its bottom rush violently the waters of Llyn y cwm. This chasm furnishes a striking feature in geological scenery an adjoining cwm, forming almost a bason, has originally been filled with waters, and formed a temporary lake. After this fissure was made, the waters, rushing violently through it into the inferior vale, produced the present lake, and left the cwm dry; and streams of huge stones lie on all sides, pointing to the hollows that lead to the chasm, exhibiting evident marks of retiring waters. On the rocks appear the Saxifraga nivalis, and the very rare plant Bulbocodium vernum. This plant, though a native of Spain, is also found far North on the cold mountains of Russia: the Lichen islandicus, Lichen tartarius, and several other species. The L. omphalodes the natives steep in urine, and form a paste, which they dry in the sun; and with the addition of alum make a brown dye. This and the L. TAR-TARIUS are so abundant, that the poor people employ themselves in gathering them for the use of the dry salters, at the low price of one penny per pound. They will, however, collect from twenty to thirty pounds a day. From these the beautiful dye called arcêll, or archil, is prepared as follows: —The LICHENS, when dry, are placed under a large indented stone, with a circular motion, and bruised; they are then thrown into capacious vats, and mixed with lime and urine. Here they are permitted to remain six months, but stirred every day; and the materials thicken as the humid particles evaporate. In this part of the process the substance appears like mire; afterwards like husks of grapes. When it has acquired the latter consistency, it is cut small, dried in a spacious room, sometimes reduced to powder, and packed in barrels for use; the most beautiful colours, such as purple, pink, greys, and pompadour, are obtained from the composition.

The two Glyders are connected by a long narrow strip of land called Y Wa un oer, or the cold mountain flat. On one side, in a deep hollow, is Llyn y Boch Llwyd, and on the other, at the foot of the Trevaen, Llyn Ogwyn.

The Trevaen is a conical hill of singular appearance, from the rugged and uncouth stones that lie upon its sides. It introduces you to the Glyderbach, out of which it is supposed by some to have been originally formed. The area of the summit of the little Glyder is covered with huge columnar stones from ten to thirty feet long, in an inclined direction, supported by others; some confusedly piled together, others flat, and others erect, and stones lying horizontally upon them. One stone, about twenty-five feet long and fifteen wide, is poised upon a large upright one, serving for a *fulcrum*, so that a small weight at the extremity will move the opposite end. Others of less dimensions are so nicely poised as to become rocking stones in the wind.

These broken masses[12] almost wholly cover the sides of this mountain; vegetation and even earth has deserted it, while unwieldly disjected fragments and bare glaucous rocks stare the traveller in the face; and through various fissures numerous streams rush down in continual roar to the lakes beneath.

Many of the upright fragments are pentagonal, with one of the sides narrower than the rest; and others, lying in the shape of cromlechs, almost give them the appearance of art. Some of the stones upon the summit are equal to those

---

12   A phenomenon called *Doear Dorr*, or rending of the earth, is frequent amid these mountains. It is occasioned by quantities of water, collected during the rainy season in cavities, on the sides of the mountains; this, in time, becomes so considerable as to burst through the surface or shell, and carries fragments of rocks, &c. into the vale below. By this considerable hillocks are removed from their place, and sometimes havodtys swept away. This is observed to happen during *thunder-storms*.

of Stonehenge. How these came here, and from what cause, is a question that involves difficulty. Were they the strata of the mountain laid bare by the continual rains and storms that assail it, their position would have assumed a greater regularity.

Mr. Pennant supposes, "this and its neighbours to have been thrown up by some mighty internal convulsion:" (*Vid. Snow. p.* 152,) and the finding, as he says he did, pieces of lava, confirmed him in this untenable opinion. It would have been more probable had they been in the valley; falling from the mountain they might fortuitously have got into these singular positions; and examples might have been adduced in support of the opinion, from places where heaps of stones, augmented by the accession of others falling on them, have appeared with some regularity. An instance of this occurs at the foot of Glyder vawr, on the margin of Llyn peris; where several huge fallen fragments have formed a cell; in which formerly a person resided, and it now serves for a sheep-fold. Many of the stones are similar in their position and appearance to those large groups on the sea beach where the tide is strong; and as they have most of them marine shells imbedded in them, they rather support the opinion of *the action of water than the action of fire.* To this I will add that I have never been fortunate enough to observe, in the course of my route, lava,[13] or any thing that could possibly be construed into *volcanic matter.* Mr. Aiken has made the same observation: the learned naturalist Mr. Llwyd made it many years ago; (*Vid. Phil. Trans. No.* 334:) and I can add the testimony of a gentleman, whose name, were I permitted to use it, would add honour to these pages, and who has travelled over most of the table-land in Wales. He affirms, *that he never could discover any volcanio matter, nor the least symptom of the action of fire amidst these mountains.*

His observation on Mr. Pennant's idea, that Llyn du Arddu in Cwm Brwynog has been the crater of a volcano is, *that every thing in the vicinity, so far from encouraging such an opinion, evidently indicates the retreat of waters towards the bowels of the earth.* The stones about the borders of the lake, and up its steep sides, lie in a circular form; and some in the Cwms still marking the channels by which they descended to the lake below. A sketch of this curious fact he has been so kind as to furnish me with.

---

13 Mr. Pennant must have alluded to small fragments of granitell, where the feldspar and iron having been decomposed, had left a cellular appearance, not unlike some specimens of lava; but there is, on a close examination, an *essential difference:* The pores of these are larger towards the interior, whereas those of lava are larger towards the surface. Lava affects the magnetic needles, and its specific gravity does not exceed 8. *Vid. Kir. V. II.* Horneblende is so altered by the atmosphere, as frequently to put on the appear ance of volcanic matter.

We must have recourse therefore to the scriptural account of the deluge; when the strata of the earth, being broken up and reduced to a chaotic state, fragments of distant hills might have rested thus at the subsiding of the waters. Numerous instances of this sort, where separate masses of stone lie upon the tops of hills and mountains, may be seen in Yorkshire, Derbyshire, Devonshire, and Cornwall.

It might have been expected, after the elaborate investigations of the learned Kirwan, respecting *basaltes* and other stones, asserted to be produced from subterraneous fusion, that we should have heard no more of the matter; that the volcanic gentry would have quietly resigned the property to be restored to its right owner, and permitted Neptune to be re-instated in his ancient demesne. But Error, like Proteus, when recognised in one shape, readily assumes another, and impudently appears again at the councils of Truth.

Infidelity will side with any, rather than with the Mosaic, account of things. It supposes that the present world arose by gradation, from the bottom of the sea; or that it was projected from the sun[14] by the violent concussion of a comet against it, and owes all its irregularities to vol-

---

14 This was not new; it was only a plausible modification of the eccentric conjectures of *poor old Whiston*; who thought that the present earth was the remains of a fiery comet, which, by having its orbit changed by a collision with the sun, gradually altered its nature, till it became what we at present see it!!!

canic explosions. (*Vid. Buffon.*) And many, fascinated by the ingenuity of such remarks, and imbibing an attachment to new systems of geology, involuntarily become the dupes of Infidelity.

Not feeling at present any symptom of hydrophobia, I cannot conceive why the internal parts of the earth may not abound with water as well as fire; and, if the common sense of the unprejudiced miner be consulted, who generally has much more experience of these subterraneous regions than systematic writers on the subject, his answer would be, that he has much more to dread from the inundations of the one than the depredations of the other.

When we hear a modern Heraclitus[15] positive-

---

15   This Philosopher flourished in the sixty-ninth Olympiad, in the time of Darius Hystaspes, before the year of Christ 500: He held, that *"Fire was the primum mobile, and grand parent of all things; generating continents and oceans by rarefaction and condensation; and, by an inverse movement, reducing all things again to their original state,"* &c. &c . *Vid. Plutarch, p.* 1, 3.

Whether Dr. H. is acquainted with the works of this antiquated sage, or has only heard of them by some French translator, I know not; but his theory is a very simple modification of the doctrines of the Italic School. What could have been the Doctor's motives for reviving this obsolete system of geology is not apparent; except it was the same which induced Erostratus to set fire to the temple of Diana at Ephesus; or it can be found in the answer, which a despicable Frenchman once gave to his companion, who remonstrated with him on the great impropriety of footing a minuet down the middle aisle of St. Peter's at Rome; *"On doit faire quelque chose pour se distinguer."*—Notoriety should be the French motto, in all ages.

ly asserting, under the profession of Christianity, that "*the present* earth arose from the ocean, and that new continents are forming by the action of fire, at the bottom of the sea, to rise in their turn; and thus the terraqueous globe *has been, and will be, eternal*"—Is this a moment for the friends of Revelation to hesitate, whether they will adopt the language of inspiration, or the bold conjectural assertions of these pretending empyrics in the Science of Physics?[16]

The side of this mountain, and its opposite Moel Siabod, for the long narrow vale of Dyffryn Mymbr, in which are the two small lakes of Llyniau Mymbr. These occupy the entrance of the vale, at the extremity of which stands the small village and church of Capel Cerrig. This dreary tract was once covered with thick forests of oak and beach.

Leland, in his *Itinerary, V. v. p.* 42, says, The best wood of Caernarvonshire is by Glynne Kledder, and by Glyn Llughy, and by Capel Kiryk, and at Llanperis. Many of the stools are still visible, and shew that the trees must have been of very large size. At present it is destitute of wood.[17] The

---

16 Those who have not read the theories of Buffon, Whitehurst, and Hutton, would find their time not misemployed, to see what Catcott has collected upon the subject in a small treatise on the Deluge, printed in 1761, and sold by Prince, in Oxford. To which they would do well to add De Luc's *Geological Letters.*

17 "The causes (says Leland) be these ; first , the wood cut down was never copissed; and this hath become a great cause of

venerable oaks are no more. Avarice and disspita-
tion have combined to despoil these alpine tracts
of their sylvan beauty and friendly shade; and,
instead of planting upon land that will bear neither grass nor corn, which *œconomy* would dic-
tate, the great proprietors of North Wales seem
emulous which shall the speediest and most effectually divest of timber his respective domain.

This plan of stripping the country of one of
its great sources of wealth, and a total inattention at the same time to the encouragement of a
spirited and profitable system of husbandry, will
operate powerfully in diminishing the value of
estates; and the baneful effects of such impolitic
conduct will be sensibly felt before the cause of it
is perceived. In Leland's time there was very little
corn raised except oats, barley, and rye, lest the
deer should destroy it. There is less perhaps now
raised in this district from the inability of the

---

destruction through Wales. Secondly, after cutting down
wooddys the gottys hath so bytten the young spring, that it
never grew, but like shrubbes. Thirdly, men for the nonys
destroied the great woodis, that they should not harbour
theves." *Vol.* V. *p.* 77.

At a variety of periods mines of different kinds have
been discovered and worked; and as little coal was found,
these must have caused a prodigious consumption of wood.
Whole forests were denudated, till the resources became
inadequate to the unceasing demands, and the mines were
at length neglected for want of means for the reduction of
the ore. This is the grand reason of so many of the apparent
worked-out mines, seen over the face of the country; which,
if fuel could be obtained at an easy rate, would again unbos-
om their treasures to the spirited adventurer.

farmers to till and manure the land sufficiently to ensure a profitable crop.

The farmers are chiefly dairy men; and make their rents from butter, wool, and lambs: they possess a few small cows, numerous sheep of diminutive size, and herds of goats.[18] These roam wherever inclination leads, confined by no fences; and frequently, unattended by a shepherd, are obliged to have recourse to their own exertions, against their formidable enemies the foxes, who here assemble în troops; and the ravens and large birds of prey, who from necessity, in this grainless country, become carnivorous. The sheep themselves appear quite different animals: instead of assembling in large flocks, they form gregarious parties, generally consisting of ten or twelve; of which number, while feeding, one stands at a distance as centinel, to give notice of approaching danger. If the guard perceive any thing making towards the little flock, he turns and faces the enemy, and permits him to advance within about one hundred yards. If his appearance be hostile, and he continue to advance, the guard then warns the party by a shrill whistling noise, till they have all taken the alarm, when he joins them in the rear,

---

18 These, from a pride that has invaded the farmers here, are on the decrease. It is considered less trouble, and more genteel, to have a greater number of sheep; though, in many cases, goats are found more profitable; yielding a rich milk, being more hardy, always procuring their own maintenance; and frequently are foster mothers for their children, as they are amidst the alps of France and Switzerland.

and they all betake them selves to the more inaccessible parts of the mountains.

During the summer months, they are followed by their owners, who leave their winter habitations, and take up their residence amidst the hills; where they erect, what are termed havodtys, or summer dairy houses. These are merely huts like the cottages before described, not unlike the ones occupied by the farmers of Switzerland. The furniture is equally simple with the building; a few stones supply the place of chairs, and bundles of rushes along the sides are in lieu of beds. Here the men pass their time in tending their flocks, or in harvest work; while the women milk the cattle, and are occupied in their dairies: they milk both sheep and goats as well as cows. A goat yields daily about two quarts of milk, the sheep one. Of these they make butter for sale, and cheese for home consumption.

Their mode of living is very simple: Baracyrch, with a little hung smoke-dried goat, forms their principal food; while their drink consists of whey, or butter-milk, and a few bottles of *cwrw*, preserved as a cordial in case of illness. They are, as may be expected from their plain and humble way of living, a hardy race; and free from many of those chronic diseases which are the offspring and concomitants of luxury and dissipation. If medicine is deemed necessary, the vegetables in the vicinity furnish it; and it is administered by the advice of some skilful and *venerable matron*.

The season over, on the approach of the cold, they return to their *hên drefon*, or winter habitations, where they enjoy the produce of their summer labours, and employ themselves in domestic concerns. It is usual for the head of the family to be skilled in, and to exercise every trade necessary, for their mode of life; as that of mason, carpenter, smith, wheelwright, shoemaker, taylor, &c. in which occupations the rest of the family assist him; and it is not a little gratifying to observe with what varied ingenuity he performs the several operations of handicraft business.

The Bottoms consist of meadows abounding with some tolerable grasses, as FESTUCA OVINA, AGROSTIS CAPILLARIS, &c. but too often mixed with a variety of the CAREX & JUNCUS, with numerous ORCHIS's and ASPHODELS, which render the scanty crops of hay still less valuable from the badness of the quality.

The vales were now enlivened by these indefatigable mountaineers, busy amidst their haymaking; seizing the opportunity which a dry day afforded to secure it. Some were loading sledges, some with horses and panniers, and even men and women carrying it away upon their shoulders. The continued rains had almost spoiled the crop, and they would have been deprived of great part of this by the violent hurricanes, had it not been for the ingenious precaution which hard necessity has taught them; that of making very small cocks, and placing a broad flat stone a little inclined over each; which serves the double purpose of keeping them steady, and defending them from the wet.[19] I wished them success, while I lamented, that patient industry should be so ill repaid; as, after all the anxiety and labour, to have only a spare crop of coarse and ill-made hay. However, it was the reserve for the sustenance of their cattle, during the long winters generally experienced here, and the sole dependance for their preservation.

Winding round the base of the lofty Siabod, to the southward, the fine lake of Llyn y Gwynnan stretches along the vale, about a mile in length, and half a one in breadth, with thick woods, (a pleasing rarity,) exhibiting the hoary spray of its numerous waterfalls, that rush down the rocks into the lake, to great advantage. A broad stream connects this with Llyn y ddinas, of equal extent, still confined by mountain-barriers, with a narrow strip of grass land on one side the streams, flushed by rains, roared down the craggy steep

---

19 Whirlwinds, or small tornadoes, are very common: they commence by a distant rumbling noise, similar to that which precedes earthquakes in the West Indies; and are seen advancing up the Cwms and hollows in a circular direction, and carrying fern, rushes, moss, slate, &c. with them; their hay, if unprotected, and frequently the summer dwellings. Mr. Jones, agent of the mines at Llanperis, relates, that some time since, some workmen he had employed to erect a wall on an adjoining hill were terrified by having their wooden boxes, in which they carried their provisions, snatched up suddenly by one of these eddies, and carried sixty yards high, which soon after fell, shattered to pieces.

on the other side; and in foaming eddies marked their course across the surface of the lake.

This is the much-admired varied vale of *Nant Hwynant*. The vast mountains that surround it, its transparent lakes, the numerous streams that water its verdant meads, the wild Avon Glas Llyn tumbling down the side of Snowdon from the lofty Ffynnon Las, its picturesque fall, and the hanging diversified woods, combine to entitle it to the appellation, *Residence of Beauty*. In this vale rises the remarkable elevation of *Dinas Emris*, clothed on all sides with wood, which makes a distinguished figure in British story. The sides are very steep, and two large ramparts of stone are still visible.

Here[20] hapless Vortigern is said to have secured himself after the disasters that followed his impolitic treaty. A small hollow in an adjacent rock, is called Cell y Dewyniaid, or Cell of the Diviners, the at tendants on the court of this British Prince. Among these the celebrated Merlin bore a distinguished part; whose story, while it serves to amuse, will give some idea of the credulity and pusillanimity, the vice and cowardice, of this early period of our history.

Vortigern, finding himself unable to cope with the Saxons, whom he had invited into his kingdom, had recourse to magic, to resist their

---

20 Gwrtheyn is said to have attempted building a castle here. This is the Welch name of Vortigern. *Vid. Evans, Diss. de Bordw,* p. 36.

arts and counteract their treachery. The oracular advice was, to build an impregnable fortress
in Snowdon; the plan was resolved on, and the
building begun but, as fast as the materials were
collected by day, they were removed by an invisible power by night.

The magicians were again convened. To throw
an air of mystery over impossibility, they asserted, that no building would stand that was not
sprinkled with the blood of a child, born without
the assistance of a father.

The kingdom was searched; for metaphysical
coalition, in an age when every thing was believed,
was not deemed improbable. At length a trivial accident brought the marvellous being to light. Two
boys were quarrelling, and one was overheard to
call the other an unbegotten knave. The boy and
his mother were instantly taken before the king:
she confessed that her child was supernaturally
begotten by an Incubus. The child was adjudged
to be sacrificed; but he, puzzling the wise men
with his questions, and giving a rational account
of the failure, he was spared; obtained his liberty,
and afterwards took the lead in the train of Necro-
mancers. The explanation he gave, doubtless put
into his mouth by the contrivers of the scheme,
was, that the fortress was erected in a deep morass; so that, as soon as the heavy stones were laid,
they sunk beneath the surface.

Ambrosius, (for that was his original name,)
was the son of a noble Roman, and his mother

a vestal virgin; she, having broken her vows to save her honour and life, invented this fable of a supernatural father; which the ignorance and credulity of the times easily admitted.[21]

He was called *Myrddin Emrys*; the name of Myrddin was patronymic from *Merlinus Ambrosius*; the sirname he took from the Congress of Magicians that decided on his fate; and to distinguish him from another Merlin, (Wyllit) born in Scotland.[22] He was an able mathematician, astronomer, and chymist;[23] whereby he was able to perform wonders in the eyes of the vulgar, and to give a probable prognostication of future events. Hence he was supposed, like Bacon, to have had an illicit connection with the spiritual world; and all he did was attributed to magic. Numbers of prophecies were attributed to him, the divulging or explaining of which was prohibited by the council of Trent.

---

21 *Vid. Nennius Eulog. Brit, C.* 42.

22 *Vid. H. Llwyd Cam, Brit. p.* 65.

23 Like the Tuscan sages, he was through life considered the son of a Genius; and like them was the author of prophetic visions, declarative ofthe prosperous or adverse events of his country. It was the policy of the British princes to command the bards to foretell, in poetic strains, their success in war, to incite their people to deeds of bravery; for which cause the vulgar supposed them real prophets. Hence their great veneration for the prophetic bards, Myrddin Emrys, Taliesin, and Myrddin Wyllt, &c. There are many of these prophecies still extant; and the custom of prophecying did not cease till Henry VII's. time; the reason of which is sufficiently obvious.

I have now been traversing one of the most wonderful parts, and worthy of observation, in the three kingdoms;[24] which, in point of romantic scenery and variety of productions, is not perhaps to be equalled by the boasted wonders of the Rhetian alps. The views are grand, picturesque, and pleasing: they exhibit a rich variety both of the sublime and beautiful. Here is nothing of art, so diminutive in the scale; but pure simple nature, wildly and capriciously sporting, in the formation of her gigantic productions, grotesque rocks, towering hills, and extensive lakes, agreeably interspersed and lying in their bosoms; whence the most limpid brooks and romantic streams the eyes ever beheld roll their salubrious waters down the sides of the mountains, or meander in pleasing murmurs through the distant vales; and then fall in beautiful cascades over rocky wears; while the dense foliage of the over hanging wood just permits the observer to ken the whitened foam of these agitated waters: Again, meeting with farther obstruction, they obtain new strength by accumulation, and dash headlong down some dreadful precipice into gloomy excavations beneath; where, thundering and roaring, they contend amidst impending dissevered fragments of rock, which, by their impetuosity, they frequently dislodge, and hurl with resistless force and deafening noise to the vale below.

---

24 Near the walls of a farm-house in this vale grows the FUMARIA CLAVICULATA.

In this varied country the mountains seen far off put on a pleasing appearance; but, on a nearer view, they inspire terrific ideas. The species of grandeur, which accompanies the idea of immensity at a distance, charms the sight; the heart feels absorbed in delight, while the eye ranges over this extensive chain of enormous and adamantine masses, rising one above the other in lofty gradation. The succession of soft and lively shades, whose tints are tempered by passing clouds, affords pleasurable sensations; and makes this native wall of rocks partake of the beautiful rather than the sublime.

But the mind of sensibility cannot take a nearer view of these same scenes without experiencing an involuntary terror. The almost-constant snows, steep and inaccessible ascents, gloomy caverns, resounding torrents, that precipitate themselves from the summits, the dark forests that here and there clothe their sides, and the enormous fragments detached by time from their foundations; all unite to impress the ideas of awe and apprehension.

It is in scenes like these, far away from the fascinating allurements and dissipating examples of public life, that the mind becomes unshackled from the world; regains its native freedom of election; and, smiling at the insignificant objects which hitherto engrossed its affections, nobly wings its flight and gains the skies. Absent from the destructive snares of folly and dissipation, I feel my own littleness and importance the view of the one dethrones my pride; the view of the other ennobles and elevates my thoughts; the one disarms me of all self-consequence and self-exaltation; the other points to the Deity, and discovers my alliance with the Divine Nature. I feel gratitude arise towards the Supreme Being, for bestowing upon me an imagination which renders these scenes of grandeur and silence grateful to my heart. I see the hand of God in these stupendous objects. Alone, I feel his secret presence guide my steps; confess that he is about my paths and about my bed; and hope I shall learn to acknowledge him in all my ways.

The manners of the inhabitants of this alpine tract partake of the nature of the country. They may be rude, but they are generous: the severity of their sky renders them hardy; while the pastoral life mingles a degree of softness in their character. These alpine Britons, who have seen no better houses than their own self-built huts; no other country but their native rocks; and no other sky but their own atmosphere, darkened by clouds and deluged by storms; conceive the whole world to be in like manner formed of the same rough materials.

The heavens do not, however, here always put on those unfriendly appearances. The tempest does not always rage, nor the forked lightnings strike the mountain's brow. The storms subside; the sky becomes serene; and the chearing sun again exhilarates the dreary scenes with his enlivening beams. Such are the Cambrian's head and Cambrian's heart: kindness succeeds to anger, and generosity to savage fury.

From history and observation it is evident, that the inhabitants of this country are not of a degenerate cast; their sentiments are elevated, and their feelings warm. Boldness and intrepidity are innate. A spirit of liberty still warms their bosoms; and they would trample tyrants and tyranny under their feet.

An inviolable attachment prevails to their country they love their king, and they are grateful to Providence, who permits each individual to live peaceably under his own vine and his own fig tree.—Happy Cambrians! may the follies of refinement, or the vices of luxury, never interrupt your repose!

Your's,

J. E.

Letter IX

Bangor

DEAR SIRS,

he distance from Caernarvon to Bangor is nine miles, of as delightful road as the fancy could possibly imagine. The views, whichever way the eye ranges, are diversified and picturesque; to the right the alpine scenery we had just left arose in sterner grandeur, flanked by the lesser elevations, with the varied Cwms, that separate the chain into so many distinct mountains, terminating in wooded vales, behind which the aspiring summits recede in the back ground from the view. On the left the Anglesea shore, with its numerous inclosures and rich plantations, intermingled with the seats of Plas Coch, Plas Newydd, and Plas Llanidan; and the Menai, opening with all the grandeur of an American river, till hid by the thick woods of Vaenol; where is the house of Mr. Smith, an eminent mansion of that name. Nothing can exceed the beauty of the Menai, covered with small craft, and winding to the North-east; as it appears in the different vistas of the woods which cover its margin. Its waters have greatly the advantage of a river; those are frequently muddy at the return of tide, while these always retain their transparency, and that green hue and sparkling brilliancy which are the distinguishing beauties of *Sea-Water*.

As we descend the hill of Vaenol, the sylvan scenery opens and exhibits the neat little City of

BANGOR

So called from *Bon chôr*, (*i . e.* good Choir.) It lies in a narrow valley, between two low ridges of slate rock, open toward Snowdon on the South, and about half a mile below the town to the North, expanding into the beautiful bay of Beaumaris; the low towers of whose Castle are visible from the beach, the noble mansion of Lord Bulkley, at Baron Hill, rising majestically behind. At a distance, Puffin's Island, and the high promontory of Orme's Head, are seen to guard the entrance of the harbour; the vast Penmaen mawr, and a line of villages with cultivated fields, abounding in wheat and barley, lie stretched along the shore. This place, at present so small, was once so considerable as to be called *Bangor vawr*, or the Great.[1] It was defended by a powerful castle, built by Lupus, Earl of Chester the scite of which is still visible on a precipitous hill, about half a mile to the eastward of the City, and the form may now easily be traced by the remaining foundations. This is all we could learn of its history.[2]

The present Bangor however arose from one still greater and more ancient, *Bangor Iscoed*, in Flintshire. Among other books we consulted for guidance in our route, was *A Walk through Wales*. We entered Bangor with an enthusiastic ardour, to see the divine river with the elegant bridge; and, more especially, the ruins of its far-famed monastery, where a hundred fresh Monks celebrated the praise of GOD every hour, day and night, (*Vid. Gildas,*) in conjunction with those of Glastonbury and Salisbury. Conceive the surprise of the party, when, on a survey of the place, we could not find sufficient water to be termed a trickling rill. In some instances we found our author accurate, and were much pleased with

---

1   These are evident traces that this was once a city of considerable extent. It probably covered the whole of the rising ground now lying between the present town and the Menai. In ploughing, ruins of buildings are frequently discovered .

2   It was occupied as an entrenched camp by the Danes, and afterwards by the Oliverian forces, in their route towards Caernarvon.

the brilliancy of his descriptions; but we were at a most perfect loss how this majestic river could have been here in 1797 and not in 1798! Examining our maps, it appeared, that no such river had been known to run here for more than two centuries; nor any bridge been heard of, save one projected a few years ago by the Irish travelling this way, to be built over the Menai; but the scheme, being opposed by the people of Caernarvon, was quickly relinquished.

A geographical friend suggested, that the author might have meant Bangor in Flintshire, a small village situate in Maeler, on the Banks of the Dee, through which the river famed in song is known to flow, and over which a handsome stone bridge of five arches forms a communication between the counties of Flint and Denbigh. This suggestion led to an inquiry how the learned antiquarian of Bath could have committed such a palpable blunder.

One of our party, more shrewd than liberal, did not hesitate to pay the author the same compliment which Johnstone paid the traveller to the source of the Nile; "Sir," says he, "the pedestrian Tourist has never been West of the Severn;" but, finding he was acquainted with the intelligent landlord of the Three Eagles, I was still at a loss to conjecture the cause of so evident a misnomerin topographical description. Taking up Dr. Darwin's *Zoonomia*, the mysterious business was unravelled. In Chap. XIX. on *Reverie*, the ingenious author observes,

> When we are employed with great sensation
> of pleasure, or with great efforts of volition, in
> the pursuit of some. interesting train of ide-
> as, we cease to be conscious of our existence,
> are inattentive to time and place, and do not
> distinguish this train of sensitive and volun-
> tary ideas from the *irritative ones* excited by
> the presence of external objects; though our
> organs of sense are surrounded with their ac-
> customed stimuli; till at length this interest-
> ing train of ideas becomes exhausted, or the
> appulses of external objects are applied with
> unusual violence, and we return with surprize
> or regret into the common track of life.

It immediately occurred, that this might have
been the case with the author in question. Having
the History of the Massacre of the Monks strong
in his recollection, and his mind wafted back to
the period when cruelty and devotion were the
grand characteristics of the age, he might have
been at the Three Eagles, refreshed himself at
Hutchins's, and left Bangor before he was able
to attend to the objects around him. And let him,
who is inclined to smile at the doctrine, recollect,
if he has never been guilty of the like from the
force of prior impressions, and in instances more
important to happiness; for oft

Our *waking dreams* prove fatal.

The British churches, as they had received the doctrines of the Gospel from apostolic hands, so for centuries they were jealous of preserving them pure, and transmitting them untainted to their posterity: and till the sixth century, they in a great measure retained their primitive integrity. But at length, St. Austin, with the innovations of Rome, arrived in the island, and endeavoured, by intreaty and force, to unite the British churches with the see of Rome. In some degree he prevailed, but the errors of that church were not so fully received by the Clergy of North Wales as those of England, as appears by their uniformly rejecting the unscriptural injunction of celibacy to the priesthood; the Clergy being married through the whole period, and readily and unanimously embracing the primitive principles of their churches, when the Reformation restored them the liberty of reassumption. But the infraction of their privileges was resolutely withstood by the British Clergy; and, if they were not all perfectly pure in their morals, for Gildas unmercifully accuses them, yet, as a body, they stood forward like men of principle in the cause, and defended it with a determined vigour, becoming persons who were contending for the faith once delivered to the Saints. The Bards united in their efforts, denouncing woe on such of the Clergy as were remiss and neglected their duty in so perilous a time, when their temporal and spiritual privileges were in danger of becoming a prey to the avarice and rapine of unjust invaders.

Taliesin has left this curious fragment.

Gwaer offeiriad byd, nis ánghreifftia gwyd,
  Ac nis Pregetha.
Gwae ni cheidw, ei Gail acefyn fugail
  Ac nis areilia.
Gwae ni cheidw ei ddefaid, rhay Bleiddie Rhifeuniaid,
  Aî ffon gnwppa.

Woe to the Priest, at eve or morn;
Neglects to preach, or weed his corn,
  And root out all the tares.
Woe to the shepherd that's remiss
In watching of his flock, and is
  Unfaithful in his cares.
Woe be to him, that doth not keep,
With shepherd's staff, his harmless sheep
  From Romish wolves and snares.

This spirited resistance brought down upon them the revenge of Rome. St. Austin and his Coadjutors had obtained considerable influence in several of the Saxon Courts. Edelfrid, King of Northumberland, having obtained an advantage over the Strath Clwyd Britons, was instigated to turn his arms against the Welch, who were at that time in possession of Chester.

On his arrival near that city, his army being drawn up in front of the enemy, he perceived a body of men, without military appearance, stationed in a place of security. Struck at the novelty of the sight, he inquired into the cause, and was told, they were the Monks from the Monastery of Bangor, who had come to offer up their prayers for the prosperous event of the day. Enraged at an opposition so singular in its nature, and stimulated with an hatred for a religion, that threatened the destruction of Paganism, Edelfrid commanded his army first to assail this defenceless and pious troop, who had already fasted and prayed three days. Twelve hundred of these unfortunate religious were cut in pieces, and fifty only of the whole number present at the battle escaped the enemy's sword.

After this cowardly act, the Saxon Prince marched to Bangor, and, with a barbarism worthy only of Goths and Vandals, destructive of those arts which soften and improve human nature, he entirely laid waste that ancient and celebrated seminary of religion and learning, and committed to the flames its valuable library. Edelfrid then attempted to penetrate into Wales, but his passage over the Dee was disputed at Bangor by the Prince of Powis, who gallantly sustained the charge, till relieved by Cadvan, King of North Wales, Meredydd, king of South Wales, and Bledrus, the Sovereign of Cornwall.

When the confederate Princes had joined their forces, they called in religion to their aid. Dinawd, the Abbot of Bangor, delivered an oration to the army; and, before the action commenced, gave orders, that the soldiers should kiss the ground, in commemoration of the Communion of the body of CHRIST; and should take up water in their hands out of the Dee and drink it, to the remembrance of his precious blood. Animated by this act of devotion, and stung with resentment for the disgrace and injury they had lately received, the Welch encountered the Saxons with great fury, entirely defeated them with the loss of ten thousand men, and obliged Edelfrid, with the remains of his army, to make a speedy retreat into his own country.

There was something singular in the event of that day, as an act of retributive justice, and as it severely punished, in the sight of Bangor, the recent and wanton desolation of its Monastery. These events are differently detailed by historians, but there is no doubt as to the authenticity of the facts, since they are admitted by all, without a single exception; and they serve strongly to prove what inveterate rancour there is in the human heart against real religion; and that, when its enemies endeavour to suppress or oppose it, they generally aim the weapons of their malice at the persons of its *Ministers*.

After this massacre, which happened A. D. 503, the remaining Monks were dispersed. Some of them were collected under Daniel, son of Danawd or Dionothus, at this place, where he founded a college for the education of youth, and gave it the name of Bangor, from whence it was removed. A church was soon erected, and it was made a Bishop's See, by Maelgwyn, and Daniel consecrated Bishop of it by Dubricius, Archbishop of Caerleon. *Vid. Rowland, p.* 153.

The church was endowed with lands and franchises by Maelgwyn, A. D. 550, who is related to have been so struck at the criminality of his past life, that he resolved to devote the residue to the cloister. But the pleasures of the world, to which he was too much addicted, induced him to relinquish the design, and again to return to the affairs of court, and his former habits of criminality.

The Deanery was founded by Iago ap Beli, A. D. 603, and further endowed by Anarawd, A. D. 878; and still further by Edgar, in the reign of Howel ap Jefaf, who is said to have built a parochial church, dedicated to St. Mary, behind the palace. The cathedral was destroyed by the Saxons, 1071. It was rebuilt by King John, A. D. 1212. In 1402 it was burnt and pillaged by Owen Glyndwr, and lay in ruins for near a century. The choir was restored by Bishop Deny, and the present body and tower built by Bishop Skeffington, 1532. The tower was to have been raised to twice its present height, but the Bishop's death prevented the execution. Indeed the mixed and ornamental architecture mark the time of Henry VII. It is built cruciform and consists of a large nave, transept and choir; but the effect of the transept is lost on one side by a new Register Office, lately erected, which greatly disfigures the external appearance of the building.

Among the remains of eminent persons that lie here, are those of Gryffydd ap Cynan, who died A. D. 437; but no vestige of the shrine remains. Beneath a simple arch lies the body of Owen Gwynedd, the wise and valiant Prince of North Wales, who obtained this high encomium—"He died regretted by his friends, and feared by his enemies, A. D. 1167." Part of Bishop Skeffington is deposited here, who died in 1530; and who, by a singular will, directed, that his body should be interred at Beaulieu, of which monastery he had been Abbot, and his heart deposited at Bangor, before the image of St. Daniel.

The choir is fitted up in a style of neat and simple elegance, by the munificence of the present prelate, and ornamented with a good organ, the gift of Dr. Thomas Lloyd, 1779. The service of this cathedral is performed with reverential decorum, and a true solemnity of devotion; and a regulation has been made by the Bishop, to accommodate all the inhabitants of Bangor and the environs. The service is performed in Welch at seven o'clock in the morning, in English at eleven, and in Welch again at four in the afternoon.

The chapter consists of a Dean, three Arch-deacons, two Precentors, two Vicars, six Minor Canons, six lay Clerks, and eight Choristers, with an income of 2000l. per annum.

The Bishop's palace is to the North-west of the cathedral, and was rebuilt by Bishop Skeffington; and though it has of late been greatly improved, it is far from being so magnificent as those of his episcopal brethren in England.

I had to lament, that a trifling dispute with his Chancellor had driven the present Diocesan from his residence; and with little prospect of his return. While I regretted the cause of his absence, I was induced to ask whether any motives of private pique or improper conduct on the part of an individual, could justify a christain Bishop in the dereliction of his solemn and impartial charge? leaving his Clergy to their own discretion, unsupported by his zeal, and without encouragement from his example? and this at a time too, when, with a laudable regard for discipline, he was enforcing parochial residence among his Clergy with the most rigorous exaction? It is to be hoped, his Lordship will speedily recover from all selfish considerations, and, placing the petty reflection of a single opponent's insolence or injuries in the scale with the weighty appendages of a mitre, will be induced to return to his cathedral, again animate his diocese by his presence, and be a blessing to his neighbourhood by his wonted liberality.[3]

---

3   While this work was going to press, the bishop died, as it is
    said, of a *broken heart*. It was with pleasure and indignation
    I received from an impartial adherent to truth, resident on
    the spot, an account of the real cause of his iniquity which
    raised the persecution and pleasure at the integrity of prin-
    ciple and rectitude of conduct which provoked. Dr. Warren
    was an instance of a Christian Bishop being cruelly persecut-
    ed, driven from his charge, and hunted like a beast of prey,

The house called the Friery, stood at a small distance from the city, founded 1276, or as Tanne says by Tudor ap Gronvw, Lord of Penmynydd, 1297. It was probably a house of Minor or Franciscan Friers, as was another at Beaumaris, founded by Llewelyn, 1230, and dedicated to St. Francis.[4] A grant of it was made by Edward VI. to Thomas

in a country where Christianity is protected, and established by law, and at the close of the *eighteenth century*. Too honest to bethe toad-eating tool of men, vulgarly denominated *the great:* and too holy to forego his solemn engagements, and make the patrimony of the church a treasury for electioneering bribes; he was pursued with every engine that malice could invent, or money procure. He was represented as a monster of iniquity, though as innocent as a lamb; and the fortitude and resignation with which he long bore the taunts and threats of his enemies, was only exceeded by their malicious industry and relentless fury. Their hatred was inexorable, their revenge insatiable. Vile reports, paragraphs in newspapers, and periodical publications; anonymous pamphlets, ridiculous caricatures, and menacing letters of assassination, were some of the instruments made use of; and from the affair of *Amlwch Church*, till the day of his death, he had not a moment's respite. And what had he done? Impartially might hehave summed up his defence, as one did of old, "*Est mihi supplicium, causa fuisse pium.*" Heis gone, where thewicked cease from troubling, and the weary are at rest. And I would charitably recommend to the relentless persecutors of the good Bishop, be they *noble* or *ignoble*, seriously to prepare to meet the injured prelate at that tribunal where there is no respect of persons: and where impartial Justice alike awards to the injurer and the injured their respective retribution.

4   "A Priory of White Friers, by Bangor, dedicated to Jesu." (*Vid. Leland.*) But for this we had not known whether they had been black, white, grey, crutched, begging, or preaching friers, of this ramified order.

Brown and William Breton, who gave it to Doctor Glynn, to convert into a free school, 1557. It has long been in high repute, as a training seminary for Oxford, and Trinity College, Dublin. A very handsome school-house has been lately erected, and the present master is the Rev. P. Williams, of Christ Church College, Oxon, with an income of £400 per annum.

At a small distance from the city, is one of the six ferries into Anglesea, called *Borth*; which being considered the safest, is more used than all the others. There is a good inn on this side for the accommodation of passengers, beautifully situated in hanging gardens on a rock, that overlooks the Menai on the shore grows abundance of the COCHLEARIA OFFICIALIS, C. DANICA, PAPAVER CAMBRICUM, LICHEN FUSCUS, L. LANATUS, L. CŒRULESCENS, BRYUM VERTICILLATUM, BYSSUS AUREA, and ASPLENIUM LANCEOLATUM; and on the rising ground, between the city and the ferry, the HYPERICUM ANGUSTIFOLIUM, and GALLEOPSIS VILLOSA.

The situation of Bangor renders it peculiarly eligible as a place of residence. There are a number of genteel houses belonging to the clergy and gentry who reside near; and the whole being white washed, and covered with slates, have a neat and comfortable appearance. The variety of views and pleasant walks, the sea, the vicinity to Caernarvon, and the great Irish and London road passing through the place, are inducements not usually met with together.

Free from the bustle of larger, and the intrigues of more polished cities, it seems fitted for social retirement: where the mind may have leisure for investigation and reflection, and occasionally find relief from its weariness in the relaxation of friendly intercourse.

Struck with the place on my entering into it, a closer observation of the distinct parts that formed the agreeable whole, served to confirm my opinion, and rivet my attachment: and with all the enthusiasm of Horace for his favourite Tiber, I exclaimed,

> Banchôr Arvona positum colono,
> Sit meæ sedes, utinam senectæ.

I wished to take up my abode in this highly favoured spot; to give free range to my partialities for natural history, in a country that afforded such opportunities for its pursuit; and only regretted that the duties of my station called me to a more public situation.

I had forgot to inform you that we put up at the Three Eagles; where we met with good accommodations and the most pointed civility from our host, Mr. Hutchins; whose urbanity of manners, and extensive information will induce those, who have once experienced it, to make an effort to spend their halting day at Bangor.

About a mile below the city, on the shore, is a considerable salmon snare: it is formed by posts driven into the ground, at certain regular distances, and the intervals closed with watling or wicker work. The fence, which forms a snare, is about ten feet high, and six or seven hundred yards in length, of a semicircular shape. The fish roll in with the flood tide, and, as it ebbs, they are fatally debarred returning to the ocean, by this ingenious device hundreds of salmon, with immense quantities of other fish, are frequently taken at one tide. This fishery is the property of Lord Penhryn; but is let to fishermen at a very considerable rental.

The Menai abounds with eels, crabs, lobsters, cockles, perewinkles, limpets, and other shell fish. Informed that many of them were within our reach, the tide being out, we determined to satisfy our curiosity.

The beach is covered with large stones, washed up by the violence of the tide: under many of these there are cavities filled with water; in which are secreted quantities of eels, crabs, &c. which were discoverable on turning over the stones. The taking them is attended with some difficulty, owing to the slippery quality of the one, and the griping faculty of the other; but, at the same time, affords a pleasing and profitable amusement. A large assortment was the result of our diversion; and a second edition of the pleasure, devoid of the toil, was furnished by the delicious repast.

So prone is man to neglect, if not to despise, the good within his power, that you will not be surprised to hear, the poor of the neighbourhood do not take advantage of this constant supply which Providence has thrown in their lap.

Another walk furnished us with new scenes for observation. Two miles from Bangor is Aber Cegid, a small creek, through which the Ogwyn empties itself into the Menai, fordable at low water; on this creck a new port is fast rising into consequence, formed at the expence of Lord Penhryn, (and called after his name) for the advantage of his Lordship's slate quarries, which are four miles above at Dolawyn, near Llyn Meirig, in the mountains of Ogwyn. The situation of *Port Penhryn* is convenient, being well sheltered by the Anglesea shore, and vessels of three and four hundred tons burthen ride securely close to the quay, to take in their lading; there were vessels now here from London, Bristol, and Liverpool; but the chief trade is with Ireland; this is made the grand depôt of the slate trade; and spacious warehouses are erected for that purpose; the hills from whence they are procured are some of those secondary mountains that form the first parapet of the Snowdon chain. The slates are of all sizes, from large tomb-stones and slabs for pavement, down to the smallest size used for roofing; they are distributed into the respective sizes and qualities, according to the scheme, and sold at the following prices, for *money only.*

		£.	s.	d.
Duchesses	per 1000	3	10	0
Countesses	ditto	2	0	0
Ladies	ditto	1	0	0
Doubles	ditto	0	11	0
Singles	ditto	0	5	0
Parents	per ton	1	6	0
Rags	ditto	0	18	0
Kiln Ribs	per yard	0	0	3

Near the port a large manufactory of cyphering slates, ink-stands, and other fancy articles, is carried on by an agent of his Lordship's, through whose politeness we obtained the above statement, and the following account of the process of the manufactory.

The rude slates from the mines are first reduced to shape and size by a small edged tool, similar to a plaisterer's hatchet, the slate being previously placed on the edge of an iron plane, fixed vertically; they are then taken to the scraper, who, with a small piece of thin steel, takes off the imperfect laminæ, and reduces the surface to a level; they are passed into other hands, who grind them with a flat stone; after wards polished by the actions of water and slate-powder; and being stained with a black water-colour and framed, are piled up in grosses for exportation. They are distinguished into two sizes, large and

small, price of the large, 5*l*. per gross, and the
small 2*l*. 6*s*. ditto. To such a degree of proficien-
cy have the Welch arrived in the manufacturing of this article, that they are able to undersell
the Dutch, while the quality is much better. The
slates imported from Holland are always rough,
and of an indifferent colour on one side, while
those of Wales are equally coloured and polished
on both a sure criterion of the two manufactories.
At a small distance from the port, a handsome
building attracted our notice: it was Roman luxury accompanied by Roman taste; an elegant set
of hot and cold sea-water baths, with dressing,
tea-rooms, &c. the light is admitted through a
beautiful dome at top; they exhibit, in their design and execution, the taste of the architect, and
the liberality of the owner.[5] The building, for the
boundage of the daily tides, stands far out, and
a communication is formed with the park by an
amazing high carriage terrace, whence the surrounding views on the Menai are seen to great
advantage. Entering the park, the turrets of the
noble mansion of Penhryn appear, standing on
the summit of a hill, formerly embosomed with
a grove of venerable oaks, which have now given
place to more modern plantations.

This was once a royal residence, and the present mansion is supposed to have been erected
upon the scite of a palace occupied by Molwynog,

5   This was the ingenious *Wyatt*, and the building, terrace,
&c.is said to have cost 30,000*l*.

prince of North Wales. In 987, it was levelled to the ground by Meredydd ap Owen. Llewelyn bestowed it upon Yardyr ap Trahaiarn; and in the reign of Henry VI. it was rebuilt on a smaller scale by Gwilim ap Gryffydd. In Leland's time it was inhabited by a Mr. Powel; and in the reign of Elizabeth it was the property and residence of the celebrated naval commander Piers Gryffyd, who so nobly distinguished himself in the defeat of the Spanish Armada.

The present possessor is Richard Pennant, created September 16th 1783, *Baron Penhryn*, of Penhryn, in the county of Louth. His lordship married 1765, Ann Susanna, daughter of Lieutenant-General Warburton, of Winnington, in the county of Chester, in whose right he posesses a moiety of the estate. It must be a drawback upon his lordship's happiness to reflect, that he has no child to inherit either his titles or his treasures. The buildings inclose a large area or quadrangle, with a gateway, tower, chapel, vast hall, saloon, and other apartments. The whole has lately undergone a thorough repair; and numerous alterations, still preserving the Gothic style, have been made under the direction of that able architect, Mr. Wyatt. An old drinking horn is preserved as a relic of the former hospitality of Penhryn; it is considered as very ancient, but the initials P. G. &c . tend to a conjecture, that it is not older than the time of Elizabeth. It is a large ox's horn, enriched with silver, and suspended by a chain of the same metal. Among the ancient Welch, according to the *Leges Walliæ*, the following distinctions prevailed: 1st, *Y Corn ydd y fo y Brenin*, or the prince's horn; 2, *Corn y Cyweithas*, or that by which the domestics of the palace were assembled;—and 3d, the *Corn y pencynydd*, the chief huntsman's, (*vid.* 311.) On festive days, it was a favour granted to the chief officers to drink out of the prince's horn, and to the inferior domestics out of those belonging to the superiors. The etiquette of the ceremony was, that its contents (strong metheglin) must be quaffed *at one tip*; and the horn blown by the person who drank last, to show there was no flinching. Such horns were in use among the Saxons, Danes, and Scotch, and most northern nations. Johnson mentions one preserved at Dunvegan, the seat of Macleod; "An ox's horn hollow, so as to hold two quarts, which the heir of Macleod was expected to swallow at one draught, as a test of his manhood, before he was permitted to bear arms, or could claim a seat among the men." (*Vid. Journ. to the Heb.*)

The south entrance into the park is by a grand gateway in the style of a triumphal arch, and corresponds with the magnificence of the mansion. The river Ogwyn, which used to extend its waters over a wide stony bed, is confined within narrow limits, and the different falls in it form pleasing cascades, which are seen from the front of the house, through vistas cut for the purpose, in the plantations; in it grows the CONFERVA FLU-

VIATILIS. His lordship, with a spirit of gratitude, and with a view of recommending an article that produced him a princely in come, has inclosed his park with *palisadoes of slate* they are cut into strips of five feet long and about six inches broad, and are fastened to the railing by wooden pins.

On a small eminence, just above the banks of the Ogwyn, stands the very neat structure of Llandegai church; it is built cruciform, the tower resting upon four arches in the centre of the building; the style is perfect Gothic, and marks the age of Edward III. The church-yard is inclosed by a slate fence round the bottom of the conc-shaped hill; which, with the neatness of the edifice, and the perspicuous situation, gives it a pleasing appearance; it is celebrated for being the burial-place of Archbishop Williams: a mural monument,[6] with the figure of the prelate

---

6 On sight of this monument, Dr. Davis felt himself poetically inspired, and produced the elegant lines preserved in Dodsley's collection, Vol. 6.

After lamenting over the fallen honours of the degraded Prelate, he breaks out in an animated apostrophe.

Could not thy Lincoln yield her pastor room,
Could not thy York supply thee with a tomb?

And ends with this pleasing moral.

Envied Ambition, what are all thy schemes,
But waking misery, or pleasing dreams;
Sliding and tottering on the heights of state,
The subject of this verse declares thy *fate*.
Great as he was, you see how small the gain,

in his archiepiscopal robes, kneeling before an altar, is placed over his remains. This great man was long the subject and the sport of fortune for a series of years he successively enjoyed her favours, was exalted to the see of Lincoln, became lord-keeper of the privy-seal, and was made metropolitan of York; while in the former station, he was tried by his peers, and being found guilty of subornation, suffered imprisonment from 1637 to 1640. After being liberated, he was raised to the archiepiscopal see of York: being shortly after banished, he died at the house of Sir, Roger Mostyn, of Gloddaeth, in 1650, aged 68. Mr. Pennant has said, "that he must be considered as a wise, rather than a good man;" he is charged with being haughty, highly resentful, and his character fraught with duplicity; the protest he made in the House of Lords[7] is produced as a proof of the former, and the advice he gave his unfortunate master,[8] with regard to the Earl of Strafford, of the latter.

A burial so obscure, a muse so mean.

7 In 1641, on the debate for taking away the votes of Bishops in the House of Peers, he, by an impassioned speech, induced eleven Bishops to join him in the protest against all Acts that should pass the House during their forced absence; for this they were impeached of high treason, and doomed to eighteen months' imprison ment, but soon after released upon bail, The Archbishop was banished his diocese during the disturbances in the county of York.

8 His advice to Charles was, in case the King could not win Cromwell by promises and fair treatment; to have recourse to stratagem, to secure his person and put him to death.

It must be confessed, that in his political conduct the archbishop discovered too much of the cursed doctrine of Machiavel, "*a public and a private conscience;*" but it should be remembered, that he lived in times when political and moral order were trampled under feet when the spirit of party ran so high, as to overwhelm the consideration of strict justice: and the want of charity and honour were lost in the provocations of injury, and the prevarications suggested by the sudden impulse of self-preservation, He retired, in the latter part ofhis life, to the peace ful retreats of North Wales, devoted his life to meditation and prayer, and is said to have met death with a fortitude that must have been inspired by a believing hope and a resignation, that bespoke the faith ofa Christian,

I am,

Yours, &c.

J. E.

Letter X

DEAR SIR,

L eaving Bangor, with regret, as we proceeded towards Conway the country increased in the richness and variety of the views the Menai here begins to expand itself from the harbours of Beaumaris and Conway into the Irish sea, beyond the jetting promontories of the great and little Orme's Head: the lofty Ogwyn stretching away to the east ward, the sullen Penman-Mawr in front, and the variety of shipping to and from the harbour of Liverpool in the distant offing, beguiled the time till we found ourselves in the small, but celebrated village of Aber, at the entrance of a glen, that runs in about two miles, bounded on one side by a mountain covered with woods, and on the other by a tremendous slate rock, called *Maes y Gaer*. In the upper part of the glen, a semicircular rock presents itself, over which, in wild uproar rolls an impetuous mountain torrent, consisting of a double fall, the lowest of which may be about fifty feet, and forming a broad and white sheet of water, whose dashing foam produces a snowy spray or dew, not unlike the Stanbauch observed by travellers amidst the Alps.

The pleasing situation of the inn, under a group of mountains rising in proud pre-eminence above each other in the back-ground, while Anglesea displays her wooded shores in front, may induce the traveller to spend a day at

ABER

Near the village is a conical mount, on which for merly stood a castle, the palace of the princes of North Wales; in digging lately, some remains of its foundation were discovered: it was here Llewelyn received the summons to deliver up the principality to the crown of England, upon the three qualified conditions advised by the Archbishop of Canterbury, and which produced the spirited memorial, which, for its animated and eloquent diction, might have reflected credit on a more polished age, and at once discovered the oppressive measures pursued by Edward, and the injurious treatment the Welch experienced from their haughty neighbours. (*Vid. Powell.*)

This is one of the ferries to Anglesea: when the tide is out, the Lavan sands are dry for four miles over which the passenger has to walk to and from the channel, where the ferry-boat plies; these, frequently shifting, render it highly dangerous, and several in stances have occurred of persons having been lost, attempting to cross them. As many are under the necessity of adventuring, a wise and humane precaution has been adopted: the large bell of Aber is rung constantly during foggy weather, to direct those coming from the island by its sound to that line across the sands which is esteemed the least perilous.

Passing the small village and church of Llanvair Vychan, a vast promontory, rising abruptly, like the Rock of Gibraltar, from the ocean, presents itself in tremendous majesty, and with its grey and weather beaten sides, forms a fine contrast to the verdant meads and fertile fields of the surrounding country.

The celebrated Pass of

PENMAN MAWR,

Was justly once the terror of the traveller; the mountain, protruding itself into the sea, afforded but a very narrow passage along a shelf on its side for the terrified traveller: under his feet were showers of rude stones that impeded his progress: beneath, some hundred fathoms down, the roaring ocean: and, above his head, the over-hanging precipice, that momentarily threatened to overwhelm him, or hurry him headlong down the craggy steep. The danger, from the steepness of the mountain, and the crumbling strata under his feet, increased with his progress, and one false step in different parts must have inevitably proved fatal; it was long a terror to the neighbourhood, and the winter evenings were fearfully occupied in reciting the dangers and the accidents of Penman Mawr.

In 1772,[1] an application was made to Parliament, and a generous aid was granted for the purpose of improving and securing this part of the road to Holyhead. A voluntary subscription, in which the city of Dublin bore a distinguished part, was also added; and under the judicious management of that able engineer, Mr. Silvester,

1   The road could only have been repaired at this time, not entirely made as some state, it being defended by a wall towards the sea at a much earlier period. "We went over the famous precipice called Penman Mawr, which fame has made abundance more frightful than it really is; the rock is, indeed, very high, and if any one should fall from it he would be dashed in pieces; yet, on the other hand, there is no danger of falling; and besides, *there is now a wall built all the way* on the edge ofthe precipice to secure them. Those who have been at the hill or pass of *Enterken*, in Scotland, know very well the danger there is much greater." *Vid. a Tour in Great Britain, printed by Strahan*, 1725.

what was deemed beyond the power of human art to remedy, was speedily effected; the road is widened a proper breadth for carriages to pass each other, by cutting the solid rock; while the side towards the sea is secured by a wall built upon a series of arches, meeting the irregularity of the precipice, with circular holes at regular distances, to take the great quantities of water that descend from the mountain in rainy seasons. One obstacle, however, yet remains, that will probably for ever baffle the efforts of ingenuity: the sides of the mountain in some places rise nearly perpendicular the whole of the height;[2] but, in others, they project over the present road, and many disjointed masses, of precarious tenure, threaten to crush the traveller to atoms. The strata, having its earth washed away by torrents, and rended by severe frosts, fragments at intervals fall, and, for a time, render the road utterly impassable: lapses of this kind are not unfrequent, and men are employed to separate these huge masses in pieces, by blasting with gunpowder to facilitate their removal; numbers of such were now lying in the road of several tons weight each; it sometimes happens, that the goats, skipping from crag to crag, to browse the alpine shrub, detach fragments sufficiently large from the space which they pass through to prove fatal to persons passing at the time; the traveller, therefore, can-

---

2   Caswel, who was employed by Mr. Flamstead to measure its altitude, reported it 1545 feet above the beach at low water.

not divest himself of all fear, nor absolutely feel himself secure from danger.

On the summit of a hill called Braich i ddinas, rising out of Penmaen, are the ruins of a castle, the fortifications of which were capable of containing 20,000 men; the remains of walls are still standing, and a well that supplied the garrison is constantly full of water, furnished by the condensed vapour of the mountain. A very faithful description of this is given in Gibson's edition of Camden, Vol. II. p. 804.

This was considered the strongest post possessed by the Welch in the district of Snowdon: it was of great magnitude, and so strong by its natural position, that a hundred men might have defended themselves against an army; in *that age* it was deemed impregnable, and here it was the remains of the Welch army were posted pending the negotiation between Edward and Llewelyn.

The mountain abounds with the CRATOGUS ARIA, but we sought in vain for the Nondescript Plant, which is called AFALEUR PREN, whose fruit resembles a lemon, and is said to grow upon the top of Penmaen; we were informed that continual attempts have been made to transplant it from this elevated situation without effect; the last attempt was made by Lord Bulkley; it was transplanted into his garden at Baron Hill, but soon dwindled and died. This failure might be accounted for from a general error not only of *Horticulturists* but Botanists themselves, that plants which are the inhabitants of hills and mountains require a *dry* soil whereas, on the contrary, most alpine plants delight in a *wet* soil: their element is water, not to mention the abundance of rain, and the constant oozings of numerous springs, the *habitats* of many are the PEAT BOGS, with which the sides and summits of uncultivated hills constantly abound. It is time this fundamental mistake was removed from the regions of Botany.

In this vicinity are a variety of Druidical and Roman remains: Cromlechs, Carnedds, Meini hirion, old forts, &c. and the whole parish of Dwygyvylchi furnishes abundant matter of speculation for the learned antiquary.

A small rivulet of the same name divides the little from the great Penmaen, and the hollow which used to be a ravine is nearly filled, and a bridge thrown across the stream. Ascending the laborious steep of Sychnant, and leaving Castell Caer Lleion to the left, we descended a hill for two miles, and entered, through the *Porth ucha*, the town of

CONWAY

It stands upon the river Conway, called by Ptolemy Conovius, and which, at high water, is here a mile over. The river rises out of Llyn Conwy, at the southern extremity of the county, in the mountains of Penmachno; the name *Kynwy* signifies the great or chief river, and it perhaps deserves this appellation, as it is one of the noblest streams of its length in Europe in the course of twelve miles it receives so many rivulets as to be able to bear ships of burthen; and for small craft is navigable to Llanrwst Bridge. Camden says this river abounded with a species of muscle (*Musculus niger & omnium crassissima, & ponderosissima* of Lister) called *Kregin diliw,* producing valuable pearls.[3] According to Pliny, they were fished for and held in high repute by the Romans. A breast-plate, studded with British pearls, having been dedicated by Julius Cæsar to Venus Genitrix, and placed in the temple of that goddess at Rome.

It is a prevailing opinion, that Sir Richard Wynne, of Gwedir, presented Queen Catherine with a pearl taken in this river, which has a place to this day in the regal Crown.

These have either lost their celebrity or the muscle has emigrated to other shores, as no such pearl fishery is heard of here. The present town, like Caernarvon, arose out of the ruins of one more ancient, the Conovium of Antoninus, vestiges of which are discoverable in the name and situation of the small village of *Caer hên, i. e.* the old city; a Roman hypocaust and bricks with LEG. X. upon them, alluding to the Xth, or Legio

---

3   Mr. Pennant terms this shell-fish *Mya margaritifera*. Pearls are a disease in the fish, similar to the stone in the human body; on, being squeezed they will eject the pearl, and sometimes they cast it spontaneously on the shore.

Antoniana, that served in this island under Ostorius, have been discovered, evincing that this had been a Roman station.

Out of the ruins of this, Edward I. A. D. 1284, built the present town at the mouth of the river, hence called Aber Conway;[4] to this scite he might be led, not only by the convenient and defensible situation, but from the example set by Hugh Lupus, Earl of Chester, who had fortified it about the year 1098.

The town is nearly triangular in its shape whether this had any reference to the *form of the Welch harp*[5] could not learn; it is probable the king paid more attention to the security of the place, than to the idea of complimenting his new, but refractory subjects; and that the form was prescribed by the situation it was surrounded by handsome lofty walls, one mile and a half in circumference; defended by twenty-four round-towers, and had four gates, Porth ucha, Porth issa, Porth y Castell, and Porth y Felin. From near each end of the walls, on the side towards the river, two curtains, terminating with the watch towers, ran a considerable way into the river to prevent the approach of an enemy at ebb tide: one of these only at present exists; the other, with both the towers, has long since perished.

---

4   Its original name was Caer Gyffin, from the stream that flows into the creek on the west side of the castle.

5   *Vid. a walk in Wales.*

The base of the triangle runs along the river, at the furthest angle of which, upon the verge of a perpendicular slate rock, stands its magnificent castle; the architect is said to have been the same who planned that of Caernarvon: if so, he seems to have reserved the greater portion of his skill and taste to bestow it here; a more noble fortress, in point of strength and beauty, was never erected.

The form ofthe castle is oblong, bounded on one side by the river, on another by a creek, and the other two sides face the town: its walls are nearly entire, and its eight massy towers, with turrets issuing from the tops of each, that give an air of lightness and elegance, are standing; fragments of the stair-cases are still remaining in one of the large towers is an ornamental window, forming an arched recess, adorned with fluted pilastres, called the ariel, and said to have contained the toilet of *Queen Eleanor*.

Another of the towers forms a curious ruin the avarice and folly of some of the inhabitants having led them to excavate the slate rock which formed its base, occasioned a vast fragment of it to fall on the beach the parts still preserve the circular shape, and exhibit a hardened composition of stone and mortar, eleven feet thick. The upper moiety remains entire, apparently suspended in air above the head of the spectator.

Within are two large courts: some traces still point out the principal rooms; the dimensions of which have been given by Lord Lyttelton, and elegant views of them may be seen in Grose.

The great hall, emblem of the founder's magnificence, is one hundred and thirty-nine feet in length, thirty-two broad, and of a proportionate height. The roof was supported by eight gothic arches, six of which are still standing; six windows towards the country, and three towards the court, conveyed light to this noble apartment: underneath were the Magazines for the supply of ammunition in time of war, and the demands of hospitality in time of peace.

Viewing this spacious castle, with its apartments, halls, refectories, kitchens, cellars, and once splendid establishment, the mind is naturally led to reflect on the luxury of its inhabitants; and we seemed hurried back to that remote period which witnessed the convivial scenes of its prosperous days. But these are gone—

> No more its arches echo to the noise
> Of joy and festive mirth; no more the glance
> Of blazing taper through its windows beams,
> And quivers o'er the undulating wave,
> But naked stands the melancholy walls,
> Lash'd by the wint'ry tempests cold and bleak!
> That whistle mournful through the empty hall,
> And piece-meal crumble down the whole to dust.
> BRUCE

The castle was furnished with two entrances, well contrived for security. The one a winding narrow stair-case up a steep rock from the river, ending in an advanced work, and defended by small round towers at the other side was a similar work, from which a drawbridge was occasionally dropped, over a deep pass, towards the tower. The judicious situation of the castle, its ingenious plan, and the amazing thickness of its walls, might have reason ably induced the founder to consider it as his *impregnable fortress at Conway*.

While surveying these magnificent ruins, and indulging in those reveries which fallen grandeur never fails to excite in the reflecting mind, we were suddenly roused by the sound of martial music, accompanied with frequent shoutings. Struck with surprise, and aided by the suggestions of fancy, we began to conjecture we might be touched by the magic wand of some invisible power; that the events we had been contemplating were about to pass in review before us; and that we must become the affrighted spectators of the accomplishment of one of Merlin's prophecies. Listening with the attention of stupor whence the sounds proceeded, and what they might mean, the loud sounding drum and shrill toned fife were reverberated in distant echo from the roofless walls. The ideas of war and carnage now rushed forcibly upon the mind: the aweful ruins in heaps before us-the thought that we were upon reputed fairy ground, where erst the witching elves were used to sport-all tended to increase our embarrassment, and raise us from astate ofalarm into that ofsilent astonishment! During a short interval we gazed upon each other, and, fixed as statues, seemed the luckless subjects of some wizard spell.

Recovering a little from our panic, we procceded with faultering steps towards that part of the castle whence the sounds proceeded, and, on entering the outer area, we discovered the cause of our laughable consternation.

The Irish rebellion, and the landing of the French, were the general topics of conversation through Wales. The very idea of *invasion* had roused a power to repel it; and it afforded an opportunity of discovering, that the spirit which had so successfully for centuries opposed our Edwards and our Henries, and bade defiance to the usurping power of England, was not lost; the bias only was changed. The very women offered to take the occupations, usually filled by the men, that they might have leisure to learn. the military exercise, and be properly prepared to meet an invading foe.

The infantile strength and spirit was called forth; and their youth had actually taken up arms before they were able to bear them. A company formed of a hundred and twenty boys, from ten to sixteen years, enrolled under the title of Welch Volunteers, were now assembled to exercise; while some, still younger, were learning to beat the drum and blow the fife, under the tuition of a few old soldiers.

This developement, though ludicrous, was highly gratifying; and amply compensated for the few unwelcome moments that preceded.

A similar disposition appeared in most of the towns through which we passed. At Bangor a considerable corps promised to rival this. A subscription amongst the neighbouring gentry served to purchase drums, fifes, light arms, &c. and, every encouragement was given to a spirit, the more meritorious as it appeared at so early an age; and when the hour of future danger might arrive, promised to become the defence of the country, and tend to the preservation of its peace.

It is but just here to remark, from the most attentive observation, that a general and almost unanimous spirit of loyalty pervades this people. However, in the hour of historic enthusiasm, they may mourn over the fallen greatness of their ancient princes, and lament in bardic strains the lost independance of their country; yet, enjoying the blessings of English jurisprudence, they yield the most prompt obedience to its injunctions; and feeling the benefits of an equal execution of the laws, under the auspices of our beloved Sovereign, whose milder virtues form an amiable contrast to those of his ancestors in the eleventh and twelfth centuries, they evince a due allegiance to the King, and the strongest attachment to the Constitution ofthe country. And should the question ever be put to the test, (which may the

great Author of peace avert!) there is every reason to believe that the throne of England would
not find more faithful friends, nor more strenuous adherents, than those residing amidst the
mountains of Cambria.

Few ofthe remarkable events which it is probable must have befel this, like other fortified
places, are recorded in history. It was appointed the rendez vous of the forces belonging to the
ill-fated Richard, destined to oppose the usurper, Bolingbroke. On his return from Ireland, the
king found forty thousand assembled in his behalf under the Earl of Shrewsbury. But the king's
enemies were too subtle for him; Percy, Earl of
Northumberland, with a small train met him at
Conway, with the solemn assurances, that Bolingbroke only wished to have his alienated property restored, and the ancient privileges of Parliament confirmed.

The King appearing to distrust the Earl's professed good intentions, Percy, to remove all suspicion, attended at high mass, vowed fidelity, and
swore allegiance at the *altar*. Caught in this wily
and deeply-iniquitous snare, the King accompanied Northumberland out of the gate; but about
Penmaen Rhos the King perceived a band of soldiers, bearing the banners of Percy. Surmising he
was betrayed, he would have returned; but Percy,
snatching the King's bridle, forcibly conducted
his course. The poor King had but just time to
reproach the Earl with his perjury; telling him,

"that the GOD he swore by that morning would do him justice at the day of judgment;" before he found himself a prisoner; and at Flint was delivered into the hands of his cruel enemy, Bolingbroke!

It was held for King Charles by Sir John Owen; was besieged by General Mytton, 1646, and the town taken by storm, August 15. The Parliamentarian General, with an inhuman severity against the Irish, seized on all that were in the place; and, having caused them to be tied back to back, ordered them to be flung into the sea. What provocation led to such a sanguinary measure is not said. Be it what it might, the character of Mytton cannot be cleared from the aspersion of savage barbarity, whether the business arose from himself, or superior orders left to him to execute. The castle held out three months longer, and surrendered by *capitulation, Nov.* 10.

The beauty of that fortress led the besiegers to forbear offering it any great violence: but, after having escaped the ravages of the civil wars, it experienced great depredations from the hands of loyalty. In 1665, in consequence of a grant from the King to Edward, Earl of Conway, he ordered it to be stripped of its timber, lead, and iron; which was sent to Ireland under a pretence, that it was for the King's service.

By this *Vandal-like act* the magnificent pile was nearly reduced to its present condition . It is now held of the crown by a private proprietor, O.

Holland, Esq. at the annual rent of 6s. 8d. and a
dish of fish to Lord Hertford whenever he passes
through the town.

Mr. Holland, with singular taste and becoming spirit, has planted, and laid out in walks, a
small rising hill near the mouth of the Conway;
commanding an extensive and delightful prospect up and down the river, the sea, Anglesea,
&c. whence the best view of the town and castle
is to be obtained; and has given it the classic and
appropriate name ofthe *Welch Arcadia.*

The situation of the town of Conway, upon a
rock verging to the water, with the opposite side
of the river well wooded, the promontary of Llandudno, and various scenery ofthe winding stream,
render it a most beautiful place to the beholder
without; and scarcely a more miserable-looking
place can be conceived than it appears within.
Many of its buildings are in ruins, others uninhab-
ited; and vacant spaces in the streets shew where
others have stood. Edward the first made it a free
borough. The Mayor, for the time being, was constable of the castle. At present it is governed by
one Alderman, a Recorder, Coroner, Water Bailiff, and two Serjeants at Mace, chosen annually.
It formerly enjoyed the same privileges, with respect to juries, as Caernarvon. It retains, however, very little of the ancient splendour, when its
inhabitants obtained a pre-eminence of distinction above the other towns that shared the royal favour. Sir John Wynne observes, "They were

styled the *Gentlemen of Conway, the Lawyers of Caernarvon*, and the *Merchants of Beaumaris*." Formerly there was an abbey of the Cistercian order, founded by Llewelyn, 1185, dedicated to the Virgin Mary and all Saints, some traces of which are still to be seen.[6] This prince had amply endowed it with lands both in Caernarvon and Anglesea; but after Edward had erected the castle, and drawn up regulations for the government ofthe town, jealous of the monks, he removed them, granting them the township of *Maynan*, near Llanrwst; he, however, acted in this case with justice and humanity, reserving to them all their lands and privileges, and bestowed upon them the right of presentation to the Conventual church of Conway; and while he confined them by an injunction to this district, he granted them additional immunities, (*Vid. Dugd.*) The revenues, at the dissolution, were estimated by Speed at 1791. 10s. 10d. It was granted, in the reign of Elizabeth, to the Wynnes; and an old house, built out ofthe materials still in possession of the family, is all that remains of the abbey of Maynan.

The church stands in the centre of the town, but is no very elegant structure: Gryffydd ap Canan ap Owen was interred here A. D. 1200; habited in a monk's cowl, according to the superstitious fashion of the times; "because (says *Powell*, p. 220.) the monks and friars had delud-

6   It is now used as a stable, and consists of an arched stone roof and Saxon door, hence called the *Stoney*.

ed the people into a strong conceit of the merits of it, and had firmly persuaded them it was highly conducive to their future happiness to be thus interred."

A singular instance of fecundity is recorded on a plain stone: "Here lyeth the body of Nich. Hookes, of Conway, gent. who was the forty-first child of his father, William H. Esq. by Alice his wife; and the father of twenty-seven children: who died the 20th of March, 1637."

In Castle-street is a very old house, having a singular window, with several coats of arms of the Stanley family; one an eagle pouncing a child; it is called the college, and inhabited by a few poor families; it might perhaps have been a school, endowed out of the abbey lands at the dissolution of the house. Near the market-place is a very large building called Plas Mawr, or the great mansion, built by Robert Wynne, Esq. of Guedir, 1585;[7] the Greek inscription over the gateway Avex, Arx, and the letters. J. H. S. X. P. S. in the front of the building, lead me to conjecture, that it was a house erected for charitable purposes; the inscription calls upon the reader to support the institution, or at least to abstain from any sacrilegious alienations. The initials, which may be read, *Jesus hominum salvator Christiani populi salus*, favours the idea that it was an hospital for the re ception of the infirm, as well as the indi-

---

7   The arms of England over the door indicate that it was erected under the royal patronage.

gent. Within are numbers of rude stuccoed arms
of the patrons; and swans, owls, ostriches, crows,
and bears with ragged staves, the supporters of
the arms of Dudley, Earl of Leicester, adorn the
walls and ceilings.

Prior to the Reformation, the poor depended
upon the monasteries and the alms of the religious for their support; afterthe dissolution,
in Henry the 8th's time, this support being removed, many statutes were pass ed and regulations adopted for the relief of the distressed
part ofthe community; public hospitals, as St.
Bartholomew's, &c. were erected in London and
other places; these having been soon found inadequate to the relief required, proper laws were
enacted and new appropriations made in Elizabeth's reign these laws were revised, a new plan
was suggested, that of a general parochial rate
adopted, and the maintenance of the poor began
to wear the appearance of a system.

This building, therefore, might probably have
been one of those built by subscription for the
same purpose as that of St. Bartholomew's in
London; it is at present occupied by a few families, who, we were informed, paid rent for their
miserable accommodations.

The poor are more numerous and more
wretched in their circumstances here than in any
part of North Wales; the want of employment
daily increases their number and adds to their
distress; there is no kind of manufactory and lit-

tle maritime trade; we found many of these poor creatures on the beach,[8] gathering the different species of *fuci*, commonly called sea wreck, thrown up by the tide, or growing upon the breakers; the wreck vegetates and clings about the stones of the rocky beach till it grows to maturity, which it does every second, or at furthest every third, year, when it is gathered for the sake of the ashes. This wreck they place in a kind of square fire-places, made on the sand, and burn to a state of liquid, which being stirred with an iron rod, dries into a cake, and when cool appears like cinders, and is called *barilla*, or impure fossil alkali; in this state it is sold to the manufacturers of soap and glass.[9] It has, of late, become a great article of export; the expence of gathering, burning, &c. is about 1*l.* 11*s.* 6*d.* perton, and the price for which it is sold from 3*l.* to 5*l.* per ton, according as it is more or less freed from sand and gravel. This, under proper encouragement, might be advantageous to the poor ofthe neighbour hood; but, at present, the necessitous *Kelper*, obliged

---

8   On the shore grows the CHENOPODIUM MARITIMUM, GERANIUM MARITIMUM: and, at a small distance, the delicate LATHYRUS SILVESTRIS, and L. NAPELLUS exhibited their beautiful crimson flowers.

9   It is a very curious fact, that the ashes of all plants, growing at a distance from salt water, afford the vegetable alkali or *potash*; while such as grow near the sea, or on the borders of salt lakes, afford the fossil alkali or *soda*; if, however, these same plants be cultivated in the interior of the country they produce potash only. *Vid.* Jacquim. *Chym.*

to sell the produce of the day to procure sustenance for himself and family, cannot avail himself of the advantage of a proper market; this the purchasers know, and the price they proffer is so small as hardly to be a proper equivalent for the necessary labour; the industrious only, therefore, will engage in this laborious undertaking, and to them necessity alone can be the incentive to industry.

Though the river is a mile over when the tide flows, at ebb it is not more than fifty yards, nor more than eight feet deep; spring tides rise from fourteen to eighteen feet, so that vessels of three and four hundred tons may ride close to the town; the port, though well sheltered, is not safe in its entrance, owing to the shifting sand banks: its present trade is very inconsiderable: slates, copper from the Llandudno mines, lead and calamine from the mines between this place and Llanrwst, and potatoes, constitute its principal exports; the imports are still more inconsiderable.

A ferry to the opposite shore, once considered as royal property, now belongs to the Mostyn family. Conway, being a great thoroughfare to and from Ireland, enables it to support three or four good inns, but when the road, now making through the Ogwyn mountains shall produce a saving of ten miles in the distance from Llanrwst to Bangor, this advantage will cease. We put up at the *Bull's Head*, and had the fair damsels to wait upon us mentioned by a former tourist. (*Vid.*

Walk in Wales.) But it will be more interesting
to the excursive traveller to be informed, that,
though he will meet with very decent accommodations, yet he will be soon convinced, from the
different species of charge and civility, that he
has now left the track of simple honest life, and
got into the great Irish road; where extravagance
in the guests has produced avarice in the hosts,
and where the frequent recurrence of greatness
and folly has procured, for the more humble and
modest traveller, the reception of indifference.

"Ther is, by Conway, on the hither side of
Conway water, an arme like a peninsula caulled
Gogarth, leying against Prestholme, and ther be
the ruines of a place of the Bishops of Bangor."
Leland.

This rocky peninsula, a neck of land about
eight miles long and three broad, stretches out
in a north westerly direction, forming a horn of
the bay of Beaumaris, and shelters the harbour of
Conway. The parish of Llandudno extends about
four miles, in which is the promontory or cape,
called the *Great Ormeshead*; this was formerly an island. Leland says, "This Commote (i. e.
Credine) partely be Conway ryver, partely by the
Se, is yn a maner as insulatid, and one way owte
of Denbigh land; the way is Over a made causey,
over a marsch often over flowen." (*Vol.* V. *p.* 49.)
There are persons still living in the neighbourhood, who say they can remember when thep-
resent marsh,which forms the communication,

was usually washed over by high tides; the whole is chiefly composed of schistose and calcareous strata.

Passing the shell of a large house, belonging to the Mostyns, a few years since, gutted by fire, at a small distance stands *Bodscallen*, a seat of Sir Thomas Mostyn the situation is commanding, and the house embosomed in venerable woods. It is a place of great antiquity, being mentioned in the records of Caernarvon, and from the ruins of a castelet near the present house, appears to have been a place of residence at a very remote period.

About a mile further is Gloddaeth, another fine seat of Sir Thomas's, on the slope of a very extensive lime-stone hill, now covered with fine modern plantations, and the plain beneath planted with forest trees; while the walks on the declivity are directed by the flexture of the hill, those on the plain are straight, diverging from a centre, in which is placed a statue of Minerva. If we take into the account the variety of rich and uncommon views arising from contrasted hill and vale, wood and water, the sportive lucubrations of nature, and the magnificent efforts of art, and then include every thing that can embolden or soften the landscape, we have the walks of *Gloddaeth*, which may justly vie with any thing of the kind in the three kingdoms.

The house was built in the reign of Elizabeth, and is famous for its library of ancient learning. The parish-church of Eglwys Rhos is a little below the woods, celebrated by the death of Maelgwyn Gwynedd; who, with a weakness not singular in his time, fled here to avoid the *vad felen*, or yellow fever, which raged over great part of Europe, supposing the pestilence would not be permitted to enter the sanctuary; but the prince was the subject of a prophecy "whenever a strange spectre appears on the marsh of Rhianedd, if Maelgwyn Gwynedd sees it he will die." He soon fatally discovered that, not withstanding the suggestions of ignorant or designing men, the atmosphere follows the regular laws of Providence, and that to expect miracles in individual concerns, when the common remedial causes are sufficient to counteract the evil, or the consequences are not of the utmost importance to the cause of religion, originates in folly and ends in presumption. The old canon is as just in religion as in scenic propriety.

Nec Deus intersit, nisi dignus vindice nodus Incideret. HOR.

On the summit of two small hills, near the shore, are the ruins of *Diganwy Castle*: the walls crossed the valley between the hills, and running up the sides formed a communication between the castle and the keep; some remains of these and the vestiges of a round tower are still to be seen. This is famed as having been a Roman station, and is conjectured by Camden to have been the *Dictum* where the *Nervii Dictenses,* under the late emperors, kept their reserve guard; it was called by Tacitus Caer Cangorum, from the Cangi, and corrupted by the English into *gannoc.*

The variety of brass instruments[10] dug up in the vicinity favour the conjecture of this having been a British, rather than a Roman station. In the sixth century it was a residence of Maelgwyn, and for centuries after alternated with Caer Segunt, in the honour of being a royal residence. A. D. 818 it was destroyed by lightning, and, as accidents arising from natural or incidental circumstances are generally construed by superstition into presages of national calamity, Diganwy ceased, from that period, to be the seat of royalty. In 876 it was considered a very strong post, but after being destroyed by Llewelyn was restored to consequence by the Earl of Chester, 1209. In 1211, King John, after vowing vengeance upon his son-in-law (Llewelyn) was compelled, by the Welch, to make a disgraceful retreat from this place. Henry III. fared still worse. In 1245, encamping his army near Diganwy, he began to rebuild its ruined castle; but the Welch did not remain unconcerned spectators of a transaction so hostile in its nature they so harassed his army

---

10   Ancient British weapons, called by the Romans *Jacula Armentata,* which the Britons used from their chariots in war. *See a particular account of them, with figures, in Mona Antiqua, p. 86.*

by continual skirmishing and cutting off the necessary supplies, that Henry was glad quickly to
return to England, cordially sick of his. Welch
expedition; *Pow.* 265. In 1257 it was besieged by
Llewelyn, and 1263 finally taken and destroyed by
that prince. During Welch independence, it was
considered by the English as a station of great
military importance; situate on the coast, it was
open to receive continual supplies for the army;
and commanding one of the principal passes into
Wales, its garrison was able to restrain the excursions of the Welch; and from its strength as
a fortress it secured a safe retreat for the English
army on the of disaster or defeat emergency

Near Llandudno are two copper mines, one
the property of the Mostyns, and the other
worked by a company of Liverpool; the ore is, for
the most part, a green *carbonate of copper*, (the
malachite, 1st variety of Kirwan,) found between
the limestone strata: but at present the veins discovered are so thin as to afford but small quantities ofore, and consequently the mines are of no
great value.

LLANDUDNO

This village, which is small and ill built, is subject
to a very serious inconvenience; in hot weather,
the springs, which supply the inhabitants with
water, become dry, and they are obliged to have
recourse to the brackish wells in the marsh be-

low. From Llandudno to the Ormeshead is an elevated down, covered with sheep, extending for four miles, but not more than one in breadth; the promontory consists of high cliffs of various heights, abounding with large caverns, which afford shelter for innumerable birds, such as pigeons, gulls, razor-bills, ravens, guillemots, corvorants, and herons. On the loftiest crags lurks the peregrine falcon, the bird so high in repute while falconry continued a fashionable amusement. The eggs of many of these birds are sought after as delicious food, and considered as a great treat to the Epicurean; the price procured for them is a sufficient inducement for the poor to follow the adventrous trade of egg-taking: but, in this as in the pearl fishery onthe coasts of Persia, the gains bear no tolerable proportion to the danger incurred. The adventurers having furnished themselves with every necessary implement for the business, while the sun affords assistance by his beams, enter on the terrific undertaking: two, for this is a trade in which copartnership is absolutely necessary, take a station; he, whose turn it happens to be, or whose superior agility renders it eligible, prepares for the rupestrian expedition a strong stake is driven into the ground at some distance from the edge ofthe cliff, to which a rope of sufficient length to reach the lowest haunts of these birds is affixed fastening the other end round his middle, and taking the coil on his arm, and laying hold with both his hands, he throws himself over the brow of the cliff; placing his feet against its sides, and carefully shifting his hands, he gradually descends till he comes to the abode of the birds; then, putting his left hand into the hole while he suspends himself with the other, he takes possession of its contents, carefully placing the eggs in a basket slung at his back for the purpose; having despoiled all the nests within his extent of rope, he ascends by the same means to the edge of the cliff, where his partner, whose duty hitherto was to guard the stake, crawling on hands and knees, affords him assistance in doubling the cliff, which otherwise he would be unable to do. Dangerous employ a slip of the foot or the hand would in an instant be fatal to both instances have occurred, where the weight of the one overcoming the strength ofthe other, both have been precipitated down the craggy steep, and their mangled carcases been buried in the ocean: but these are rare. To a stranger and by-stander this occupation appears more dangerous than it really is in persons habituated to bodily difficulty the nervous system becomes gradually braced, and the solids attain that state of rigidity which banishes, irritability; while the mind, accustomed to scenes of danger, loses that timidity which frequently leads to the dreaded disaster. To the person whose heart palpitates in the near approach to such heights, it must appear a presumptuous employ, and daily instances of its fatality might be expected: but fact demonstrates the contrary, and serves to prove how much we are the creatures of habit, and to what an extent difficulty and danger may be made subordinate to art and perseverance. The ravens and falcons take their stations here from its vicinity to the island opposite, called Puffins' Island, from the great quantity of puffins that frequent it during the summer season. The puffin, or coulterneb, *Alea arctica* of Lin. is the most extraordinary bird that frequents the coasts of Britain its body is not larger than a pigeon's, but its bill is of an uncommon size and shape; it is flat with the edge upwards, and said to resemble the coulter of a plough its legs are placed so far back that it moves awkwardly, and with great difficulty gets upon, the wing. During the winter months these birds frequent the northern parts of Europe: about May they begin to arrive on our coasts: a few days after their arrival they prepare for breeding, by burrowing in the ground, in a winding direction, for the depth of eight or ten feet, and if they happen to get under a large stone they consider themselves still more secure; in this fortified retreat the female lays one egg, relying upon its courage and strength of bill, with which it bites terribly, to ward off the attempts of the hostile foe. After the young are excluded the shell, the fierceness of the parent is incredible: no bird nor beast will venture to attack them: sometimes the sea-raven, Jacobson informs us, will dare to be so rash, but generally he forfeits his life for his temerity: the meeting affords a most singular combat; as the raven approaches to put his talons upon the young puffin, the parent catches him under the throat with her beak, and darts her claws into his breast; the raven, wounded, screams most dismally for quarter, but the of fended bird is deaf to the intreaty, and makes directly for her proper element, the ocean, where the raven is quickly drowned, and the puffin returns in triumph to the nest: yet, it sometimes happens, that the invader is the victor, and the raven destroys both the parent and her young; this, however, seems no more than retributive justice. The puffin is, in similar instances, an aggressor, and it is but just that the unprovoked invader should, in turn, be a sufferer from undeserved invasion; the puffin, frequently too proud or too idle to make a retreat for itself when it finds one already made, without the least pretence but superior power, disposseses the poor rabbit of its subterraneous habitation, and, to prevent further annoyance, destroys the inhabitants; in these unjustly acquired seats the young puffins are found in great numbers when arrived at full growth, they are generally fat, and esteemed a delicious *bonne bouche* by those fond of high eating: to others their flesh appears rank and fishy, from the nature of their food: the old ones go fishing during the day: these, half digested in the stomach, are reduced to an oily matter, which is ejected from the old one's into the mouths of the young: it is during these excur-

sions that the ravens are most successful in prey-
ing upon the young puffins. When wanted for the
table, they are dug out ofthe burrows, or hunted
by ferrets.

The migration of the old birds takes place early in autumn, and about the latter end of August
the whole tribe is seen assembling to take leave
of their summer residence it sometimes happens,
that those who had met with the loss of their first-
laid eggs, owing to the delay occasioned by laying
others, have their young in a backward state: but,
if they are not fledged at the time of migration,
they are left on land to shift for themselves. At
this period the harvest of the falcon commences:
he keeps guard at the holes of the late-hatched
puffins, till pressed by hunger they are under the
necessity of going abroad in quest of food, and
then fall an easy prey to their wary enemy.

On an eminence called *Dinas* is an ancient
fortification, consisting of a wall of prodigious
thickness round the summit of the hill; within
are large circular caves, which Mr. Pennant supposes to have been the rude habitations of our
ancestors; not improbably one of the places of
security, to which the Welch, during the perilous
times that frequently attended the invasions of
their country, sent their women and children.

Near this is the wonder of the neighbourhood,
the Maen Sigl, or *self-moving stone*; a huge,
massy, rude stone, that has sometimes been seen
to move when no one was near it in this case it

is considered by the common people as the portentous harbinger of disastrous events, and some are preserved in the traditional recollection of the inhabitants as a confirmation of the opinion. It is, from its rocking, stiled Cryd Tudno, St. Tudno's Cradle; the base ofthe stone is upwards, and its point of contact with the ground so narrow as to render it moveable with a slight degree of pressure; in violent hurricanes this, from its excellent poise, may be seen to move by the force of the wind; the conjecture is well founded, which supposes these stones (for there are many such through Wales) were anciently instruments of imposition. The Druids, by their arts, deluded their votaries into an opinion that, as the ministers of the Most High, they were endued with miraculous powers, and to sanction these unfounded pretensions, they engaged as auxiliaries deception and falsehood; but such, in all ages, is the state of the uninformed mind, that to obtain unreasonable and implicit credit requires very little more than unqualified arrogance and boldness of pretension. The people believed their priests possessed a supernatural power of moving these stones, and supernatural power is supposed to be accompanied by supernatural wisdom. The stone is surrounded by a foss, with a narrow path leading to it, intended to keep the vulgar at a venerable and convenient distance, and give additional solemnity to their oracular decisions. Similar deceptions are, to the present day, practised bythe modern

Druids, the Brahmins of India;[11] and similar stories of religious juggling disgraced the history of Christianity, and defiled the sanctuary during the dark ages; but real religion looks down with the most scornful derision upon such deceptions; she wants no foreign aid; she is intrinsically adequate either to defence or conquest; she asks not the emblazoning of falsehood; she delights not in meretricious ornaments:—sufficiently amiable in her native dignity, to the attentive observer she shines in all the untarnished splendour of truth; and sufficiently powerful in her motives, she pours into the serious inquiring mind irresistible conviction.

Two miles from Gloddaeth, on the shore, is a small singular building, having three windows and a door, with a vaulted roof, covered with pebbles in stead of slate, called St. Trillo's Chapel inside is a well, formerly much esteemed for the sanative virtues ofits waters; it was supposed to have been the constant residence of the saint, the clergy of that time chiefly living in an *Eremitishmanner*; half a mile farther is the parish church of Llandrillo, and near it the ruins of *Bryn Earyn*, where, anciently, was the *Llys*, or palace of Maelgwyn Gwynedd. Adjoining the shore is Rhos Vynach, or the Marsh of the Monks, once belonging to the abbey of Conway; where is a considerable and profitable wear, forty pounds worth of fish having sometimes been taken at two successive tides. The bishop and the vicar of Llandrillo, as

11   *Vid. Bernier Voyage de Cachemire.*

the coparceners in the estates of the abbey, share the fish of every tenth tide between them. It would seem by this, and some other instances, that fish, though included by some among the animals *feræ nature*, were formerly tythable, and were considered not as a *personal*, but as a *prædial* tythe; and notwithstanding the decisions of lawyers to the contrary, the nature of tythes and the history of their payment serve to evince to any impartial judge, that formerly almost all tythes were *prædial*, and those only were *personal*, which, from the spirit of the times and the lenity of the clergy, have long ceased to be paid; the restrictions upon the canon law by different statutes have almost rendered it useless; the decisions, in tythe cases, have almost uniformly tended to curtail the rights of the church, and to impoverish her ministers; and, unless some powerful provision be made to counteract the consequences, at no very distant period the church will be left without sufficient emoluments to support a regular and decent ministry.

The peninsula, though a small tract, furnishes a delicious treat to the Botanist, and from the number, as well as the variety of its plants, Gogarth may deserve the appellation of the *Botanical Garden of Cambria*. In the vicinity of Gloddaeth he will find CYSTUS MARIFOLIUS, C. HIRSUTUS, RUBIA PEREGRINA, THALICTRUM MINUS, ARENAREA VERNA, SCROPHULARIA VERNALIS, POLYPODIUM CAMBRICUM, VERONICA MONTANA, V. SPICATA,

Scilla verna, Potentilla verna, Silene nutans, Lysimachia thirsiflora, and Geranium sanguineum.

Near the Ormeshead, Salicornia herbacea, Cystus helianthemum, Oryganum majus, Anthyllis vulneraria, and the much admired, though rarely seen Chlora Perfoliata.

On the Sands, Eryngium maritimum, Crithmum maritimum, Arundo arenaria, Schilla verna, Elymus arenarius, the gaudy Chelidonium cornicularum, expanding its large yellow flowers, while the elegant little plant the Rosa spinosissima, with its rich profusion of blossoms, was actually exhibiting what poets have feigned for the Cyprian Queen, *beds of roses*.

This shore is also ornamented with the most beautiful indigenous plant of Great Britain, the Pulmonaria maritima, whose red and blue flowers form an elegant contrast to its undulated glaucous leaves.

Thus, my friend, have I led you through the flower garden of Wales; but flowers, by many, are regarded as objects too trivial for the consideration of philosophy; I need not observe to you, that every thing must be great which has God for its author; that these, insignificant as they may appear, display a richness of colouring and elegance of design, which art in vain attempts to imitate; and which evidently demonstrate the divine wisdom; nor does the whole creation afford more splendid objects for examination, than the structure of plants and the economy of vegetation; they who practise this study experience how delightful it is, it leads the mind up to its Creator, and seems to restore man, even in his fallen state, to a participation of that felicity, which, in a state of innocence, he enjoyed in Paradise. Yes, the humble and neglected weed can raise our thoughts as effectually to heaven, as the most resplendent planet, and till we have learned habitually thus to think of both, we have not learned to think properly of either; the contemplation of Nature should always be scasoned by a mixture of devotion . A discovery of superior excellence in the works of creation should produce admiration of the Author; and the consideration of their utility ought to incite the most profound adoration for the great Parent of Beneficence.

I am &c.,

J. E.

Letter XI

Dear Sir,

aking the turnpike road that lies on the right bank of the river, we proceeded towards Llanrwst. The Conway winds through a luxuriant vale, bounded on one side by moderately rising hills, and on the other by the eastern termination of the Snowdon chain; a lofty barrier, sometimes clothed with wood, sometimes exhibiting horrid precipices, with now and then a gaping chasm, down which an alpine river dashes its impetuous waters to the Conway.

Here Nature, in her rudest form, gave a delicious softness to the humble vale—

Where gentle Conway glides in darken'd streams,
And peaceful sends her waters to the sea.[1]

The harvest had been protracted by the late incessant rains; and the people were now busy in gathering heavy crops of hay; which the swells in the river had threatened to deprive them of. The sun smiled upon their labour, an air of cheerful joy appeared upon every countenance, and the song of hilarity gave additional spirit to the animated picture. At Porth Lwyd the scenery becomes highly picturesque. The irregularities of the mountains continually changing their face from barren crag and fissured rock, to verdant down and wooded hill; while the opposite ones,[2] rising in gentle slopes from the meads, furnish a constant variety to the admiring eye. The bridges of Pont Porthlwyd and Pont Dolgarog, are neat stone structures over their respective streams, issuing from Llyn Geirionydd and Llyn Cwlid. These, rushing over the barrier, form two immense falls; the former nearly surrounded by woods, and its perpendicular descent upwards of a hundred and eighty feet. The lake of Geirionydd

1   When the elegant Gray styled it "Old Conway's foaming flood," he must have meant, when a high spring tide has been met by a South-west wind.

2   These consist of *shale*, those of Snowdon of *slate*.

is famed as having had the residence of Taliesin upon its banks. The infant story of this Prince of British Poets, who flourished in the sixth century, is so singular, that I must give it you. It is not unlike the discovery of Moses.

Gwyddno Garanir, a petty king of Cantre'c Gwaelod, the inundation of which was before noticed, had granted to his son Elphin the profits of a salmon wear; who not finding it successful, or at least not producing sufficient to counterbalance his extravagance, grew melancholy; and the fishermen attributed the misfortune to the Prince's dissipation and riotous mode of living. While the Prince was attending the wear and lamenting the smallness of his income and the straitness of his circumstances, his men espied a coracle with a child in it, wrapped in a leathern bag, exposed on the water by the cruelty of some unknown mother; the father was supposed to be better known.

The Prince, when the child was brought before him, felt compassion, and ordered every care to be taken of him. After this Elphin flourished. Taliesin received an excellent education, and became the most celebrated bard of that period. When grown up, the accomplished foundling was introduced by Elphin to his Father's Court; where he presented a poem to Gwyddno, entitled, *Hanes Taliesin*, comprehending, in a masterly style of poetry, his own history; and, at the same time, another to his patron, to console him for past misfortunes, and to exhort him, under all present troubles, to trust in Divine Providence.

This is a fine moral piece, and artfully addressed by the bard in the character of an exposed infant, prophesying the future prosperity of his benefactor: and, like a *true poetical* prophet, he is mindful that the events should confirm the declarations of prophecy. *Vid. Spec. of Ancient Welch Poetry.*

This beautiful ode, styled *Dyhuddiant Elphin*, or Elphin's Consolation, is preserved in E. Evans's collection; and a very poetical translation by a Welch lady, was printed 1780, in quarto.

Near the village of Trefriw, the river makes a sudden bend; the tide seldom reaches farther, and the depth of water only admits of vessels of burthen to this place. From its vicinity to the woods, a number of small vessels are built here, and sent down to Conway at the equinoctial tides. Small boats and numerous coracles are seen both above and below Llanrwst bridge, occupied chiefly in fishing. These the *Vitilia navigia* of Pliny, took their name from having been made of the skins of beasts, called coria. At present they are formed of wicker work, about five feet long at the broadest end, four feet wide, and two feet in the prow, and covered with a piece of tarpauling, or tarred canvass. A piece of board is placed across the centre, on which the fisherman sits with a small paddle in his hand, and himself strapped upon the seat. With so slender a security do these people commit themselves to the perilous wave in quest of fish; as they generally use the drag, two go in company; with the left hand they manage the net, and with the right, the paddle; at the same time taking the leading ropes in their teeth. It is curious to observe with what adroitness they preserve the balance (the loss of it would be fatal,) while managing their nets. In the season they take quantities of salmon and smelts, with other fish; and when the labour of the day is past, taking their vessels out of the water, and strapping them on their backs, they carry them home, and lay them in front of their cottages to dry till the next voyage. These vessels are still more curious, as the rude efforts of our ancestors to obtain the sovereignty of the ocean; and whoever feels a conscious pride in living in an age, when the very elements are made subservient to the arts of commerce; and belonging to a country, whose maritime fame is the envy of the world, cannot but with pleasure survey this infant origin of the British navy. Prior to the Roman Invasion, the ancient Britons discovered their skill and courage in crossing the channel in these precarious vessels; and gave auspicious omens of their future and invincible prowess on their native element, the ocean.

Passing Llyn y Craig, the highest point to which the spring tides flow, a small distance from Trefriw, we entered, over a handsome bridge of three arches, the town of

LLANRWST

This bridge, which divides the counties of Caernarvon and Denbigh, is a very handsome structure, built A. D. 1636, at the expence of Sir Richard Wynne, groom of the bed-chamber to Charles the first, while Prince of Wales, from a design of the English Palladio, *Inigo Jones.*[3] On the centre of the parapet are the arms of the Wynne family, and the ostrich plume, a compliment to his royal master. A proof of the excellence of the building may be obtained by a person standing at one centre, who may perceive the whole fabric shake, by a blow given at the other. The centre arch is the portion of a larger circle than the two outer ones; and the segment consists of a chord less than the diameter.

A plate of this bridge is given by Mr. Pennant, who observes, "That the middle arch is fifty-nine feet wide; two are extremely beautiful, and mark the hand of the architect, the third differs greatly, having been rebuilt in 1703, by a very inferior genius."

The difference did not strike me, and had I seen this remark before, it would have led me to have been more particular. I have an engraving of it in my possession, by an architect, where

---

3   His real name was Ynir, but after he had travelled into Italy, according to the fashion of the times, he changed it into Ignatius, or Inigo. He is said to have been a native of this part of Wales.

the exact dimensions are professedly given thus:
—Centre arch, sixty-one feet in the span, chord
twenty-four feet at low water: the two outer arches, span thirty feet and a half, chord fifteen feet;
length of the bridge one hundred and seventy
feet; diameter of the piers, ten feet; width of the
bridge, fifteen feet.

Between two such respectable authorities, who
shall decide? Till I have again seen the bridge I
must say, *Non nostrum inter vos, tantas compo-
nere Lites.*[4]

The views, both up and down the river, are pro
digiously fine; and the whole country, from the
source to the mouth of the Conway, is an animating picture, which justly lays claim to being one
of the most picturesque in Wales.

Llanrwst, though the principal town of this
part of Wales, is not remarkable for the elegance
of its buildings, or the spaciousness of its streets.
Though not a large, it is a populous town, with a
good market-hall, and a well endowed free school,
in the gift of Jesus College, Oxon; and carries on
a small trade in harp making. The market is well
supplied, and reasonable.

We entered the town on the market-day,
Tuesday; and were not a little entertained at the
variety of articles that might be purchased in it.
The adjacent towns and villages do not abound
with shops of every description, as in England;

---

4   Latin: "Tis not for us to end such great disputes." Virgil,
     Eclog. III. —Ed.

the market day, therefore, is the time for buying in supplies for the week; and the market is filled with the luxuries as well as the necessaries of life. Few men are to be seen; the business being conducted by *women*; and we could not refuse admiring the spirit of industry manifest on these occasions. No person is idle—no hand in pockets, or in fold, is seen, but both the buyer and the seller are employed in knitting; and hundreds may be seen going and returning, earning their subsistence as they walk along.

How different is this from the manufacturing poor in England, where attendance on a fair, or market, is a general pretext for squandering and idleness. Indeed œconomy, as well as industry, the two grand hinges on which the happiness and comfort of the lower classes in society turn, may be learnt from all the movements of this people.

The living is a rectory in the patronage of the bishop. The church, situate near the river, is dedicated to St. Rystyd, Archbishop of London, 361; and lays claim to considerable antiquity. The ground was given, and probably the church erected, by Rhun, son of Nefydd Hardd, one of the XV. tribes of North Wales, to expiate the murder of Prince Idwal, perpetrated by the father of Rhun. The time ofits erection may therefore be fixed A. D. 1160. On the floor are several brass plates with figures of the Wynne family; so beautifully enchased, as to reflect the highest credit on the obscure artists, Sylvanus Crew and William Vaughan. Nor would the execution, visible in several of them, disgrace the present æra of the fine arts. But neither Crew nor Vaughan are recorded on the list of Fame.

> Full many a gem of purest ray serene,
>   The dark unfathom'd caves of ocean bear;
> Full many a flower is born to blush unseen,
>   And waste its sweetness in the desart air.
> GRAY.

In the corner of a chapel is a stone coffin, with an inscription, importing, that it was removed from the abbey of Conway, its ancient place of sepulture; and contains the body of Llewelyn ap Jorwerth. An ancient tomb incloses the remains of Howel Cotymor, grandson of the Knight of Bettws, and the original owner of Guedir. On the tomb lies the figure of a Knight in armour; the inscription round is, *Hic jacet Howel Cotymor, ap Gruff(yd) Vychan ap Caruffe am(e)m.* An ornamental gallery brought from the abbey of Maynan, displays some curious carved work of considerable merit.

The church, which is a good gothic building, is disfigured by outside shutters to the windows kept shut, except during divine service; a custom prevalent through this part of Wales, and understood to be a necessary precaution, for preserving the windows against the depredations of ball players; ball playing being an amusement to which the Welch are passionately devoted. The

Guedir chapel, founded by Sir Richard Wynne, from a draft of Inigo Jones, intended as a burial place of the family, is an ornamental building, and discovers the hand of a master.

Two miles from Llanrwst is a large slate mountain, the highest part of which is called Craig y Gwalch, or the Rock of the Falcon, once covered with oaks; which, from many of the stools remaining, appear to have been in no degree inferior to those which enjoyed a deeper soil. Here is a subject of useful inquiry, how these huge forest trees could radicate and flourish on the *bare rock?* If vegetables do not receive all their nourishment by their leaves, then these must have derived some nutritive matter from the strata beneath, through latent fissures.

Near the base of this mountain stands *Guedir*, with extensive woods in the back ground. From the date over the gate-way, it was built in 1558, by John Wynne, Esq. grandfather of the famous Sir John, author of the Memoirs. It consists of two courts, a greater and a less; and exhibits a specimen of a noble mansion for a country gentleman in the days of Elizabeth. It has been observed, that this house took its name from having been the first house in Wales that had glass windows. At this Mr. Pennant feels indignant, and derives it from Gwaed-dir, *i. e.* Bloody Land; from the battles fought here about 610, by Llywarch Hên; or the cruel battle fought near, between Jevaf and Jago, and the sons of Hoel;[5] he calls in the testimony of a bard to prove, that the use of glass was known in Wales for centuries before.

Respecting the use of glass, there can be no doubt at a much earlier period. But at that time it was not in *general* use in England; and is not to the present day in North Wales. It is probable, therefore, that a large mansion with numerous windows, which, from the situation of the house, would exhibit the brilliant rays of a departing sun to a great distance, might induce the common people to change the name from Gwaed-dir, to Gwydr, now Guedir.[6] A chapel, a neat building in the gothic style, and overshadowed by a very large Spanish chesnut, stands near the scite of the old house; where service is performed four times a year.

Guedir lately became the property of Sir P. Burrel, (now Lord Guedir, or Gwydr) in right of his wife, *Lady Willoughby de Eresby*, eldest daughter to Robert, late Duke of Ancaster.[7] The woods are extensive, and consist of a great vari-

---

5   Hywel Dda was their uncle. Ieuaf and Iago were sons of Idwal. —Ed.

6   There is nothing to prove that the old house was not glazed; and that from this circumstance it might have derived its name some centuries before.

7   This lady is possessed in her own right of the office of Lord Great Chamberlain of England, which is executed by her husband. By her father's side, she is descended from the ancient family of the Berties; and by the female, from *Owen Gwynedd, Prince of North Wales*. Vid. *Hist. of Gued.* Ram.

ety of forest trees; oak, ash, elm, firs, sycamore, beech, &c. Among its plants, the RUBUS IDÆUS, and VACCINIUM ULIGINOSUM, are abundant.

Ascending the opposite acclivity, which forms the eastern boundary of the vale of Llanrwst, we got into the road; winding through an extensive wood of sapling oaks, interspersed with beech and chesnut;[8] the elegant spruce, the pensile birch, and the rich scarlet berries of the mountain ash, added a pleasing variety to the sylvan scene. The opposite rocks and woods of Guedir, the people busy with their hay in the little vale, the meandering river, and the sun darting his resplendent rays through the intervals of shade, formed a landscape peculiarly soft and pleasing. But we were not long before we experienced the effects of contrast: obtaining the summit of the hill, which is five miles long, nothing but a desart heath presents itself to the disappointed view. It is a barren morass, circum-

---

8 The FAGUS CASTANEA is frequent in the woods in Wales, and seems to have been much more general in England formerly than it is at present. There are many remains of old decayed chesnuts in woods and chases. Many of the old buildings of the metropolis are formed of this timber; and Fitzstephens, who gave a description of it in the reign of Henry II. speaks of a notable forest of these trees, which grew on the North part of it. Ducarel recites a grant of the tythe of its fruit in the forest of Dean, made by this monarch to the abbey of Flexley. It is an agitated question, whether this beautiful and profitable tree be or not a native of this island? After all that has been adduced on the negative side, by the Hon. D. Barrington, Pennant, and others, I cannot but conclude with Evelyn and Collinson, that it is indigenous.

scribed by naked dark brown mountains, which give it a sombre air of melancholy grandeur. As far as the eye can ken, the prospect is relieved by no variety; nor is the view interrupted by a single object that can awaken curiosity. Not an inclosure, not a hut, nor the most distant trace of the country being inhabited. The very cattle, as though prognosticating famine if they staid, had forsaken it; nor was one of the feathered tribes heard to chaunt his aerial song. Scarcely any marks of vegetation, save here and there a few species of carex, peeping through the black earth; with SCIRPUS PLAUSTRIS, and C. CŒSPITOSUS, ERIOPHORUM POLYSTACHION, AIRA CORYOPHYLEA, JUNCUS CONGLOMERATUS and J. SQUARRORUS, all pointing out the incongeniality of the soil.[9]

Making the best of our way we at length discovered a few turbaries, which intimated human beings were at no great distance; and further on we discovered some poor people with sledges, dragging away the peat and turf that had been recently cut in the distant bogs.

Alas! said I, even these refuse spots, these blanks in the map of nature, are not unattended to! The misery that takes refuge in the neighbourhood is glad to ask for some consolation from the scanty productions of this dreary waste!

---

9   A visible declivity is apparent in this extensive flat, and it might without much expence or difficulty be drained, and quickly improved but expence and difficulty are relative terms, and have a very different meaning in different places.

The mind alive to the beauties, is sensibly affected with the seeming defects in Creation, and gradually becomes in unison with the objects, and the scenery around it. We found ourselves enveloped with gloom, but were at length relieved from it, by the venerable plantations which encircle an old mansion of the Wynne's, called Voelas Hall, occupied by the Hon. Mr. Finch, who married the heiress of that family.

An artificial mount is to be seen here, on which formerly stood a castelet, destroyed by Llewelyn the Great. A remarkable column bears a very obscure inscription, part in Latin and part in Welch. All that can be collected from it is in the last line, importing, that *the excellent Prince Llewelyn lies buried here.* This must have been Llewelyn ap *Sitsylt*, who was assassinated 1021; about the place of whose sepulture history is silent. Llewelyn ap Jorwerth having been publicly interred in the abbey of Conway; and the third and last Llewelyn being slain near Bualt. Several other small pillars, were standing, with illegible characters, in the time of Camden.

Two miles to the right is Ispytty Evan, where. formerly stood an hospital of St. John of Jerusalem. This was an asylum for travellers in this wild country during the inhospitality and perils of war; formed under the protection of the knights of this order, who held the manor, and made the precincts a sanctuary. After the abolishing of the order, the privileges passing to other hands, the place became the terror of the country; exempted from regular jurisdictions, it became a rendez-vous of the abandoned and the desperate from every quarter, and was literally converted from a house of penitence and prayer into a den of thieves; a set of banditti ravaged the country far and wide with impunity, till, by the prudence and perseverance of Meredyth ap Evan, in the reign of Henry VII. they were completely extirpated.

After a long interval another charity arose in this place, but not out of the ruins of the former. Captain Richard Vaughan, a poor knight of Windsor, erected and endowed, A. D. 1600, an alms-house for six poor men, with a weekly allowance for bread and coals.

We descended to the small village of Capel Voclas, and passing a bridge over a stream tributary to the Dee, we came to some low unprofitable boggy meadows, where several farmers were mowing their ill-conditioned grass: the mode of performing this is very different from that we had been used to witness the scythe is much longer and broader than ours, which the mower lifting up in nearly a vertical direction, strikes at a distance from his body with all the strength he possesses, as though he were striking at a monster whose attack he dreaded and whose escape he feared; it appears awkward to a beholder, yet it is reasonable upon two grounds; the intermix ture of rushes, &c. in this coarse herbage renders it difficult to cut, and frequent failures in the crop will not admit of going *regularly* over the ground. They have a peculiar mode also of sharpening the scythe: a piece of board, three inches wide and about eighteen long, narrowed at one end by way of handle, is covered over with a composition of pounded gritstone and hog's-lard; this is used as a common whetstone for all the cutting instruments used in husbandry. The stone is brought in lumps from the foot of Snowdon, and sold in the market at one penny per pound. Wishing them favourable weather for housing their scanty and hard-earned crops, we soon reached the solitary inn of

Cyrniogeu

Hearing that three chaises and a post-coach were kept at this inn, we promised ourselves that we should meet with a few comforts to console us after our melancholy day's excursion; but we found, on entering, that the *external* and *internal* of places, as well as persons, are too frequently at variance; we could not procure a single article of a quality that even hungry appetites could cordially relish; and I would advise the future traveller, who intends to call at Mr. Rowland's, to be provided with a portable cordial, to chear him under the chearless reception at the Inn of Cyrniogeu.

Three miles further we reached Cerrig y Druidion, famed, in Camden's time, for some remains of Druidical worship, whence it originally took its name; the Antiquary will now find himself disappointed, for these sacred reliques have long since been removed by the hands of interest, and made subservient to erect ing a wall round a farm-yard; they consisted chiefly of cromlechs and kistvaens, or stone chests; and a particular account of them is given by the learned annotator of Camden, II. 813.

The road now became less dreary, and a few cultivated farms gave a gleam of hope, that we were once more approaching an inhabited country; unacquainted that there was any thing peculiarly worthy of observation before we should reach Corwen, we suddenly came upon a scene as grand as it was unexpected.

Pont Llyn Dyffws

A bridge of one arch, about fifty feet in the span, is seen bestriding a deep and dismal chasm, through which the hoarse-sounding torrent, the Glynn, rushing down into a deepened bed, roars over the disjointed rocks beneath, and, lashing the rocky sides that check its impetuosity, rolls its angry waters to the Dee. The stupendous fissure, full two hundred feet deep, is overhung by large forest trees, whose spreading branches, intermingling from the opposite sides, throw a darkened shade over the awful scene, and the eye dreads to follow the maddened torrent through the profundity of its horrible bed.

A bold cataract, above the bridge, gives you sufficient notice that you are near, and the hoarse rumblings of the water, heard in distant murmurs down the dark and wooded glen, give an additional effect to this truly sublime scene.

The road from Bala to Ruthin here joins that of Llanrwst, for which purpose the bridge was built; it winds round the side of the hill on a rocky shelf, with a wall towards the ravine, while the rude perpendicular mountain lifts its tremendous head with overhanging crags, that serve to heighten the colouring of the terrific picture; and I may venture to affirm, that the *coup d'œil of Pont yr Dyffws* is not inferior to *Pont Aber Glaslyn*.

We crossed the Dee over an old stone bridge of six arches, where its dark and deep waters are archly contrasted with the wooded banks as it flows through the narrow verdant vale of Edernion, and soon found ourselves again in Merioneth, at the small town of

CORWEN

The only inn is the Owen Glyndwr, to which we were directed by a huge figure painted on a sign, having large eyes and a long beard, much like the Saracen's Head, meant as a likeness of the hero of the vale, who still lives in the remembrance and affections of the people of Corwen. The decent accommodations, and the pointed civility of the people, made this a comfortable retreat. Wishing for every kind of refreshment, after a long and toilsome day, I inquired for a *Tonsor*; after waiting till the supper was ready, and my patience nearly exhausted, I discovered that my meaning was not comprehended; the girl, supposing, from the time of the evening, and the custom, of the place, that I must wish for the soothing sounds of music to lull me to repose, introduced a blind harper: I smiled as you may suppose; to have shewn any symptoms of disapprobation would have been calling my own taste in question, and an unfair requital of her well-meant intentions. I retained the village minstrel, and on further explaining my wants, was informed, there was no barber within many miles; that a woman shaved at Corwen, but she supposed my honour would not like to be shaved by a *woman!* Smiling at the haughty ideas our sex were supposed to entertain of the fair, and the humble opinion she had of her own, I readily acquiesced. The girl, who understood me rather from my looks than my language, hastened her steps, and, in a few minutes, a tall stout damsel made her appearance, about twenty five, of a fair and ruddy complexion; who, with the apparatus in her hand, and a smile upon her face, in broken English addressed herself to the company. In the one hand was a pewter jug containing hot water, in the other a case of razors and a shaving box wonder not at the latter, the accommodation of more polished countries; it was a present from a gentleman, whose beard she had taken off with so much dexterity and ease, as to leave an impression of gratitude upon his mind, and he had, as a token of it, made this useful acknowledgment. She proceeded to the work. Entertained with the novelty of the thing, and the perfect good humour of the operator, expressed in smiles and the softest sounds of her language, my beard was removed before I wished, shall I say? certainly before I expected. On inquiry, I learned that *Magdalene Hughes* was the daughter of a creditable person of the town, possessed, at his death, of a small property, which, while the family remained together, was sufficient to keep them, but that some were married and some dead, and she was left with an aged mother, and had taken up this odd, but profitable trade, as a means of procuring subsistence for both. I never had my beard more easily removed; but, independent of this, from the consideration of the latter circumstance, the man of sensibility will never pass Corwen without contributing a small gratuity to this dutiful daughter of affliction. I presented her with a small piece of silver on the occasion, and we soon learnt the happiness this unexpected event produced was not confined to herself. The generosity of this simple people appeared in this, as in many other instances, of too liberal a nature, to be confined within the narrow limits of self. The joy of the unadulterated Welsh character is the joy *of social participation*; the harper, who had been playing for us during the hour of supper, was now enlisted in the service of Magdalene; her young acquaintance in the town, and the servants of the house were invited to the feast; the mistress of the house, entering into the spirit of the occasion, contributed her mite also; the merry dance and chearing cwrw went round to an advanced hour, and we had the pleasure of witnessing a large portion of inoffensive mirth, produced by an inconsiderable gratuity. Early in the morning we were awaked before we wished by a number of voices singing; the cause of this unwelcome serenade we found, a congregation of Dissenters assembled in a chapel opposite the inn, before they went to their respective employments, to pray for the prosperity of their country, and supplicate the Divine Being for a speedy restoration of peace among the ambitious and contending powers of Europe. This matin service was performed for this patriotic purpose at the same hour once a week. There was something so truly philanthropic in this work of supererogation, as some might be inclined to term it, that, however we might differ in some points from this people, this called loudly for imitation, and we could not help furnishing our quota of approbation.

The town is neat, but very small, situate on a rising ground on the southern bank of the Dee. The church is a neat cruciform structure, in a highly romantic situation, immediately under a

vast rocky cliff, the abrupt finishing of the Ferwyn; it is dedicated to St. Julian, archbishop of
St. David's, who was esteemed the godliest man
and greatest clerk of all Wales; he died 1089.

On the south side of the church stands a cross,
which the vulgar call *the sword of Glyndwr*; the
shaft is let into a flat stone with four supporters;
in its present mutilated state it measures four
feet eight inches; it might have been originally
six; it would then answer, in shape, to a coffin
lid, or one of those grave-stones in that shape, so
frequently found in church-yards. As the place of
Owen's burial is uncertain,[10] it might be conjectured that his remains lie under it; but the mark,
representing a sword, is one of those crosses that
marks the interment of a *monk*, or a person of
some *religious order*.

A neat building stands on the same side of the
church-yard, a monument of the judicious munificence of a private gentleman, called Corwen
College.

It consists of six dwellings, with endowment
for the support of six widows of poor clergymen,
possessed ofthe cure of souls at the time of their
decease, in the county of Merioneth, by William
Eyton, Esq. of Plas Warren, Shropshire, who left

10   A marble slab is shewn in the cathedral of Bangor as his burial-place, but this is highly improbable: the guardians of the
church would hardly permit the body of its *incendiary* to
obtain a place of distinction within its walls. It is said, that
he was buried at Mannington, in Herefordshire, where he
died, at the house of his daughter, A. D. 1415. *Vid. Pennant.*

by will, 1709, a sum for this purpose; but, from some cause, the building was not finished, according to the inscription over the entrance, till 1750. The endowment was originally sixty pounds, but is now doubled; this sum, by a singular circumstance, is at present enjoyed by *one*. A proviso was made in the will that the widows should keep the building in repair; and if, at any time, there should be less than the number, those resident to share the residue of the income; it was now occupied by only one, a Widow Stodart, who, with an otherwise friendless sister, lived toge ther in a degree of affluence.

A small building, adjoining the church, contains the parish-hearse it is a light caravan with two wheels; the body, like that of a hearse, is hung upon springs, and painted black; a person is allowed a salary out of the parish rate to keep a stout horse: when informed of the time of burial, he is to proceed to the house of the deceased with his vehicle, and move with the body a solemn pace to the place of interment; this must strike every person as much more decorous than the common practice of remote country parishes in England, where the dead are frequently carried in a common dung-cart, or the coffin swung across a horse's back, who hastens to get rid of his load. A decent respect for the dead has, in all ages, been considered as a mark of a polished people; in this respect the Welsh shew a great degree of refinement, no people being more attentive to the solemnity of funeral rites.

A manufactory of woollen cloths, from the wool of the neighbourhood, has lately been commenced at Corwen, and promises to employ the numerous poor of the neighbourhood; it produces white coarse goods, bought up by the Liverpool merchants for the use of the colonies. The rocks about Corwen, abound with the LICHEN PROPOSCIDENS and RUBUS CHAMÆMORUS, called MWYAR BERWYN, or the BERWYN MULBERRY: *anglicè* DEWBERRIES, or CLOUD BERRIES; they are considered by the natives as powerful antiscorbutics, and held in high estimation for tarts, &c. &c.

Fronting Corwen is a British post called Caer Drewyn it is a circular wall on the summit of a steep hill, about a mile and a half in circumference, with the remains of circular habitations within, now in ruins. Mr. Pennant supposes this to have been one of those strong holds where the Welsh placed their women, children, cattle, &c. as a safe-guard, and considers it one of those chains of posts that began at Diserth and ended at Canwyd; but, from this place having no supply of water, I should rather suppose it to be one of the temporary entrenched camps, where they halted for a night or two till they were able to regain strength, to recommence their depredatory warfare.

Owen Gwynedd is supposed, by Lyttelton, to have occupied this post while Henry II. was encamped on the opposite side of the vale; the king had assembled all his choice forces on the

Berwyn, and strongly entrenched them by felling the woods and taking every possible precaution against ambush and surprise. Both armies, for a considerable time, lay in sight of each other; but the Welsh, well acquainted with the country by their light troops, cut off the king's supplies of forage and ammunition, and so harassed them by skirmishing, that the king was glad to withdraw to England in chagrin and disgrace, without having struck a single blow. (*Vid. Powel, p.* 190.) The place of encampment may still be traced by a rampart of earth between the church of Corwen and the village of Conwyd.

This was afterwards the retreat of the celebrated Owen Glyndwr, whose memory is highly revered in this neighbourhood, long the scene of his exploits and his hospitality. The family name of this extraordinary character was *Vychan*; he was styled *Glyndwr*, or Glyndwrdwy, from his possessions lying principally in the vale ofthe Dee, (Dwrdwy) commonly called the vale of Llangollen: some remains of his private palace are still visible at a place called Sychnant, about three miles from Corwen. He was fourth in descent from Gryffydd Vychan, the surviving son of Gryffydd ap Madoc, Lord of Bromfield and Yale, whose résidence was at *Castell Dinas Bran.* By his mother's fide he was allied to the North-Wallian Princes, from which descent he afterwards derived his claim to the throne of Wales.[11] Writers vary about the precise

---

11   Leland thus reckons his genealogy: "Lluelin ap Jorworth

time of his birth; it must have been some time between the years 1349 and 1354. It is a common idea, that extraordinary characters have their births ushered in by extraordinary events or uncommon appearances; his father's horses were said to have been found standing in the stable up to their bellies in blood the night previous to his nativity. Holinshed relates this as a presage of this *arch-rebel*'s future cruelties: while the Welsh considered it as an omen of the just *retaliations* he would make upon their cruel oppressors; Owen encouraged this idea, as a mean of securing the enthusiasm of the people in his favour; and, it is not unlikely, in endeavouring to persuade others, he had persuaded himself into a belief of its reality. Shakspeare finely delineates this mixture of superstition and vanity, when he puts the description of his birth into the hero's own mouth.

> ————————————————"At my birth
> The front of Heaven was full of fiery shapes;
> The goats ran from the mountains, and the herds
> Were strangely clamorous in the frighted fields;
> These signs have marked me extraordinary;
> And all the courses of my life do show,
> I am not in the *roll of common men.* "

Endued with great military genius, a spirit impatient of controul or provocation, with the late

---

Droyndan, Prince of al Wales, had Grifith; Grifith had Lluelin; Lluclin had Caterine; Caterine had Eleanor; Eleanor had Helene, mother to O. Glindoure. "

disgrace of his country strong upon his mind, he was prepared for those arduous scenes of difficulty and danger which the circumstances of the times unavoidably laid before him. In the reign of Richard he had been a favourite at the English Court; and evidently, from principle, was attached to the person and inte rests of that monarch; for he followed the fallen for tunes of his royal master; and, after the king's death retired to his patrimony, full of indignation at his Sovereign's wrongs, and with an ardent desire to revenge them. His resentment against the usurper, Henry, Duke of Lancaster, was exasperated by private grievances as well as by public wrongs; as might naturally be expected, he incurred the frowns of the new court; and, it was not probable, that any prior or present grievances, belonging to partizans of the late king, should be redressed; it was more probable that *new ones* would be added; and every engine of deceit and malice be put into action to entangle, in the mazes of the law, so powerful an antagonist to the new government. Aportion of Owen's lands were seized by Lord Grey, and, shortly after, by designedly omitting to summon Owen, as a baron, to attend the King, insult was added to injury, and a pretence of forfeiture, as weak as it was wicked, was set up, to alienate the remainder of his patrimony.[12]

---

12   On the attainder being issued against Owen, Henry IVth sold the lordship of Glyndwrdwy to Robert Salisbury, of Rûg, in which family it still remains.

In the very unsettled state of the public mind, especially among the Welsh, and the just plea they might have to throw off the English yoke, from the late unjustifiable usurpation, the danger might have been foreseen by the most shallow politician, of urging a person of such abilities and interest as Owen into desperate measures; it might have been expected, that the ambition of Owen, fired by revenge, would induce him to throw off allegiance from a power he considered unlawful; and which, hitherto, had only been exercised to rob him and his friends, and oppress his country. It required little penetration to discover that this would be a signal for a general revolt and insurrection through the principality. The prognostications of *Trevor*, who advised temperate proceedings, but in vain, were quickly verified; the Welsh, instigated by their bards and minstrels, who recited their accumulated wrongs, the virtues of their princes, and their present hero, in alternate song, rallied round the standard of their new leader, and, calling to mind the prophecies of their ancient bards,[13] looked up to him with all the confidence of enthusiasm, as a miraculous personage from Heaven, who should revenge the blood of their country, and restore to

---

13   They awakened the people to the recollection of the feats performed by their ancient Princes; represented Glyndwr as a descendant from them, and now their rightful Prince; expounded the hitherto mysterious prophecies; and asserted, that in this extraordinary man was to be expected the completion of every prediction of the oracular Merlin.

it, once again, its lost independence. Surrounded by a people ardently breathing for liberty, and at the head of a formidable army, his first act was that of just retaliation. He seized upon the lands and person of his chief enemy, Lord Grey,[14] and, on the 20th of September, 1400, he was publicly proclaimed Prince of North Wales. The insurrection now became general, and the Welsh, except within the influence of the royal garrisons, entirely threw off the English yoke. So formidable indeed was the rebellion now considered by the English, that the King thought it necessary to march against Owen in *person*; but, after endeavouring to dislodge him from his fastnesses among the mountains, and losing the flower of his army in the attempt, he returned to London in chagrin and disgrace. Taking advantage of this interval, Owen over-ran South-Wales; taking many of the castles, garrisoning some, setting fire to others, and destroying by fire and sword every thing that opposed the execution of his designs.

The King, having recruited his army, and filled his treasury by contributions, again took the field against this arch-rebel; but with no better suc-

---

14 Reginald was kept a close prisoner, and probably severely handled by Owen. The king wished to obtain the liberty of his favourite: Owen demanded ten thousand marks for his ransom, and the king's son, with other nobles, as hostages for the payment; the king, at length, complied with the extravagant terms of redemption, and Reginald was set at liberty.

cess. Want of victory was, in this case, defeat; for every day Owen acquired new friends and additional strength. The year 1402 was the meridian of his glory, He completely subdued his great enemy Grey, who had again appeared in arms, and forced him into a matrimonial alliance with one of his daughters. Having thus secured him, he proceeded to an act, which, however politic it might be considered from the urgency ofthe times, yet cannot its atrocity ever be wiped from the escutcheon of Glyndwr. Under pretence that many of the clergy had favoured the cause of Henry, unheard, and with a total disregard to innocence or guilt, he adjudged them to the sword, and sacrilegiously sacked and destroyed the cathedrals of St. Asaph and Bangor. Owen was now become the hope of his friends and the terror of his enemies. The repeated trump of victory had roused the dormant spirit of the most indifferent parts of the country. And by his past experience, and the influx of additional troops, he became still more formidable from an invasion of the North, by the Scotch, which created a powerful diversion in his favour. He was not only able to over-run great part of the principality, but to make predatory excursions, and levy contributions to the banks of the Severn. Victory trod close upon the heels of victory; and the English, beaten and discomforted in every quarter, to cover the disgrace of total defeat, attributed the causes to the incantations of witches and wicked sprites, enlisted under the banners of the British Chieftain. Owen judiciously encouraged an idea so calculated to inspire his own army with courage, and throw dismay and terror among the troops of his enemy. The Prince of English Bards, while he pourtrays the vanity of Owen, makes him vaunt ingly boast of his connection with the spiritual world:

> Where is he living, clipt in with the sea
> That chides the banks of England, Wales, or Scotland,
> Who calls me pupil? or has read to me?
> And bring him out, that is but woman's son,
> Can trace me in the tedious ways of art;
> Or hold me pace in deep experiments?
> I can call spirits from the vasty deep.

Owen's affairs began to wear so prosperous an aspect, that he assembled a Parliament of the principal gentlemen who espoused his cause at Machynlleth.[15] His title to the principality was here formally acknowledged, and the crown placed upon his head. He entered into an alliance with the Percies of Northumberland, and

---

15 Here he narrowly escaped assassination, from a snare laid for him by his brother-in-law, David Gam, a professed friend, in the pay of Henry. But the plot being opportunely discovered, Glyndwr escaped . He spared his life from affection for his wife, butkept him in close confinement for ten years.

Powel says (p. 316,) that he was released upon his solemnly promising to be true and loyal to Glyndwr in future; that David basely fled from his engagements, and Owen retaliated by burning his man sion, but Gam escaped.

with Mortimer, in the name of his brother the Earl of March; and this triumvirate, like the old one of Rome, placing their geographical instruments before them, divided the empire amongst them. The effects of this coalition, however, was not friendly to the cause of Glyndwr. Two armies arrived under the command of Mortimer; and a third, under Percy, tried to form a junction with Glyndwr, and encamped in the vicinity of Oswestry. Henry, with true military skill, sensible how important it was to his cause to prevent, if possible, this junction, hastened by forced marches to engage Percy, at the risque of being surrounded by a detachment from the allies, whom he overtook and defeated near Shrewsbury. This cast a gloom upon Owen's atmosphere for some time; but, spurning fear and trampling on difficulty, he entered into an alliance with Charles, King of France; by whose assistance, with troops and money, he renewed the war with redoubled vigour; and was so successful this campaign (1404), that the English were driven from every post; the Principality was alienated from the Crown of England, and Welsh independence appeared firmly re-established. The next year the atmosphere was again darkened with clouds, and Heaven seemed to frown upon his affairs. The English troops, led by the wise and intrepid Henry, Prince of Wales, proved invincible; and the Welsh, as though suddenly bereft of their usual spirit, yielded in several pitched battles to superior discipline, and became an easy conquest to the enemy. The spirit of Owen himself, who had hitherto borne up against adversity, and shaken off difficulties like dew-drops from a lion's mane, seemed broken; his principal friends dispersed; and he was obliged to wander from place to place, accompanied by a few trusty partizans, amidst the retired and secure parts of the woods and mountains. Shortly after this, Owen's fortune again revived. He received fresh succours from France; and we find him at the end of the year 1405, at the head of a powerful and well-appointed army, encamped on Wobury Hill, in the parish of Witley, near Worcester, the suburbs of which he burnt. The King was constrained to go a *fourth time, in person,* against this formidable enemy. Here the French, unequal in valour to the English, shamefully gave way at the beginning of the day; and the allied army experienced a most terrible defeat. Owen, with the remnant of the Welsh, made good his retreat to the mountains of Wales; and feeling the indignation which the brave always experience at the sight of cowardice, sent the French troops home, and begun to turn his attention to internal defence. From this period his affairs began rapidly to decline; his forces were not only weakened by the late disasters, but also by the defection of the whole district of Ystradt Tywy. Though possessed of sufficient strength to retain his fortified positions, he was too weak to meditate any thing beyond defensive measures.

Though his career was stopped, and his army almost dwindled to nothing, yet the spirit of Owen was not utterly depressed; for in opposition to a grant of lands made by Henry, consisting of estates belonging to the adherents of Owen, he was not behind the King in an ostentatious display of regal power. He granted a pardon to one John ap Howel ap Jevan Goch, "Anno principatus nostri VI, datum apud Kevn Llanvair Xo die Jan. *per ipsum principem.*" On the seal was the portrait of Owen, seated in a chair of state, bearing a sceptre in his right hand and a globe in his left. Having lost his principal fortresses, Owen, though he had acquired some additional followers, was unable to do little more than make prædatory inroads upon the Welsh Marches. Numbers of his friends, wearied with the length of the war and the hopeless prospect of final success, at length deserted his standard; and he was constrained to confine himself to the most difficult passes and defensible positions amidst the mountains. Still, though the power of our hero was reduced, his spirit was far from being subdued. He yet possessed the Alps of Wales, in which he remained invincible, because inaccessible; though so closely blockaded, as to cease to be formidable to the neighbourhood.

Here, with a determined bravery, he maintained his position in spite of the whole force of England, till long after the death of Henry. When Henry V, wishing to have his mind and his troops disengaged, to chastise the French; and finding Owen and his adherents still in a respectable state of defence, who, in the absence of his troops, might annoy the heighbourhood, condescended to enter into a treaty with him. The tenor of which was a free pardon for him and his followers; and an act of oblivion and general amnesty for the whole kingdom. Whether the hero deigned to negociate is not said; probably his death, which happened about this time (1415), interrupted its completion. If this event[16] took place, as stated, at the house of his daughter, there is reason to suppose that he did. The treaty was, however, again renewed by the same Minister, Sir Gilbert Talbot, with the son Meredydd ap Owen, February 24th, 1416; and by his closing with the terms, peace was restored to both countries, after an undecisive struggle of *fifteen years.*

I have given a short sketch of the exploits of this extraordinary character, because they are little known; and because the events of the time of Henry the Fourth, as they stand in the English history, are obscure without it.

Yours, J. E.

---

16   He died September 20, 1415, aged 61.

Letter XII

Chirk.

DEAR SIR,

e now entered the far-famed vale of Llangollen or Glyndwrdwy; and rambled for miles upon the banks of its still more celebrated river. The lofty Berwyn stretched its high table land to the right, while the left was formed by gentle slopes and verdant meadows.

As we proceeded, the mountains put on a bolder aspect; and the valley, with its river, assumed a more varied shape. No longer the tranquil stream we before admired, it swelled and foamed with all the turbulence of rage, grew impetuous, and forced its passage over its uneven bed in the form of an unbridled torrent. Consistent, however, with its capricious character, it takes a devious course; one while receding from the view and seeming to flow in peaceful silence, at another it appears rolling over shelving rocks, while its wood-fringed margin heightens the effect of the hoary wave.

The road sometimes ascends the acclivity of the mountain, and then suddenly drops into the lengthened vale; while the opposite side of the river consists of moderately wooded hills, that present themselves in all the luxuriance of forest foliage, interspersed with numerous villas of the gentry, and white-washed cottages of the more humble inhabitants; which give additional charms of life and spirit to the varied landscape. Descending into a rich bottom surrounded by woods, where a crystal stream issuing from a fissured rock into a natural bason below, we saw a number of females assembled to wash their linen; which they performed by first laying it to soak in the bason, then beating it with a piece of flat board on a portion of the rock, and rubbing the more delicate articles with their hands in the running stream: then spreading them on the turf to dry. This brought to our recollection a similar mode of washing in a more polished country; which must recur to him, who has ever led his devious steps to the banks of the Seine. Or should it be refused protection under the roof of

refinement, it has at least got the sanction of antiquity: it was the custom of ancient Greece.

Homer describes Ulysses and his companions,
as seeking in the course of their route

————The cisterns where Phoecian dames
Wash their fair garments in the limpid streams,
Where gathering into depth, from falling rills,
The lucid wave a spacious bason fills:
The mules unharness'd, range beside the main,
To crop the verdant herbage of the plain.
Then emulous the royal robes they lave,
And plunge the vestures in the cleansing wave:
The vestures cleans'd, o'erspread the shelly sand,
Their snowy lustre whitens all the strand.
POPE.

To persons who have seldom been beyond the
precincts of a city, this may appear a very singular custom; but it must be admitted an eligible
one, where fuel is scarce; and at least conducive
to cleanliness and salubrity.

From hence the boundary to the left opens in
the small, but beautiful vale of *Egwest*; through
which a rapid stream from the mountains of Yale,
flows into the Dee. The variety of the scenery increased every step as we approached Llangollen.
The Dee widens, and irregularly flows over its
shelving bed, and exhibits its bottom dry, except
at time of flood, in various places. It consists of
laminated slate rock, making an angle of about
thirty-two with the plane of the horizon; but frequently rising into ridges of a sufficient height

333

to interrupt and divide the stream of the river. It at length forsakes nearly the whole of its bed, and contracting its waters into a narrow channel, throws them with velocity over a ledge of rock through a single arch of the beautiful bridge of *Llangollen.*

This bridge consists of four pointed, or angular arches, the widest not more than twenty-eight feet in the span. Built by John Trevor, Bishop of St. Asaph, in the year 1346, and is considered by the Welsh, as one of *Tri Tlws Cymru,* or, The three Elegant Things of Wales.

The town is small, on the southern bank of the river, and has nothing to boast of, save a good parish church, dedicated to St. Collen, an Irish saint of eight descents from Mathalwch, Lord of Cwl, in Ireland, who lies buried here: and a well endowed free school. The houses are meanly built, and the streets narrow and without pavement. But Llangollen derives its consequence from the celebrity of its vale, the beauties of its surrounding scenery, and the interesting objects of antiquity in the vicinity. And perhaps no place is more justly famed; where the sentimental and refined lover of nature may have full scope for the indulgence of imagination.

At a small distance, overlooking the town, is a very neat building in the cottage style, fitted up with great taste by the present occupiers, the Right Hon. Lady Eleanor Butler and Miss Ponsonby. The former was sister to John, late Earl of Ormond, and is aunt of the present Earl.[1] The latter is of the noble family of the name in Ireland, and cousin to the present Earl of Besborough.

An extent of about two acres includes every thing graceful, as a confined pleasure ground. It is an elegant villa in miniature, and justly entitled to Miss Seward's appellation, "The Fairy Palace of the Vale."

These ladies, united by sisterly affection, congenial talents, and endued with virtues and accomplishments, calculated to adorn more public scenes, retired early from the gay world, and chose this recluse spot for their constant residence. Avoiding every appearance of dissipation, they lead a life as retired as the situation.

While we lament that such examples of femalevirtue should be lost to society in an age of levity and vice like the present, we cannot help admiring the spirit of self-denial and command, which could inspire such contempt of the world in the youthful period of life, surrounded with the blandishments of pleasure, and the allurements of ambition.

The morning being wet, damped the ardor of our company for the proposed excursion to Llan Egwest, and Dinas Bran. Setting out alone, a walk of about a mile up an ascent, brought me to the foot of a hill of conical shape, rising suddenly

---

1   This lady is omitted in Kearsley's Peerage; but this is but one error among many. *See Titles Drogheda, Dalhousie, &c.*

on all sides from its base; on the summit of which stands the celebrated castle of

Dinas-Bran

The fragments of this ancient building rising in the clouds at a distance, are a sufficient guide to it. The thick misty rain that had fallen, rendered the ground very slippery; which increased the difficulty of climbing this otherwise arduous acclivity. But seized with the enthusiasm of an antiquary, and burning with ardor to survey the spot where Freedom's Chieftain sat in proud security, amidst oppression's storms, I resolved upon the ascent, and at length overcoming every difficulty, gained the mountain's brow.

The building, which occupies the whole of the summit, save a narrow esplanade at the top of the front escarpement, is not large. Two wells and a chapel, beside other apartments, were contained within it. The materials are the shistose stone of the neighbourhood. The form is oblong; length two hundred and ninety feet; and breadth one hundred and forty; the walls exceeding thick, and those at present standing, from ten to eighteen feet high. The side least steep was defended by deep trenches cut through the solid rock. From the breaches made in the walls, this fortress must have been exceedingly strong; and from its inaccessible situation, impregnable to every assailant but the invincible one of time. To this the mouldering ruins give ample proof of its submission:

> Beyond the same, and yet on hill full hygh,
> A castle stands, an old and ruynous thing;
> That haughtie house was buylt in Weather's eye,
> A prettie pyle and pleasure for a king;
> A fort, a strength, a strong and stately hold
> It was, at first; tho' it now is full old;
> On rocke alone, full farre from other mount
> It stands, which showes it was of great account.
> CHURCHYARD.

Here might the leaders of the brave, but over powered Britons retreat, when Glory bade them quit the field, and wait for more auspicious mo ments here securely hide while the marauding enemy burnt their towns, and laid waste their country, to meditate revenge, and form plans of just retaliation. Prior to the use of cannon, this place could only be taken by treachery, or starved into surrender. It was generally supplied with a year's provisions.

The English forces chiefly consisted of Baronial levies; these temporary troops were only formidable in campaigns; soon quitting the field, by the tenure of their service, they were ill calculated for *blockade*. Even a regular siege, if obstinate, generally sickened and disheartened the soldiers, and obliged their commanders to quit the field; not unfrequently in disgrace and infamy.

This is doubtless a very ancient, and one of the primitive Welch castles; butthe period of its erection, and by whom erected, are both buried in equal oblivion. It is said, but upon no authority, to have been built by Brennus, a Gallic general; and hence its name. Camden derives it from *bryn*, a British word for hill, and *dinas*, a fortified place, *i. e.* the Fortress of the Hill. It is more probably derived (as Lloyd observes) from the mountain stream that flows near it, called Brân ar Crow, from the colour of its waters, imitating the feathers of the bird; and it is called Crow Castle by the people. It was the seat of the ancient lords of Jâl or Yale, and probably built by one of them. In 1257, it afforded an asylum, from the fury of his justly enraged countrymen, to Gryffydd ap Madoc, who basely sided with Henry II, and betrayed his country. On his death, the guardianship of his children vested in the Crown, by feodal custom. The eldest the King committed to the custody of John, Earl Warren; and the second to Roger Mortimer. The guardianswell under stood the nature of their charge, and faithfully executed their private instructions. They procured the assassination of the children, and took possession of the estate. But Warren, struck with remorse at the foul murder of his innocent ward, spared the third son, who must also have been committed to his care; and afterwards procured for him, by a grant from Edward I, that part of Yale, strictly the Lordship of Dinas Brân. Whether the grant was only for his life, or he had no issue, does not appear. It afterwards was possessed by the Warren family, whence it passed by marriage to the Fitzalans, Earls of Arundel, and followed the succession of the Lordship of Yale. It at present forms part of the extensive possessions of the Miss Middletons of Chirk.

In 1390, a celebrated beauty resided here, a descendant from the princely house of Powis, named Myfanwy Fechan, she won the heart of a celebrated Bard, Howel Lygliw, who addressed her in a beautiful ode, preserved in Jones's collection; she is the subject of an amiable digression for the poetical authoress of Llangollen Vale:

> 'Mid the gay towers on deep Din Branny's cone,
> Her Howel's breast the fair Myfanwy fires;
> O harp of Cambria, never hast thou known,
> Notes more mellifluent, floating o'er the wires;
> Than when thy Bard this brighter Laura sung,
> And with his ill-starr'd love Llangollen's echo rung.
> SEWARD.

The time of its being dismantled is unknown. Leland, describing it as a place of great strength, says it was in ruins in his time; and relates a story of an eagle that built annually in the neighbouring rocks; and that a person used to be lowered down in a basket to take the young, who was obliged to have another basket over his head to save him from the fury of the old bird.— Vol . V. p. 53.

Looking round upon this demolished castle, once the seat of royalty and power; its walls, some in mouldering heaps, and others kept together by the fibres of the clinging ivy; with the doleful plants Sambucus ebulus, Sorbus hybrida, and Circæa lutetiana, the inhabitants of waste places, in great luxuriance; my mind was naturally filled with melancholy reflections, and the descriptive lines of Dyer came forcibly to my recollection:

——Ancient towers crown his brow,
That cast an awful look below;
Whose ragged walls the ivy creeps,
And with her arms from falling keeps;
So both a safety from the wind,
On mutual dependance find.
'Tis now the ravens' black abode;
'Tis now the apartment of the toad;
And there the fox securely feeds,
And there the poisonous adder breeds,
Conceal'd in ruin, moss, and weeds;
While ever and anon, there falls
Huge heaps of hoary mouldered walls.
Yet Time has seen, that lifts the low,
And level lays the lofty brow,
Has seen this broken pile complete,
Big with the vanity of state;
But transient is the smile of Fate!
A little rule, a little sway,
A sun-beam in a winter's day,
Is all the proud and mighty have,
Betwixt the cradle and the grave.

Passing the foot of Fron Fawr, another cone shaped hill, and crossing the Brân in the Vale of Egwist, stands the Pillar of Eliseg. It is a round column, originally twelve feet high; an improvement perhaps of the *Meini Hirion*; and which succeeded them as a monumental emblem of the dead. The inscription is now illegible, but was copied by Lloyd; and informs us, that it was erected about the end of the 7th, or beginning of the 8th century, by Cancenn; sacred to the memory of his great grand-father Eliseg.

It stands upon a pedestal, five feet diameter and eighteen inches thick; the length of the remaining shaft is six feet eight inches; of the capital eighteen inches. Folly and superstition in former times might have paid religious honours to this pillar, as a Cross; and the ignorance and fanaticism of later times, for the same reason, laid violent hands upon it, and mutilated this precious monument of antiquity.

At a small distance down the stream stands the ruins of

VALLE CRUCIS ABBEY

This was a house of Cistercians, founded A. D. 1200, by Madoc ap Gryffydd Maelar, Lord of Dinas Brân, who was buried here; as was also his son, Gryffydd ap Madoc, 1278.—*Vid. Powel*, 279.

Intended as a burial place for the family, it can be no matter of surprise, that so quiet and recluse a situation was chosen, in preference to one in a more exposed part of the country, and on the banks of the boisterous Dee. The monks, who had nothing to do in the choice of a scite, might certainly with greater abstraction and less interruption spend their time in silent meditation and prayer, for the soul of the founder; which these ecclesiastics were especially bound to do; and for which purpose the building was erected. Its endowments were increased by numerous benefactors, and at the Dissolution, according to Speed, amounted to 214l. 3s. 5d. The time of its erection was nearly the commence ment of monastic institutions in Wales. For after the destruction of that of *Bangor Iscoed*, the first we read of was that of Tygwyn, built A. D. 1146.

> After which (says Powel, 221) they mightily in creased and spread over all the county And now the fountain-head began to be corrupted, for the clergy maintained a doctrine which their ancestors abhorred as may be easily gathered from that worthy divine, Ambrosius Telesinus, who flourished A. D. 540, when the Christian faith, (which we suppose delivered at the Island of Afalan, by Joseph of Arimathea,) flowed in this land in a pure and uncorrupted stream, before it was infected and polluted by that proud and blood-thirsty monk, *Augustine*.

From hence it appears, that the churches in this part of Britain long resisted the innovations of the Church of Rome; and the monastic life was held in disrepute for centuries, after it was popular in England. What tends to confirm Powel's remark is, that the greater part of the religious houses through Wales were Cistercians; a division of the extensive order of St. Benoit, or Benedict, which had just sprung up, and was the fashionable religious order of the day.[2]

The ruins of the church and part of the abbey still remain. The church was built cruciform, in several styles of architecture; and furnishes a specimen of the ornamental Gothic of the 13th century. A few of the arches are pure Gothic, but those which support the tower, and several of the doors are *mixed and ornamental*. The East end is in the most ancient style, where the windows consist of long narrow slips, sharply pointed at top. The West end has a large window with three lancets; and under, an arched door-way. Above is a small marigold window, of an elegant fretwork, with this inscription—A. D. ADA M. D. M. S. *fecit hoc opus, Pace beata quiescat. Amen:* and under, the mutilated date, M. D . . . . This unknown person probably repaired, or rebuilt

---

2   Every thing with which man has to do, degenerates in time, the order of Benedictines became regardless of the excellent institutions of their pious founder. Robert, Abbot of Molines, perceiving this, took with him twenty -one of the most religious of his monks to Cisteux, near Langres in Burgundy; where he erected a new abbey, which he called Cistercium, and his companions Cistercians. The first abbey of this order here, was founded at Rival in Yorkshire, about the year 1131, by Walter Espeke, according to this distich:

Anglia millesimo centes anno quoque et uno,
Christi et tricesimo, micuit Cistercius ordo.

this end, the beginning of the 16th century. The pilasters that support the internal arches end in capitals of elegant foliage; and the mouldings of the arches are highly ornamental. In the North transept is a chapel, with two arches, and near it a double *bénétier*, or vessel for holy water.

Adjoining the church is the abbey. The abbot's apartment was contiguous to the church, with a small opening into it, whence he might, if indisposed, hear the service of the church performed from his chamber-A similar accommodation belongs to the Principal's lodge, at Jesus College, Oxford.

The front of the abbey was noble in its appearance. A large window, highly ornamented with stone tracery, and which reached from the roof to the ground, is still visible, with three long lancets; and over them two others, with remarkable pilasters dropping from them. Within are the marks where stood a small narrow stair-case. The cloister is vaulted, and supported by rows of low pillars; now divided into apartments, which are appropriated for cattle; a farmer occupying part of it as a dwelling house. A number of ash-trees have taken root in the area, and spread their heads high above its mouldering walls. This is said to have been the first religious house in Wales that was dissolved. It remained in the Crown till the time of James the First, who granted it to Edward Wotton, afterwards created Lord Wotton.

Say ivy'd Valle-Crucis, time-decay'd,
Dim on the bank of Deva's wand'ring flood,
Your riv'd-arch glimm'ring thro' the tangled glade,
Your grey hills low'ring o'er yon night of shade;
Deep in the vale's recesses do you stand,
And, desolately great, the rising sigh command.
SEWARD.

The situation of Valle-Crucis Abbey, in this recluse vale, surrounded by lofty hills, and secluded from the world's rude gaze by thick woods, peculiarly fitted it for meditation and prayer; and it seems truly one of those seats

Where erst Devotion did delight to dwell.

In the deep repose of this secluded spot, not a sound was to be heard that could disturb the solemnity such scenes were calculated to inspire. The mouldering walls, loudly bespeaking the frailty of all earthly things, and the sun bursting from behind a cloud and peeping through the time-worn crevices of the building, threw a tint of melancholy light; and the consideration, that it was holy ground, all tended to heighten the energy of thought. And who is there, endued with a mind to think and a heart to feel, that could thoughtless pass over ruins crumbling beneath his feet? Who, that ever knew what sympathy meant, could pass by places that have figured in the page of history, without furnishing his tribute to fallen greatness? Who, that ever felt a spark of devotion, could irreverently tread upon ground consecrated to religion, and look indifferently upon walls erected for the service of the Deity? If there be such a man, I renounce all connection, I scorn the most distant communication, with him! He is the vile, the sordid slave of earth; and is destitute of every ingredient that enters into the composition of humanity!

But what is it gives rise to these sensations I feel? Is it the building? The mossy walls, the pointed arch, the ponderous columns, the figured niche, the dim recess, the prospective gloom of the long-drawn ailes and fretted vaults? No! These, unconnected with the lapse of ages, produce no such powerful effects. Is it the recollection of the pomp and grandeur of the *Catholic worship*, once performed within the sacred walls? its music, torches, tapers, masses, processions, vesper and matin rites? No! These to the rational Christian must excite a smile, and pity for the spirit that produced them; save as they were connected with the important truths of *Religion*. Yes! yes! it is *this* lies at the bottom of all the solemn veneration I feel! It is *this* gives me the hesitating step. This excites the strong emotions of awe! This absorbs my attention, and lifts my heart towards Heaven!! There is something *immortal* within us, that, when subjects like these are discussed, or presented to our view by memory and reflection, demonstrates our connection with the invisible world. For what purpose were these walls erected? For what endowed with such a profusion of wealth? What these sacred altars? What these hallowed shrines? Where are the original inhabitants? Where the series of successive generations? Whither are they gone? What is their employment? What their pursuit? Are they still exercised with anxieties and cares; still the subjects of affliction and pain; still obnoxious to disease and death? Or, are they exempt from all these; and, having put off the body, put off every thing mortal with it? And, as they taught, entered on a land of perfect happiness, breathing ætherial air, sunshine without a cloud, and everlasting joy beaming upon their heads? Doubtless some of them are! Then what am I? What is my pursuit? Whither does it tend? Alas! said I, the age of superstition is gone; but is not the age of *religion* gone with it? Revert, ye halcyon days, when to be religious was to be fashion able! When to be devout was considered rational; and when a life of religious instruction, and devotedness to God, was esteemed the highest of all sublunary employments! Riveted in the most profound reflection, I seemed to have strengthened my connection with the spiritual world, nay almost bordering upon it; every thing around me conspired to cherish the pleasing idea, and it was not till the importunate demands of hunger reminded me of my mortality, that I could be induced to forego it. With reluctance I left the solemn scene, and, retracing my steps, joined my company at the Hands, or Union Inn.

We met with excellent accommodations, but the charges extravagantly high. This did not appear unreasonable, when we learned that mutton was 6*d.* per pound, beef 8*d.* veal 9*d.* chickens 3*s.* and 3*s.* 6*d.* per couple, and every other article proportionally dear; and that provisions of all kinds could be procured cheaper from Shrewsbury, a distance of thirty miles, including carriage and commission. The cause is obvious. The Salopian butchers drain the country of the fat, and the graziers buy up all the lean, cattle, to feed on their rich pastures for the London markets. The large purchases they make produce a partial scarcity; this prevents a regular supply, which always enhances the price to the consumer. Persons, therefore, desirous of living in Wales, from the idea of its being a cheap country, in which they may retrench, must go where the art and the avarice of the English traders have not extended their influence; where the market furnishes a supply equal to the demand; and where the produce and the consumption of the country reciprocally alternate together. They must admire the wilds of Merioneth more than the beauties of Denbigh; and rather fix their residence on the bank of the humble Dyfi than of the boisterous Dee.

A few miles from Llangollen we met with the famous boundary between England and Wales, called

CLAWDD OFFA

The kingdom of Mercia, one of the Saxon Heptarchy, including the Cornavii, Corutani, Dobuni, and Catnellani, bordered on Wales. The Welsh frequently made inroads upon the Saxons. Offa entered into, a league with several other Saxon Princes, passed the Severn with a numerous army, drove them to the mountains with great slaughter, and took possession of the flat country west of the Severn. In consequence of which the seat of the Princes of Powis was removed from Pengwern, (Shrewsbury) to Mathraval. Sensible of the great evil of these continual inroads, Offa, to mark the confines of each country, or to give the greater security to his own, caused a deep dyke and rampart of earth to be made,[3] which extended a hundred miles over rocks and mountains, and across deep vallies and rivers, from the Clwyddian bills to the mouth of the Wye.[4] It may be traced at Brachy-hill and Lanterden in Herefordshire, and is continued northward from Knighton in Radnorshire, over a part of Shropshire; enters Montgomeryshire between Bishop's Castle and Newtown; passes over Mynydd Digoll, through Liner-park, to the Severn, at Ruttington, just below the conflux of the Bele and the Sev-

---

3   A. D. 776.

4   There are marks of small artificial mounts at certain distances-along the course, which were propably the scites of forts, while it was considered as a boundary.

ern it appears again passing by the churches of Llandysilio and Llanymynech, over the horse-course above Oswestry; whence it descends to the Ceiriog, near Chirk; crosses the Dee, and the Rhiabon road, near Plas Madoc; and forms part of the turnpike road from Wrexham to Pentre Bychan; leaves Minera on the left, crosses Cegs-dog river; and at a farm near Treyddm chapel, in the parish of Mold, Flintshire, ceases to be visible. This great work still retains the name of Offa's Dyke, and is an evidence of the ignorance and barbarism of the age; having been raised with immense labour; but directed to no impor-tant use, at least as a line of defence between two hostile nations. As a mark of the boundaries, it answered no beneficial purpose; and Offa only betrayed his ignorance, when he supposed this prohibitory line would restrain the incursions of the Welsh. They smiled at his folly, despised his toils, and irresistibly carried their ravages far and wide on the English marches. So formidable were they for a long season, that a sanguinary law was made by the victorious Harold, that any Welshman who was found on the eastern side of Offa's Dyke should have his right hand cut off.— *Vide Speed's Chron.* 401.

I have been thus particular respecting this cel-ebrated boundary, because most authors have mistaken the line, and confounded it with an-other, but similar dyke, equal in depth, but not in extent,[5] to that of Offa's, called *Wat's Dyke*. It attends it at unequal distances from five hundred yards to three miles or more, till the former disappears. Even Camden describes part of one and part of the other, for Clawdd Offa.—*Vide Vol.* II. p. 698. Both are accurately delineated on Mr. Evans's map of North Wales. I am at a loss to conjecture for what purpose Wat's was made, unless, as the foss of the other was on the side of Wales, the Welsh might have used it as an entrench ment; and the English or Danes might have formed the other as a *counter barrier*. Old Churchyard notices the distinction:

Within two miles there is a famous thing,
Cal'de *Offaes Dyke*, that reacheth farre in length;
All kind of ware [people] might thither bring,
It was free ground and cal'de the Britaines Strength.
Wat's Dyke, likewise, about the same was set,
Between which two, both Danes and Britaines met,
And trafficke still; but passing boundes by sleight,
The one did take the other pris'ner streight.

This is another inducement to think that Wat's Dyke was made by the Danes; that in time of peace the inhabitants might be permitted to barter their respective commodities for mutual benefit; and the space between the two dykes be considered as neutral ground, like the frontier fortified towns on the banks of the Rhine.

---

5   It is only discoverable at Macsbury, near Oswestry, and ends at the Dee, near Basingwerk

An infringement of the laws of hospitality on the part of the Welsh, it is said, led to the sanguinary statute of Harold; and the Welsh prohibited in future the privilege of putting a foot beyond *Clawdd Offa*. On the right of the village of Chirk, on the summit of a lofty hill, projecting from the Berwyn Chain, stands

CHIRK CASTLE

The present edifice stands upon the scite of one more ancient, belonging to the Lords of Dinas Bran, called *Castell Crogen*. It was built by Roger Mortimer,[6] who seized upon Chirk and Nanheadwy, as Warren did upon Bramfield and Yale. By purchase it went to the Fitz-Alans, by marriage to the *Mowbrays*; and, after seeing a number of owners, it was sold by the son of Lord Bletso to Sir Thomas Myddleton, in whose family it still continues. The two Miss Myddletons inheriting, as coparceners, on the demise of their late brother.

The castle is square, having two courts and a magnificent gateway, strengthened at the corners with four round bastions, ending in small

---

6   A communication to the Antiquary Society imports, "that it was begun 1011, and finished 1013. The repair of the wing, destroyed in Cromwell's time, cost 28, cool.; the front is 250 feet long; the court 165 by 100; and five round towers, 50 feet diameter; Adam's Tower, 80 feet high; the wall near the dungeon 9 feet deep; and the dungeon as deep as the walls of the castle are high."

turrets. The entrance is between two round towers, by a high narrow arch, not exactly in the centre of the front; and a pair of gates of exquisite beauty, wrought in so rich a style as to be considered a wonder of Wales. The first appearance is grand, but on a nearer view the building is heavy. Among the chief rooms are a very large saloon, handsome drawing-room, and a picture-gallery, abounding with scarce and valuable portraits, one hundred feet by twenty-two, with a variety of other handsome apartments; but all are dull, owing to the windows principally looking to wards the areas of the castle. Part of it was demolished during the civil wars. Sir Thomas was long a strenuous advocate of the Parliamentarian side of the question, and a very successful officer in that cause. But, towards the decline of life, like many more embarked in the same unconstitutional business, perceived that he had been spilling the blood of his countrymen to establish the power of a faction, whose tyranny was far worse than that which he rose in arms to oppose. He now, but too late, endeavoured to make restitution, and, in conjunction with Sir George Booth, endeavoured to restore the ancient constitution and laws. But the forces under Sir George were quickly defeated by the active and vigilant Lambert. Sir Thomas took refuge in his castle of Chirk, were Lambert pursued him; and, after a few days' shew of defence, he was constrained to surrender at discretion. One side, and three towers, which Lambert destroyed, Sir Thomas after ward rebuilt in one year. The damage occasioned by the civil wars was estimated at 80,000l. On the Restoration, Sir Thomas was offered a coronet for his services and his sufferings, which he refused. This venerable pile, though its history is not so interesting as many other castles, yet, when we take into the consideration, that it has withstood the storms of warfare and of time, *for five centuries*, has much to boast of; and is, perhaps, the most perfect castellated mansion of its age in the kingdom.

The park is very extensive, reaching to the foot of the Berwyn mountains; and covered in places with lofty forest trees. The pleasure-grounds are well laid out, and the different plantations disposed with great taste. But what arrests the attention of the traveller is the incomparable and almost inconceivable view from the elevation near the house. It is impossible to imagine any thing more extensively grand; *seventeen counties*, as a natural map, spread their varied beauties before the eye of the spectator. Towards England, the plain and town of Shrewsbury, its towers and spires; the range of table land, called the Clay Hills, extending towards the Malvern Hills, in Worcestershire; the solitary Wrekin; the high land that bounds the Vale Royal of Chester: towards Wales, Llangollen Vale, Castell Dinas Bran, and the boisterous Dee; the range of mountains dividing the counties of Merioneth and Montgomery, the Clwyddian hills, and the Snowdon Chain; with mountains appearing piled upon mountains, till height and distance give them the semblance of the neighbouring clouds. Indeed, nothing can exceed the variety and extent of scenery discoverable from this *enviable spot.* Chirk is also famed in history as being the residence of a Lord Marcher; and as this is little understood, I will furnish you with a few hints relative to the subject, and should be happy if I could see a good history of

LORDS MARCHERS

It has long been a question of difficulty when these peculiar Seignories and distinct Jurisdictions took their rise.

During the time of the Saxons we hear nothing of them. The Severn was considered the ancient boundary between Wales and England till the time of Offa: what was conquered by that monarch, on the western side, was annexed to his kingdom of Mercia; and, as a portion of the kingdom of England, came into the possession of Alfred the Great. When he divided the kingdom into shires or counties, he made part of the country, west of the Severn, a county of itself, by the name of Hereford; and the residue he added to the eastern side, for those of *Worcester and Salop.* Though some of the lands were granted to the Saxon nobility, who built castles for their defence, yet they were not considered as *sole guardians of the Marches*. The crown was obliged to guarantee their new possessions, and the towns of Chester, Shrewsbury, Worcester, and Gloucester, were fortified, and kept in a state of defence, to repel the incursions of the Welsh. It seems to be a necessary distinction, that as much of Wales as was obtained prior to the Norman Conquest, the Saxon Princes obtained at their own charge, and for their own use; their subjects not being suffered to intermeddle in the affair. The word *marches* signifies the limits between the Welsh and English; and, as the country west of the Severn was put under the protection of the lords of these places, so far they might be considered lords protectors of the marches. But it was not till by grants from the crown they obtained a right of conquest, and were invested with certain palatine jurisdictions and baronial privileges from tenure and creation, that they were entitled to the appellation of *Barones Marchia*,[7] or *Lords Marchers*. They were considered, from their importance, superior to other barons, and, from the red book in the Exchequer, it appears that they were summoned to attend the coronation of Queen Eleanor, consort of Henry IIId, by the style and title of *Marchiones Marchia Walliæ*, or Marquises of the Welsh Marches. This was the

---

7   They were Barons in the true import of the word, according to the definition of the Civilians, *Merum mistumque imperium in aliquo castro oppidove, concessione principis* ."

origin of the noble title of Marquis (*Vid. Black-stone, Vol.* I. p. 398.) next in honour to a duke.

The Welsh considered themselves as an independent nation, and had uniformly refused submission to the crown of England. The invasion of England by the Normans they looked upon as a contest between two foreign nations, in which, as they had no interest, they had no right to interfere.

William, and his successors, conceiving that a right of conquest, in one instance, conferred on them a title to possession in the other, levied forces and waged war upon the borders of Wales; but, after several attempts to crush them, from the nature of the country and the military prowess of the inhabitants, proving unsuccessful, William, in the true spirit of Machiavelian policy, *divide & impera*, adopted a new mode of warfare; he issued grants to certain favourites of all the lands they should be able to conquer from the Welsh;[8] invitations were, at the same time, sent to the Welsh, possessing seignories on the borders, with ample promises annexed, and a reservation of all their rights and privileges, for the simple acknowledgment that they were dependent upon the crown of England. Little, however,

---

8   This measure, though originating in awise policy, was ground ed on the absurd idea of *forfeiture*, because the Welsh, in a more prosperous state of their affairs, had refused that allegiance which had been unjustly extorted from them by force, and to which, through existing circumstances, they had reluctantly submitted.

was done during the reign of William; his attention was taken up too much with the refractory spirit of his new subjects and the revolt in Normandy, to attend to the subjugation of Wales. William Rufus, in quiet possession of the throne, and endued with more ambition than courage, turned his attention to his father's plan; his views were seconded by two traitors, Jestyn ap Gwrgaint, Lord of Glamorgan, and Eineon, a rebellious chieftain of Caermarthen. The wickedness of these men, coinciding with the views of Rufus, infused a deadly poison into the bosom of their country. Jestyn agreed to receive the Normans into his territory if they would assist in extirpating his great enemy, Rhys ap Tewdwr, Prince of South Wales. The Normans, under their leader Fitzhamon, executed the task; but, while Jestyn and Eineon were disputing about their respective shares in the recovered territory, Fitzhamon seized the opportunity, and possessed himself of the principal part of Glamorganshire, leaving only the rough and barren mountains to the contending parties. The lands he parcelled out among the twelve knights that accompanied him in the expedition, by a feodal tenure, the right of which he vested in himself. The king confirmed him in the possession of his new conquest, with the single proviso, that he should hold the same as a fief of the empire. A way was now opened for further seizures. The fortunate issue of this adventure roused a spirit of enterprise among the Norman nobility. The king did not fail to catch hold of the ambition and covetousness of his subjects; he laid before them the strongest allurements, and influenced them by the strongest incitements to human actions, *the prospects of interest and power.*

Several barons and others, consulting the wishes of the monarch, petitioned the crown for leave to do homage and declare their fealty for any conquests they might make; divers grants were accordingly issued out, conferring upon them all the lands they should thus obtain from the Welsh, with the reservation, that they should hold such lands in capite of the king.

In the commencement, the only qualification for a Lord Marcher seems to have been a disposition for conquest, and the only restriction the above tenure; but, although conquest was the general principle in which this dignity originated, yet, in a few instances, we find a different ground for this distinction. Gryffydd, Prince of Powis, finding his situation perilous, from the meditated conquest of Wales, and actuated by motives of fear and discretion, submitted himself, with his dependent lords, to Henry I. agreeing to hold his possessions under him, paying the same obedience and fealty as the Lords of the Marches.

In like manner the territory of Mowddy became a fief of the crown.

The lordships of Bramfield and Yale, with Chirk and Nanthendwy, as appendages of the lordship paramount of Dinas Bran, became the possession of English Lords Marchers as follows:

Emma, relict of Gryffydd ap Madoc, being left with several sons, and not agreeing with her husband's relations respecting their education, being the daughter of an English nobleman, and prejudiced in favour of the English, delivered the two elder to the king's custody, under a pretence that they were wards of the crown, their ancestors having sworn allegiance to the English monarch. He committed Madoc, with his patrimony, to the care of John Earl Warren; and Llewelyn, with his patrimony, to Roger Mortimer, third son of Baron Wigmore; the former built the castle of Holt, and the latter the castle of Chirk, which were made the splendid sepulchres of these unhappy orphans. Thus did these lordships differ from some others; but in one point they all agreed; they did, and were obliged to hold of the *king in capite*. This, and renouncing allegiance to the Princes of Wales, was all that was required of the succeeding Lords Marchers.

Thus were Lords of the Marchers made and established, possessing, in all cases, except high treason, *Jura & privilegia regalia*.

A number of new grants were continually issuing from the throne, and a line of offensive posts was soon established to harass and annoy the Welsh. South Wales being defenceless by the death of the brave Rhys ap Tewdwr, favoured the designs of these military robbers; among the foremost was Bernard de Newmarche, who took possession of the three can treves of Brecknock; Roger de Montgomery next did homage for Cardigan; and his younger son, Arnulph, obtained the extensive lordship of Pembroke. The Earl of Shrewsbury did homage also for Powis, and separated the town and adjoining estates from that lordship. The Earl of Chester for Englefield and Rhyvanioc, with the coast from Chester to Conway. Ralph Mortimer, for Elvel; Hugh de Lacy, for Enos and Rhos; Eustace Cruor, for Mold and Hopedale; Fitzalan, for Clun and Oswestry; Montalt, for Harwarden; Dru de Buladan, for Abergavenny; Gilbert, for Monmouth; Fitzwarner, for Whittington; Roger le Strange, for Elesmere; Martin, for Kemes; Morris de Londres, for Cydwely and Cornwallan; and Roger Mortimer for Mochnant, (now Chirk) Cynlleth, and Nantheudwyn, &c. &c.

Thus was the last asylum of the Britons invested on every side, and invaded by their inimical neighbours; South Wales was nearly all in possession of the English and Normans, and North Wales was curtailed and reduced to the island of Anglesea, the counties of Caernarvon and Merioneth, and part of Cardigan and Denbigh.

For the better security of themselves, and the government ofthe people, the new lords erected castles, garrisoned them with their own soldiers, and built towns in the most fertile parts of the country for their English followers. It was in this manner most of the castles and towns on the borders of Wales were founded; this is evident, from the number of the one,[9] and the ancient charters, expressive of immunities to the burgesses of the other; few or none of them having purchased these of the crown till many years after; and, when that took place, which was seldom the case, they were only *confirmations* of privileges, granted them by the founders.

Among the castles built about this time, were Pembroke, Tenby, and Haverfordwest, by Strongbow and his family; Newport, by Martin, Lord of Cemes; Cydwely, by Londres; Swansea, Oystermouth, and Loughor, by the Brewises; Brewis is also said to have built Radnor, Buelt, and Rhuiadr; Blaen Llyffney, by Herbert; Cardiff and Cowbridge, by Fitzhamon, and the Earls of Gloucester; Neath, by Greenfield; Abergavenny, by Dru de Baladan; Ruthin, by Lord Grey; and Denbigh, by the Earl of Lincoln. Many of these were fortified places prior to the Norman conquest, which, being devastated by war, or injured by time, were repaired or rebuilt by the conquering lords.

The tenure by which these lords held under the king was, in case of war, to serve with a certain number of vassals; to furnish their castles with strong garrisons, with sufficient military implements and stores for defence; and to keep the king's enemies in subjection. To enable these lords

---

9   There were thirty-three in the county of Salop alone; and, in the line of the Marches, one hundred and forty.

to perform this, they were allowed to assume, in their respective territories, an *absolute jurisdiction*; their power seems to have been as arbitrary and despotic, within their several seignories, as that by which they were created. Various regulations, in divers reigns, were made respecting the nature and extent of their authority; and, doubtless, when their assistance was no longer wanting, their power was daily abridged and thrown into the scale of monarchical aggrandizement. In the 24th of Henry VIII, a statute passed, c. 9, against killing of young beasts called wainlings," (*i. e.* calves just weaned .) By this Act a penalty of 6*s.* 8*d.* per beast was imposed on each offender: and it was especially provided "that every Lord Marcher should have the forfeitures of every offender within their *seignories, liberties, and franchises royal.*"—Among the various privileges claimed under title of these *franchises royal* may be reckoned fines for non-appearance at their courts; the forfeiture of common mainprise, recognizances, mizes; a power to hold courts baron and leet, to have waifs and strays, infangthefe, outfangthefe, treasure trove, deodands, goods and chattels of felons, persons con demned and outlawed; and also wreck de mere, wharfage and custom of strangers; and, *by a stretch of privilege, perhaps,* they generally seized upon the goods and chattels of those who died intestate.

There is no record to be found in the tower, or elsewhere, of any grant to possess the authority annexed to their dignity; the king's writs, from the courts of Westminster, did not extend to, nor were they executed, in any part of Wales, except Pembrokeshire, considered as a part of England by the title of Little England, beyond Wales. There were several reasons why the high privileges enjoyed by these lords *could not be held by charter*; when the king granted a baron the lands he might conquer from the Welsh, it was not then known what he would conquer, or, whether he would eventually obtain any. The lords themselves would not be very solicitous to procure such charters, as it sometimes happened that the lands they had thus taken possession of were restored by treaty, or the Welsh recovered them by force of arms, and expelled the Marchers. A still more powerful reason alleged is, *that the immunities and rights were of so high a nature, and so united by law with the crown, that it was not in the power ofthe king to delegate or disunite them*. It was thought advisable, from the urgency of the times to suffer the lords, by connivance, to establish such regulations, and exercise such authority as they might judge necessary, for the quiet and peaceable government of the country. These jurisdictions, not being recorded as grants from the crown, if at any time questioned, might be adjudged invalid.

In the marches the English laws were chiefly administered, and the tenures for the most part were of the same nature. Some Lords, however, from prudential motives, endeavoured to soothe the asperity of conquest by permitting the Welsh inhabitants to inherit after their ancient custom, agreeably to the laws of Howel Dda; with the proviso, that nothing should be done contrary to the interest of the Lord. Among other concessions, in favour of the customs of the former inhabitants, was the use of Gavel-kind, or the law which made an equal distribution among all the male children of the property of the deceased; and the transfer of lands by a surrender in court, similar to our tenure of copyhold of inheritance.

As the mode of conveyance, as well as the law of succession, was different with the two people in some Lordships, two distinct Courts were established, in which rights were discussed according to the customs of the two nations; one called *Welsherie*, and the other *Englisherie*. In a few lordships, the double custom prevailed; where the tenants, being English, were allowed the privilege of Gavel-kind; and at the same time transmitted their lands by feoffment. This was termed, holding by *English tenure and Welsh dole*. In many places, the English customs entirely prevailed. The whole jurisprudence within their limits depended upon the will of the conquerors. But it sometimes happened, that the jurisdiction of one Lordship infringed upon the rights of another, and disputes arose about the extent of their authority. As they were all equal, these disputes could not be settled by the means of ordinary justice. It was necessary, therefore, that *superior Courts* should be erected, for the purpose of accommodating the differences. The Lords Marchers regularly held their Baronial Courts, where the inferior Lords, who held of them, were obliged to attend. The Lords of Glamorgan usually kept their Court in the castle of Caerdiff. This, by an intimation from the King, was made also a Court of Chancery for the marches of South Wales, Appeals might be made, both from the Lords themselves against others, and also from the people against the wrong judgments of the Lords, to this higher Court; and all matters of equity were to be decided in the Chancery Court of Glamorgan. A similar Court was erected at Ludlow, for the marches of North Wales. In each, a President and Council sat for the regulation of these vicegerents; and to restrain, in some degree, the oppressive hand with which these Lords too frequently tyrannised over their poor vassals. In the statutes at large, especially those of Henry VIII. much information may be found relative to the nature and power of these Courts of Presidency. Amongst other regulations in that reign, it was recommended by the King to the Welsh, to adopt the custom of other civilized nations, in taking one family name instead of the tedious manner of adding the name of several generations, by the conjunctive particle ap; and the Courts were requested to inforce *a compliance to the King's wishes.*[10] The motive assigned was, the facilitating the identification of parties in judicial proceedings; but, *in fact*, this was a scheme of policy to blend the Welsh with the English, by obliging them to drop the names of their ancestors who had bled in the cause of liberty, and assimilating them in names as well as manners with the conquerors.

From the time of the Normans these tenures in creased to the time of Llewelyn, so that the marches, which at first were no more than a line of demarkation between Wales and England, extended into the very heart of the country. On the death of that prince, in the eleventh year of Edward the First, the necessity and the grants ceased together; and after this period no more Lords Marchers were created. The Welsh submitting to Edward, he took the principality into his own hand, and conferred it on his son Edward, Prince of Wales; of consequence, all submissions were afterwards made to the Prince. The King assembled a Parliament at Rhudlan

---

10 Though the genteel people imitate the English, yet still the prejudices of the lower classes rivet them to the ancient manner of appellation. By this involute method, the Christian name of the father is the surname of the son or daughter, *e. g.* if a person's name is *Owen David Luke*, Owen is his appropriate name, David his father's and Luke his grandfather's; his son would be called *David Owen*; and David Owen's son, *William David*, &c.

Women, after marriage, retain their maiden names, which occasions great confusion to those unacquainted with this peculiarity.

Castle, where laws were enacted for the government of the country, according to the English manner. From this time, no Lord Marcher could exercise any prerogative, not confirmed to him be fore, without a special grant from the Crown. Having now effected that for which they were created, their power and consequence gradually diminished and became obsolete. Appeals were constantly made from the Courts of Presidency to the Courts of Westminster. From the statute of Wales, 12 Edward I, various statutes had been enacted with regard to the internal polity; every one of which trenched upon the power of the marchers, till the 35th of Henry VIII; when (by stat. 34 and 35, H. VIII. c. 26,) the various jurisdictions were abolished, and Wales incorporated and finally annexed by law with England. Baron, Hundred, and County Courts, were established there; and a seffion appointed tobe holden twice a year ineach county, by the name ofthe Great Sessions of Wales; in which all pleas of real and personal actions are held with the same form of process as in the Court of Common Pleas in Westminster; and writs of error lie from its judgments (it being a Court of Record) to the Court of King's Bench.

Still, however, these Lordships long retained peculiar privileges; and the Courts of Presidency were not finally dissolved till the first year of William and Mary; which then were considered, as the preamble of the act (1 Wm. and Mary, stat. 1, c. 27,) sets forth to be *an intolerable burth-*

en to the subject. The original number of these Lords was twenty-one; of whom *one only*, Abergavenny, now remains; who is, in consequence of this high descent, the first Lord *Baron of the realm*. The others are lost, either by falling to the Crown, or merging in other offices or titles; and the jurisdiction and authority, the signs by which they were known, being no more, it is difficult to discriminate these from other Lordships. They may be known, however, by the following inferences: 1st. It must have been inherited or subdued prior to the death of the last Llewelyn. 2d. It must have been held of the *King* in chief, and not of the *principality*. 3d. Any suit, that may have arisen about the title, must have been pleaded at common law in Westminster Hall. 4. All offices of other manors, that were held of the King or of the principality, were found by virtue of writs out of the King's Exchequer of Caernarvon or Chester, for North-Wales; and Carmarthen or Cardigan for South-Wales; and out of Pembroke for lands in that Earldom. But the Escheator of the marches of Wales, in ancient time, inquired of the tenure, and found an inquisition *post mortem* of the Lord *by writ out of the Chancery of England*; and, as these Lordships were not in any shire of England, the business of the inquiry was laid on the escheator of the next English county; and such escheators had the charge and survey of the Lordships marches; and such escheator was to go into any Lordship, and swear an inquest, and find an office after the death of the Lord, and inquire of the tenure and value of the Lordship. Thus have I given you a very brief out-line of the origin, power, and decline of *Lords Marchers of Wales*; necessary to be known for understanding an interesting part of English and Welsh history. Whoever wishes for further elucidation upon this obsolete subject will find much curious information in a manuscript now in possession of P. Lloyd Fletcher, Esq.[11] of Gwernhaeled, Flintshire, whence this was principally extracted.

Leaving the noble mansion of Chirk, the seat of genuine hospitality and real elegance, we crossed the river Ceriog, a tributary to the Dee, and at present the boundary between England and this part of Wales; and, pulling off our hats as a token of respect, bade a reluctant adieu to the Principality. We turned our backs upon a country which had furnished us with new scenes at every step; where Nature has been lavish with whatever tends to please and elevate the mind; where Flora sports in sweet variety, and spreads her matchless charms over Alpine heights, as well as lowly vales, in rich profusion. A country that was eminently distinguished as the birth-place and residence of the children of freedom; who, from their independent spirit and martial prowess, for

---

11   This gentleman is among the number of those whose virtues adorn distinction of rank. To the utmost urbanity of manners, Mr. Fletcher adds a liberal hospitality that lays a contribution upon the gratitude of every travelling visitor.

centuries chastised rapacity and injustice, and made oppression and tyranny tremble on the Throne. The mournful reliques of whose skill and valour furnish the Antiquary with curious objects for research; and lead the feeling mind to admire the courage that defended them, to detest the spirit that caused their erection, and to weep over the lost independence of a people, after so many struggles for its preservation. A country where a plain, honest, hospitable people, uncorrupted by wealth, and not enervated by luxury, still keep the noiseless tenour of their way; where calm content and bliss delight to dwell. Thou land of charms farewel! And ye, its envied tenants, now farewel!

I am, yours, &c. J. E.

Letter XIII

DEAR SIR,

I n my former letters I have frequently adverted to the peculiarities of the people of North-Wales; and some of their local customs have been noticed *en passant*. The design of the present is, to detail a few observations that could not so well fall in with connected narrative.

From a variety of causes, the Welsh have changed but little in their persons or manners for centuries; so that the observations of Gyraldus, in the reign of Henry II . (A. D. 1188,) will, in many respects, apply to the present inhabitants of North Wales. The modern Cambrian has the face rather broad than long, the space between the temples wide; the cheek-bones prominent; *the hair black, and the eyes dark;*[1] these, frequently accompanied with a fair skin and roseate bloom in many of the females, gives them an air of animated vivacity peculiarly pleasing, and may entitle them to be considered as beautiful, when its proper concomitant, proportion, may be wanting. The men are in general rather below than above the middle stature. They are thickset, with limbs rather small; and though in stances have sometimes occurred of prodigious strength, yet, like their ancestors, they are light and active, more free than strong; and the modern, like the ancient Briton, is not very attentive to food or clothing. The latter consists of a flannel jacket and breeches for the men; and a lindsey jacket and petticoat, with a round felt hat, for the women; while both sexes are seen to climb the craggy steep, and trip over the thorny plain naked to the knee. But they are not destitute of shoes and stockings; these they carry in their hands to market and to church; and at the next adjacent stream they sit down on a stone, wash their feet,

---

1   The author of a *Walk through Wales*, when he describes them as having *blue eyes* and *yellow hair*, must have had in view the people of the coast of South Wales; where the mixture of Flemmings, Normans, and English, has scarcely left a single trait behind of the person or character of the ancient Welsh.

and put them on. Returning, they perform the same ceremony, and lay them up again.[2] Their food is equally coarse and scanty. Oatmeal-cake or barley-bread, and potatoes; and their drink the diodgriafel. This course is sometimes varied by hung-goat, dried fish, cheese made of goats' and sheep's milk, and butter milk, grown acid from keeping. The cakes are manufactured by the mistress of the house; the meal is made into paste with water, and spread thin upon the back-stone over the fire, to bake. The colour raises a dislike, otherwise the taste is not disagreeable. Wheat flour may be found in some houses, but, as yeast is rare, there is consequently little fermented bread.

Refinement has not yet deadened the natural feelings of the Welsh, nor produced that apathy of behaviour which prevails among a more polished people. The fondness they evince for their country, and tenacious adherence to their native language, is not more remarkable than their singular attachment for each other. This spirit, which pervades the community, in individuals is most eminently displayed. Zeal for the welfare of every branch of a numerous family, which pro-

---

2   When Trevor, Bishop of St. Asaph, gave Henry the sage advice, not to provoke the Welsh to insurrection, the Lords gave for answer, "There could be no fear about such a *bare-footed rabble*." The king soon found, that it is easier to despise than to conquer an enemy; and what gave rise to the contempt was what rendered them always formidable and frequently victorious.

duces reciprocal protection and respect between the higher and lower classes, frequently calls forth a spirit into action rarely to be met with elsewhere; and has, on some occasions, been exhibited in a manner, that, to those narrow minds which make *self* the centre of every ray of exertion, would appear extravagance and romance. Take one illustration.

In consequence of the poverty of the soil and state of husbandry, the harvest is very late; and frequently, from the uncertain state of the weather, a difficulty occurs of procuring the scanty crops upon which their existence depends. It often happens, that the strength of hands is not adequate to the labour, and a poor farmer is in danger of being ruined. But there is a natural sympathy amongst the Welsh, that provides for this adverse circumstance. Sensible of the evil arising from a scanty crop badly housed, they form societies of assistance, called Cymmorthean Cynhauaf. As soon as one or two farmers have finished their own, or what portion is ready, they immediately repair, with their servants and horses, to assist their backward neighbour. This they do without any other fee or reward than their maintenance, and the consciousness that arises from the performance of an act of brotherly kindness. We have seen numbers engaged in this amiable occupation, and the pleasure they felt might be deduced from their clamorous exultation. If the sky lowers, and gathering clouds forbode a storm, likely to mar their friendly intentions, the noise increases, exertion is redoubled, and they seem more anxious to secure their neighbour's produce than their own. The desirable end accomplished, they return with shouting to the house, where, congratulating the farmer's good fortune, they express their mutual happiness in acts of cheering festivity.

It was not till I had witnessed these scenes of philadelphic labours, that I fully understood the elegant allusion of the prophet, when speaking of the pleasures of the favoured people of GOD:— *"They joy before thee, according to the joy in harvest."* Isai. ix. 3.

Nor does this strange patriotism and brotherly affection, this love of their country and their neighbour, exclude the attention to the *stranger.* That endearing affection, *hospitality*, that disinterested principle, which makes the wants and the comforts of others our own; that sparkling gem in the breast plate of humanity, still forms a prominent feature in the character of the Welsh. Gyraldus says,

> hospitality was so much the habit of this nation, by a mutual return of civilities, that it was neither offered to or requested by travellers. As soon as they entered a house, they immediately delivered up their arms into the custody of a person in the family; and if they suffered their feet to be washed by a person that offered them water for that purpose, they

377

were considered as sojourners for the night.
The refusal of this civility intimated the desire
of a little refreshment only.

Ingenuous and considerate, the present gentry
contribute to the comfort and accommodation of
the stranger; they dispense with a liberal hand
the benefits derived from their exalted situation;
and support the dignity of character derived
from their princely ancestors, by a pointed attention to those who happen to visit in their vicinity. If a person travel without recommendation,
or has not sufficient confidence to make one for
himself, he may consider the Welsh as averse to
strangers. But with it, it is only necessary *to be
known, that he is come to survey the beauties of
the country*, when he is conducted to every thing
worthy his observation, with the most zealous attention; and with an impressive welcome, in vain
expected in more refined countries. Nor is this
temper confined to large mansions, supported by
extensive domains; it inhabits the lowly cottage;
and often in the miserable habitations of penury have I witnessed its fascinating influence. The
North-Wallian peasant will bring out his little
stores, borrow of his neighbours, run with you
miles to put you in the way; and so far from ask-
ing for remuneration, will feel offended if you
offer any. This blooming evergreen, that cheers
the weary senses of the forlorn traveller, by the
beauty of its bloffoms and the fragrance of its

scent, blows throughout the year; and flourishes amidst the most barren rocks, and remotest wilds of Cambria.

High spirit and military courage are points no less legible in their character: the invincible opposition they shewed towards the victorious legions of Rome, and the centuries they supported an unequal contest with the English, placed them high on the annals of fame; and the same courage displayed when circumstances have called it into action, proves that the spirit of the Welsh is not degenerated; and that on proper occasions they will establish the legitimacy of their descent by national intrepidity. Amid these striking colours a few shades, too deeply marked, deform the national character.

National importance and family distinction too frequently descend into a petty pride, that induces the Cambrian to think more highly of himself than he ought to think. Pride of Ancestry was a principal point amongst the ancient Britons; of course they were more desirous of noble, than of rich marriages. So deeply rooted was that principle, that even the very lowest of the people carefully preserved the genealogy of their families; and were able, from memory, not only to recite their immediate ancestors, but to trace them back through numerous generations.

An instance is quoted by Mr. Pennant of the pedigree of the clergyman, Mr. Evan Lloyd, who accompanied him; and as it is a genuine copy of the form of a British pedigree, I shall give it you. "Evan ap Edward, ap Richard, ap Edward, ap Humphrey, ap Edward, ap Dafydd, ap Robert, ap Howel, ap Dafydd, ap Meirig, Llwyd o Nannan, ap Meirig Vychan, ap Ynyr Vychan, ap Ynyr, ap Meuric, ap Madog, ap Cadwgan, ap Bleddyn, ap Cynvyn *Prince of North Wales.*"

This, which arises from their mountainous situation, and living long in the same district, may be placed amongst their hereditary prejudices; and might be considered as a venial defect in the national character, as only the excess of laudable affection: since it may be observed, that he, who is attached to high rank, must feel some respect for the virtues of him who procured it; were it not for the spirit of contention which it inspires, and the condescension to useful imitation which it prevents.

A too quick sensibility renders the Welsh highly tenacious, and their spirit is prompt to rise on the appearance, or even on the slightest *apprehension of insult.* This frequently proceeds from intemperate animation to the most violent paroxysms of passion, productive of hasty expressions and undue acts of violence. This spirit, when unrestrained by whole some laws, was a constant source of massacre and slaughter; as it is now become of assaults and litigations. I wish I could thoroughly refute the appellation of *quarrelsome,* that has been frequently given to the temper of the Welsh.

Pennant acknowledges that his countrymen were in very early times as fierce and as savage as the rest of Europe; and cannot deny, but that the Welsh were to excess "Jealous in honour; sudden and quick in quarrel." And much of this irritability still exists.

This irritable disposition is too frequently called into action by the influence of Bacchus. Conviviality is apt to lead to habitual intemperance; and this is the fruitful parent of a thousand other ills: it is a vice that benumbs the energies of industry, fosters the seeds of idleness, and adds disease and want to the other calamities attendant upon poverty. Among the yeomanry it gives rise to a litigious and ruinous spirit, too often promoted by low chicanery and artful knavery.

A Welshman, if he can find in his genealogy a *Chieftain Bard*, or warrior, considers himself nobly born; the least reflection therefore on his family, especially over a jug of cwrw, infallibly subjects the libeller to a volly of abuse, if not to a direct assault: the company, as if all were interested, immediately become involved in the contest. From the injuries given and received on these occasions, arise a variety of actions: not unfrequently the attorney of the village is present, and then action and cross action are combined to fleece the contending parties. Every assizes is burthened with pleas about petty rights and petty quarrels, made the subjects of a suit; for the Profession let no opportunity slip of exciting a spirit calculated to increase the content of their purse. Attornies are consequently numerous; and it would be a low calculation to put down, for the same extent of population, *three* in Wales for one in England.

Frequently may you see the farmers returning from the Courts of Justice, abusing their ill stars, after having spent the annual profits of their farm; and sometimes the money that should have been reserved for the landlord: and this without the smallest prospect of advantage, unless the ruin of the adverse party could be considered as such; fully convinced of the folly of their conduct, but not so of the *spirit* that occasioned it.

These shades, however, are not so dark as they have been; and they seem to be imperceptibly growing lighter every day. It is to be hoped, that Religion, which seems daily to extend its benign influence, will put a stop to these feculent streams, by drying up their source; and, by eradicating the principles of vice, prevent all the consequent misery. It is but justice, however, to remark, that murder, highway robbery, burglaries, and those greater crimes, so frequent in England, are perfect strangers to the Principality.

The invidious remark of Johnson, in his *Tour to the Hebrides,*—"That mountaineers are *thievish* because they are poor; and having neither manufactures nor commerce, can grow rich only by theft and robbery;" is confuted by the honesty remark able in North Wales. Locks and bolts to doors are for the most part unknown; and where they are, seldom used and the solitary traveller passes the most dismal roads and dreary wilds devoid of fear of insult or depredation. Nor are his views rendered unseemly, or the country disfigured by gallows and gibbet. A positive proof that this people are yet uncorrupted by an intercourse with their more opulent neighbours; and that the greater crimes are the offspring of luxury and infidelity.

Among a variety of Welsh customs, those in courtship, marriage, and at funerals, cannot fail to excite attention. Hymeneal negotiations are literally carried on by the Welsh peasantry in bed. The young Strephon frequently goes several Welsh miles[3] to visit the object of his choice; either to her place of servitude, or the residence of her friends. The young couple retire to a bedroom, and between the blankets converse on those subjects which the nature of the occasion may suggest. The youth generally goes on a Saturday night, and returns to his work on the Monday morning. This familiar intercourse continues for the space of two or three years, and seldom fails to terminate to the honour and happiness of the parties.

This singular custom, which has been compared, not very happily, to the American *Bun-*

---

3   The Welsh mile (milltir or milldir), used until Edward I conquered Wales in the 13th century, was 3 statute miles and 1,470 yards long (6.17 km). —Ed.

dling, is one of those that served to mark the original British character; and among many others, remains to distinguish this people to the present day. To those who conjecture that every familiarity must be accompanied by improper ideas, this mode of making love must appear highly objectionable; and those, who consider every custom that differs from their own as founded in barbarism, will be inclined to censure it as productive of evil.

I was almost illiberal enough to suppose, so near a contact of the partics, at a time of life when passion is seldom subservient to reason, must have a dangerous tendency. An attention to facts, however, soon corrected this hasty judgment upon what has been for ages the custom of a country. Inquiring of those, who, by long residence, have had opportunity for observation, I found this mode to be as innocent as any other: that it is considered so by the parties themselves is evident from the ease with which it is conducted. No awkwardness of guilt appears in Strephon's step, nor blush of confusion in the fair one's cheek. The parents never refuse to acquiesce in it; nor do the moft fastidious of the sex offer a single objection.

It has been observed, that a custom otherwise perilous, by becoming general, loses much of its dangerous tendency; and that, what is considered as a matter of course, seldom produces improper ideas. The power of habit, sanctioned by popular opinion, may rise superior to passion; and the desire of fame above the charms that inspire it.

Such, (says an elegant writer,) is the nature of human depravity, that what is common is not es teemed a precious opportunity; what is most difficult to attain is thought the most desirable; and the fruit of stealth more delicious than that more easily and more publicly gained and privacy becomes dangerous, not because no eye sees, but be cause to privacy is ever attached the idea of suspicion. After all, depravity of conduct is generally the off spring ofimpurity of ideas; and though the reverse is not uniformly the case, yet, for the most part, he that thinks no evil, seldom commits any; and where simplicity of manners and conduct abound, the gartered motto may be more aptly used than on the original occasion,—

"*Honi soit qui maly pense.*"

By this justification of a custom that appears strange because it is singular, I do not mean to in sinuate that virtuous love is confined to the mountains of North Wales; or that degrading consequences are not *sometimes* the result of these *congressus cubiculares*; but this I may assert, that the Cambrian fair goes more frequently from the chamber of wooing to the altar of Hymen, than the more polished females to the East of the Severn.

Marriages, among the Welsh, are no less singular than their courtships. There are two kinds of marriage amongst the Welsh, distinguished under the titles of the great and little wedding; the former resembles the *confarreatio*, and the latter *de usu*, among the Romans. In the little wedding persons cohabit together; and if, after trial, they have reason to be satisfied with each other, the friends are invited to witness the intentions of the parties; and they are after considered as man and wife. If the parties, prior to this, are dissatisfied, the woman is dismissed; and such repudiation is not considered an hindrance to future marriage: but this is chiefly now confined to the borders of Cardigan.

The great wedding is thus conducted: -When two young people have agreed to enter into a state of wedlock, a friend undertakes to perform the office of *Gwahaddor*, or bidder to the wedding; who goes round the neighbourhood to all persons in nearly the same station of life. If the wedding is of the better sort of people, he carries circular letters; if among the poorer, he does it *viva voce*. The import and form of the message is nearly as follows:—

SIR,
My daughter's wedding-day is appointed to be on Saturday, the 14th instant next, at Eglwys Newydd, at which time and place I humbly beg the favour of your good company; and what further re membrance you shall be pleased to confer shall be gratefully retaliated by me, who am,

Sir, &c.

In consequence of this, or a similar invitation, the friends and neighbours for a great extent, make a point of attending the wedding, laden with presents; consisting of money, butter, cheese, &c. &c. these are carefully set down by the clerk of the wedding, opposite to each respective name, which are to be paid in the same public manner, and on the same occasions, whenever demanded. This custom is called Pwrs a Gwregys; and making the presents termed, paying Pwyddion. As an ancient usage, it is considered on refusal as recoverable by law; but a sense of the reciprocal duty generally prevents hay ing recourse to such a mode of recovery.

It has sometimes happened, that a species of matrimonial swindling has been practised; persons in distress have made feigned nuptials, to recall the presents they may have made, and obtain those of others.

The day fixed, a few, assembled for the purpose at the bridegroom's friends, proceed to the house of the intended bride, and demand her in marriage. And though the bride, attended by her relatives, has been waiting in anxious expectation of the dear summons, yet delicacy or custom throws a temporary obstacle in the way to bliss.

The friends of the bridegroom, in rude poetic strains, recite the virtues of their hero, and the eligibility of the connection; while those of the bride oppose the match in equally cogent arguments. After this shamn contest has continued the customary length, the father, or some near relative, steps forward, the bridegroom is introduced, the friends are treated; and, after a short interview, they proceed towards the church. But reluctance on the part of the fair is still shewn, who makes frequent attempts to escape; exhibiting symptoms of strong aversion to her change of state, by unmeaning tears and forced lamentations. This farce acted, she at length quietly submits; and the ceremony at church performed, they repair to the house of the bride, and proceed to celebrate the wedding in continued mirth and festivity for several days together: Sunday only puts a stop to feasting; when the new married couple sit down to receive further Pwyddion, and the congratulations oftheir friends,

The gifts on this occasion, in the case of poor people, sometimes amount to forty or fifty pounds: an essential benefit to young persons just setting out in life. Till the business of Pwyddion is over, they do not appear out, which is generally by the second Sunday; when the friends attend them to church, and the marriage is from this period *esteemed valid and properly sanctioned*.

This custom undoubtedly originated in the hospitable and affectionate disposition for which this people were for centuries famed. Nor can it be denied, that this national dowry must have acted as a strong inducement to matrimony; and been highly conducive to the strength and population of the country. It provided a permanent and never-failing fund for the use of those entering into life; which encouraged them to set out with hope, and called upon their resolution to persevere in the same ceconomy and industry that produced it.

We were sorry to be informed that this liberal custom is growing into disuse; and that population, in this already thinly inhabited country, is likely materially to suffer in consequence.

It might be expected, that those who had such singular customs at the entrance on life, would have some peculiarities on the departure out of it, Previous to a funeral it is usual for the friends of the deceased to meet in the apartment where the corpse is placed; some of them, generally the female part, kneel round it, and weeping bitterly, lament and bewail the loss of their departed friend. When it is brought to the door, one of the relations gives bread and cheese and beer over the coffin to some poor persons of the same sex, and nearly of the same age with the dead, for collecting herbs and flowers to put into the coffin with the body; sometimes a loaf, with a piece of money stuck in it, is added. This done, all present kneel down, and the minister, if present, repeats the Lord's Prayer. At every cross-way they stop, and the same ceremony is repeated, till they arrive at the church, Frequently the intervals are filled up by singing of psalms and hymns, which amidst the stillness of rural life, and the echo from the hills, produces a melancholy effect; and adds to the sombre solem nity of the occasion.

A similar custom prevails in the Highlands, which they term *Coranich*. The bier is always carried by the next of kin, and this is considered as the highest mark of piety which can be paid to the departed relative. This, as we learn from Valerius Max. *L.* 7, *c.* I,[4] was a usage among the Romans. If it happen in a morning or evening, the service is read accordingly. After the general thanksgiving, the minister goes to the communion-table, where he reads the two prayers which are usually, in other places, read at the grave; and then concludes with the prayer of St. Chrysostom and the Valete Grace. This done, he remains at the table till the nearest relation of the deceased comes up and deposits an Obituary Offering. If it be a person of consequence, the sum is a guinea or more; if a farmer or tradesman, a crown; if a poor man, six-pence: the next of kin then follow the ex-

---

4   Metellus, the conqueror of Macedon, was borne to the funeral pile by his four sons. As a mark of respect, those who had deserved well of the commonwealth were carried by the Magistrates or Senators; while persons hated by the people were carried by Vespil, lones or Sandapillones, hirelings for the purpose. To this custom Horace alludes—

                    ————————Cadaver
      Unctum oleo largo, nudis humeris tulit hæres.
                          Lib. 2, *S.* 5.

                    ————————Augustis ejecta cadavera cellis,
      Conservus vili portando locubat in arca."
                          Lib. 1, *S.* 8.

ample, offering sometimes as much, and sometimes
less than the first: the rest of the congregation, who
intend to offer silver, follow, when a solemn pause
ensues; and the rest of the congregation offer pence:
but pence are never offered at genteel funerals. The
offerings on these occasions frequently amount
to eight or ten pounds.[5] This is certainly a relict of
Popery, and was no doubt formerly intended as an
acknowledgement to the priest for praying for the
welfare of the departed soul; as a composition for
a short residence in purgatory; or perhaps for any
failure in the payment of tythes and oblations, and
is termed *Arian Rhiew*. Though still continued, it is
now only considered as a small tribute of esteem to
the memory of the deceased, and as a mark of attention to the resident clergy.

This emolument adds to the comfort of the North
Wales' clergy; and it was with conscious pride and
pleasure, that we found them more easy in their circumstances, and respectable in their character, as a
body of men, than those of the southern part of the
principality. None are admitted into holy orders at
St. Astaph or Bangor, but such as have graduated at
Oxford or Cambridge; whereas, until a regulation
adopted by the present worthy Bishop of Roches-
ter, then Bishop of St. Davids, men without talents,
education, or character, were usually ordained from
every petty school in the country. He ordered, that
in future, none should be admitted in holy orders,

---

5   Those of Caernarvon amount to little short of one hundred
     pounds per annum.

except such as had spent two or three years at one of these five schools; Cowbridge, Caermarthen, Pembroke, Ystradmeyrick, or Brecknock; and this to be immediately preceding the time of offering themselves candidates. He also at the same time enjoined, that no curate should have less than fifteen pounds for serving one church; thirty for two, &c. But it cannot be supposed that parents will send their children and be at the expense of an University education, to have an income, with labour, of fifteen or at the most, *thirty pounds per annum!!!* The Curacies in North Wales are seldom less than forty or fifty. But lest great blame should attach to the South Wales bencficed Clergy, it should be remembered, that there is a great difference in the *livings*. At the Dissolution, most of those in South Wales were good; Henry VIII. therefore distributed them amongst his favourites; and they became lay impropriations, with *unendowed Vicarages*; and had it not been for Queen Anne's bounty, halfthe churches in that country would have gone without ministers; as it is, a number of chapels have been suffered to fall into a dilapidated state. On the contrary, those of North Wales being considered as poor at the time, escaped the rapacity of Henry; and were suffered to remain in the hands of the Clergy, where, as they ought, they continue to the present day.

Your's, &c.

J. E.

Letter XIV

The state of *Agriculture* is at a very low ebb; it appears to have experienced little improvement for centuries; and the Welsh farmer has the very first principles of good husbandry to learn . Attached to old customs, and deprived, by his insolated situation, of the stimulus arising from better examples, and still more so by the shackles of penury, cultivation makes no progression, and vegetation dwindles under the hand of industry. The distinctions of three, four, and five-field husbandry, does not obtain.

The far mer possesses no systematic knowledge; he follows no determinate plan, considering only the circumstances of the day; he plows his land as it appears convenient, and throws in his sced as the weather furnishes opportunity; the quantity of acres for wheat and barley is more determined by the preceding circumstances, than by any other cause. Sa that from the observations of Gyraldus, it appears that agriculture, .if it has not for centuries made a retrograde motion, has observed a stationary point.

Their usual custom was for oats, to plow the land once in March or April: for wheat and rye, they turned it up twice in the summer, and a third time in winter, about the season of threshing. From which it appears, that they fallowed for wheat and rye, and found that fresh turned land, and a stiffer soil, suited better the mountain oats.

This ignorance in the most important concern to the welfare of a country may be referred to the following causes:—Want of *fallowing—paring and burning—neglect of sheep-folding—want of enclosures—scarcity of manures, and improper application of those they possess*—and want of water meadows.

Fallowing may be justly considered, though part of the modern system, as a proof that husbandry is not far advanced towards perfection; and the time will come when this will be as much despised and rejected as it has been extolled and practised. The Eastern farmer would smile at the idea of land standing in need of rest; and ask if it was considered as endued with animation? Through the populous and extensive empire of China no such thing is heard of.

It certainly is a serious drawback upon the profits of a farm, that one year's rent should be sunk every three or four; and may justly be viewed as a standing proof, that a knowledge of vegetation and the pabula of plants has not yet exceeded a state of mediocrity. Still *necessitas non habet leges*,[1] we must apply to practice what knowledge we have; and none will be disposed to deny, that *three good crops* are preferable to *four bad ones*. But few of the Welsh farmers have any idea of fallowing. After breaking up a portion of grass land, they follow up the first by succeeding crops, till the land, deprived of heart, (as they term it,) refuses to give her wonted assistance, being drained of every principle favourable to a profitable crop.

In many places this ruinous scheme is pursued till the weeds become predominant, and the land naturally lays itself down to grass; and a crop of couch and other unfriendly weeds turns the arable into miserable pasture. When they have thus tired out all their land, recourse is then had to the injurious custom of *burn*-breaking, or paring the sward off the land, with a broad iron instrument, in thin turves or clods, which they burn in piles, and scatter the ashes upon the lands.

---

1   Latin: 'Necessity has no law.' —Ed.

This is no modern invention of agriculture, it was the practice of the Romans; and if antiquity would sanction a practice, this would have a fair claim to excellence. See it accurately described by Virg. *Georg. L.* 1.

But it is the opinion of practical men, (*Vid. Bath Papers, V. I.*) that this custom is more detrimental than advantageous. It may destroy noisome weeds, but it injures the under surface, and leaves a portion of effete ashes, which, without some corrective, are but very ill calculated for the purposes of vegetation. That it may with skill and caution be used on deep clay soils, and on sour moors, I do not deny; but the idea of obtaining saline substances of a highly fructifying nature is erroneous; little or any salts being discoverable in the ashes of peat and turf; for nineteen out of twenty parts of the vegetable matter, the only substance separable by fire, is dissipated in air. It is only from fresh vegetables that alkaline salts are to be obtained; and the quantity in the common mode of procuring them is so small, that it would be more œconomical to purchase them in the market. If making the groundless tenacious be the object, it would be better to burn a portion of it in a kiln, and carry it upon the land. But after all, this object is better obtained by lime, without any of the disagreeable consequences that often follow burn-breaking.

This custom has received the decided disapprobation of the Irish Legislature: which has prohibited its being practised under a penalty of ten pounds per acre.

The Welsh farmer should travel through the counties of Glocester and Wilts, to see what is there done by sheep-folding; and observe how large crops of grain are produced upon bleak and barren downs, far out of the reach of any other manure. He would thence discover, that, while his flock is growing and thriving, his land, without much trouble or expence, is enriched. He would be informed how it enables a grazing farmer to cultivate a portion of barren arable land with success, by furnishing a strong manure for a certain quantity; and by the judicious management of clover-lays and turnips, an additional produce to subsist his cattle through the trying months of winter.[2]

But this desideratum cannot be accomplished without a new system of Inclosure,[3] by

---

2   It has been observed by experienced men, that sheep-folding on *grass lands* is a profitable plan. That they soon render coarse herbage fine, not by their biting so close, as is generally supposed, but by their treading, rendering the soil closer; and from the quantity of dung and urine they deposit, they occasion the inert vegetable matter beneath the surface to be developed, and new combinations are formed favourable to vegetables, that constitute a sweet and wholesome herbage.

3   The inclosures are so few, and generally near the house, that those that are become highly valuable; and it is customary to fetter all the sheep that graze near them, by confining the right fore-foot to the neck, with a rush or hay-band: yet, sometimes these accomplished leapers, impelled by hard

which the farmer would be able to keep larger flocks and herds, and to fodder them in winter. This would not only increase his wealth by the store of butter, cheese, and beef and mutton, for the market; but would, by the dung of home-fed beasts, enrich the soil. The want of inclosures deprives the farmer of the important manure from the farm-yard. The house is generally built on the side of some acclivity, and he has no idea of securing the contents of the Barton. What straw he has is used as winter food for the cattle, which are foddered as they roam over the unconfined pastures; and their dung and urine is dissipated without any benefit accruing to the land; according to the just observation, that slight manuring is equal to no manuring at all. It should be the first object of the Welsh landholders to increase the number of inclosures; and of the Welsh farmer to begin folding his sheep. By this means he would soon be possessed of more valuable arable land, and have a quantity of grass land highly productive, that would continue to improve the longer it remains.

In a country thinly peopled, and destitute of large towns, the richer manure must be scarce; and the succedaneum *sheep-folding* is not used. Still the country in various parts produces different substances, that, with judicious management, might supply the deficiency.

---

necessity, will, by a conp de main, seize upon the pasture, and disappoint the hopes of the farmer.

A knowledge of a few common principles of chymistry, and the application of them to practice, would do wonders for Wales; but these are not known, and if they were, would probably be disregarded. *Lime* is the general substitute in the in land parts, and sea-wreck and sea-sand in the parts bordering on the coast. The great error of those who disclaim the use of lime, has been that of using it on all kinds of land, without distinction; vainly expecting equal advantages from the most opposite effects. While it has proved a useful dressing to some soils, it has rendered others less fertile. To clay lands and cold wet bogs, this substance may be useful in a mechanical and chymical view. It may break and divide the argillaceous particles, and render it less tenacious by absorbing the superfluous moisture, and thus be beneficial as an *alterative*. It may, by combining with the superabundant acids with which these soils abound, decompose the vegetable and animal matter; and, by assisting putrefaction, develope other principles favourable to the growth of vegetables. In silicious soils by increasing the density andtenacity, enabling it to hold water longer, the principal food of plants, lime also may be highly beneficial. But the Welsh farmer, from having heard of the great crops obtained by *liming*, or rather from the strength of prevailing custom, and the facility with which he can obtain this substance, is fatally bountiful in its application; and from supersaturation it produces an action on the soil more violent than is compatible with a state of fertility. Sometimes it is put upon the ground in its full caustic state, and immediately ploughed in. This, from the quantity of vegetable matter lime will thus dissipate by its disengaged heat in a state of gas, that otherwise would have helped to fertilize the soil, must be highly injurious. In other cases, from the distance it is fetched, and the time it is suffered to lie upon the ground, it is slaked by the dews and rains; and being long subject to the action of the atmosphere, becomes in a great measure inert, returns to a state of carbonate of lime or chalk, and, without other assistance, only serves to increase the barrenness of the soil, Yet still with out reason, the Welsh farmer goes on, subjecting himself to increasing loss by increasing experiments; and wondering and complaining at the sterility of the soil. He loads his grass lands, with the same inattention to causes and consequences. A first or second dressing, by its meeting with other substances, that enter into new combinations with it, will afford matters friendly to the growth of the several useful grasses; but when oversaturated by its specific gravity, it falls below the roots ofthe sward, and forms a new soil, consisting of calcareous matter, several inches thick; and those who have witnessed the state of herbage upon unassisted chalk lands, need not be told how he is soon disappointed of his usual crops of grass and hay.

Sea-weed, wreck, or ware, is by some successfully applied; and when taken fresh from
the sea, and immediately ploughed in, the effects are distinctly marked by early and luxuriant crops. In barley grounds the produce has
been beyond all reasonable expectation; and
there have been instances where the value of
the land has increased in a sixfold proportion in
consequence of the judicious application of this
manure. But the generality of occupiers of land
on the coast take a convenient opportunity for
collecting it; lay it up in heaps to ferment; where
by they lose the great advantages that might be
derived from it. In this respect, sea-ware and
most other marine plants differ from other vegetable and animal manures.

To render the latter completely useful, fer-
mentation is indispensably necessary; the former, on the contrary, exhibiting the most beneficial effects in a recent state. It may be urged in
defence of this conduct, that the greatest quantity is thrown up from November to February.
But every month produces some; and reservoirs
might easily be constructed on the sea-shore, or
it might be mixed in the season of plenty with a
proportion of earth and lime into a compost; by
which means its valuable properties might be
preserved. A point of the highest importance to
the maritime farmer.

Sea *Sand* and Sea *Sludge* I shall class together, though essentially different; because they

are both used in an improper manner in North Wales. These should be used as top dressings, and in a fresh state. But the reverse is the case. Immense quantities are thrown up daily by the tide the unskilful husband men of these parts collect it at their leisure; and, drawing it out of the tide's way, lay it in heaps for months together, till successive rains have deprived it of the whole of the salts, the very principle for which it must be considered valuable as a manure.

All the reasoning in the world will not induce these obstinate farmers to change their course. Indeed it would be absurd to reason with people unaccustomed to reason. In this case, and on such subjects, *example* is the only powerful and proper stimulus. An introduction of rational English farmers, possessed of capital, would be the best and most obvious mode for the landed gentlemen to adopt, for the improvement of their estate and the melioration of the country.

I have witnessed two or three instances in the course of my peregrinations, where sensible men, perceiving the errors of their brother farmers, wait till their land is ready for the marine manure. At ebb tide they engage all the hands and strength they can, and draw the mud or sand immediately upon their arable land, plough it in, and throw in the seed. By this simple and judicious plan, the rest have the mortification of seeing these men procure decent crops from land they have given up in despair; without ever inquiring into the cause, or adverting to the method which produced it.

What Mr. Kent justly styles the greatest and most valuable of all agricultural improvements, *water mead*, is not known in this country, though peculiarly adapted for its use. The only water meadows the Welsh farmer is acquainted with, are those which nature makes, either by the river overflowing the vales, or the mountain rivulets intercepted by stones, forming catch-meadows on the sides of the hills. And though he frequently sees the advantages his pastures derive from this detention of the waters, and that winter floods which quickly subside contribute greatly to fertility, yet, inattentive to the operations of Nature, he does not profit by her instructions. Though possessed of the most convenient situation, he has not the most distant idea of the utility or possibility of bringing water upon the land and taking it off again at pleasure. To do this requires acute observation, ingenuity, and a knowledge of the proper time for its introduction and dismissal. Unacquainted with this hot bed for early grass, and destitute of the only substitute, turnips, he feels the force of an ungenial spring, and the months of March and April in this backward district are cruelly destructive to his flock, and fatal to his hopes. Obliged to subsist his ewes upon coarse, and often ill-ended hay, they soon shrink their milk, the lambs get stunted, and he not unfrequently loses a third, nay a half of his flock, for want of nourishing food at this critical season. This, in a country where the most profitable, and almost the only system is sheep breeding, must be considered as a radical defect. To remedy it, the young Welsh farmers should be encouraged to travel through the breeding counties of England, and accurately mark the difference at this season of the year between those possessed of water meadows, and those who are not; the contrast would not fail to be striking.

The landlords should stimulate their tenants by long leases, lending small sums of money to defray the expences of the work, and granting bounties to those who should lead the way in this enriching and almost necessary improvement.

From this statement, drawn up from actual observation, it must obviously appear, that the value of land must be low, and the occupiers of land far from opulent.

In Montgomeryshire, land in farms was from eight shillings to two, and that considered too dear. In Denbighshire the average price about seven shillings, in Merioneth four—in Caernarvonshire from five to ten shillings *per acre*; lands near towns, as in England, fetch high prices, according to the luxury or spirit of the place. In the vicinity of Dolgelly the price is fifty shillings; and near the town of Caernarvon, meadow land is as high as three pounds. As other documents the following advertisements of Estates for sale may serve as a clue to the value of land:—

To be sold by auction at the Eagle's Inn, at Festiniog, on Thursday the 28th . day of June, 1797, the following freehold tenements, situate in the parish of Llandecwyn, in the county of Merioneth:

Lot I. Taly lyn farm, two hundred and forty seven acres, 57*l*. per annum.

Lot. II . Onnen, one hundred and eighteen acres, 31. 10s, per annum.

On Wednesday the 27th of June, at the Eagle's Inn, in Llanrwst, the following freehold estates, situate in the parish of Penmachno, Caernarvonshire:

Lot. I. Penybryn, two hundred and sixty acres, 73*l*. 10s. per annum.

Lot. II . Bryn Idael, one hundred and fifty-five acres, 31*l*. per annum.

N. B. Extensive sheep walks belonging to all these estates.

It may be proper to remark, that by the measurable farm is considered that between walled bounds; the depasturing ground is *undefinable*. It is a common practice among the tenants of a district to meet annually, to determine what number of sheep and cattle each ought to be allowed to send to the open pastures, regulated according to the size of the farm; but the richer sort always overstock, and the poorer sell the privilege for *four-pence per head*; there is, therefore, ample room for improvement, and, to the spirited adventurer, this country holds out a spacious and encouraging field for agricultural speculation. Mountainous countries are generally enriched with a variety of mineral strata, and those of North Wales seem to possess their full share; almost every considerable mountain presents traces of lead or copper, and the country abounds with mines at work, or the vestiges of others neglected.

The principal lead mines are confined to Flint and Denbigh, while those of copper abound in Caernarvon and Anglesea; quantities of calamine are dug in some parts of Denbighshire; and there is every reason to suppose that Snowdon abounds in tin. I have several fine specimens of the common tin stone and tin pyrites, 2d and 3d species of Kirwan, from the neighbourhood of Llanberis. Little iron has hitherto been discovered, and its concomitant coal but in very few places in Flint and Anglesea. The inhabitants, who do not burn peat, have their coals imported from Liverpool, at the average price of 1*l.* 4*s.* per ton. To mining, amongst other causes, may be attributed the present uncultivated state of the country, and the immense proportion of waste lands; for it is an observation that applies to every country, where a spirit of mining is discoverable, there, in proportion, the spirit of patient industry, so necessary to agriculture, flags, and the labours of husbandry dwindle. The inhabitants generally become poor, and the face of the country wears evident marks of neglect and wretchedness; a system of adventure is generally accompanied by a spirit of gambling; and a mine discovered is considered as a fortune made. The minds of the inhabitants are called off from concerns more immediately pertinent, and engaged in delusive dreams of imaginary gains; property is called in to aid the imagination, and the aggregate capital and labour of a district that would have ameliorated the soil, and made the land a perennial source of wealth, is sunk, by diving into the earth some hundred fathoms, only to convince the adventurers that much has been spent, and, barring the failure, much might have been gained; because one mine has answered, and a few individuals have been enriched, all expect that similar pursuits must be crowned with equal success; not reflecting that where much is acquired much must have been risqued; and if but few have proved fortunate many must have failed; like the golden dreamers that support the lottery, who count the larger prizes without once considering that the very nature of a prize bespeaks a *blank*, and the larger the one the more numerous must be the other.

The peasantry, necessary to till the ground, are collected to one or two barren spots, whereby the soil is deprived of the means essential to its improvement. The poor are easily enticed to an employment, however dangerous in the pursuit, or hazardous in the issue, from the higher wages held up by the adventurers; high wages tend to corrupt the morals of the lower classes, and invariably weaken the sinews of industry; the views of the peasant are generally confined to the present hour: if he obtain more than he can properly spend to-day, he has lost the motive for labour to-morrow; idleness naturally superinduces vice; and vice is the infallible road to want and misery. It is not to be expected that these people should calculate, or that they should reflect what produces great and sudden gain to the proprietors cannot ensure certain employment for the labourers, much less do they foresee that, in case of failure, the whole will be suddenly turned adrift to seek a livelihood where it may be found; and that their families must be left in a starving state, while the land, on which the burthen must fall, is not in a condition to support it. Those who have acquired riches from the bowels of the earth and their united labours, and from whom they might expect the boon of charity, have left their residence and repaired to the seats of luxury and dissipation. Observations like these will obtrude themselves on the observing traveller, and whoever has been attentive to facts, cannot but have remarked, that wherever mines have abounded agriculture has been in a despicable state, and the lower classes generally in the most abject poverty. By these remarks it is not meant to decry the pursuits of mineralogy, so essential to our manufactures, but to place them in their proper subordinate rank, and to say, that mining should never meet with pointed encouragement till the agriculture of a country is in an improved and respectable condition.

Your's, &c.

J. E.

Letter XV

DEAR SIR,

I must not forget the language of the country, nor the enthusiastic rage for poetry and music; nor must I pass, with common and regardless eye, their bards and minstrels. The Welsh language lays claim to high antiquity, as being a branch of the Jaspian, or that dialect of the Hebrew spoken by the posterity of Japhet; it is evidently like the old Gallic, of Celtic origin.[1] Both in its formation as well as grammat-

---

1   *Vid. Mr. Bullet, Mem. sur le lang. Celt.*

ical construction, it bears a near resemblance to the Hebrew; and its affinity is further traced by the learned Rowlands in his comparative table of three hundred words, similar, in sound and meaning, to so many Hebrew ones; whence it appears to be the most primitive and uncorrupt living language in the western world.

It is rich and copious, abounding with original words, more especially technical terms, which other languages borrow from the Greek, or express by circumlocutions; and, from its aptitude to form *verba sesquipedalia* by composition, which are not, owing to the change of consonants, harsh in sound, and are highly significant, it is peculiarly fitted for poetry and oratory; its accent, like the Hebrew, being chiefly confined to the Penultima, produces sometimes a sameness, but, at the same time, a dignity of sound; the multiplicity of consonants gives it an appearance of uncouthness to the eye, but, as these are not all pronounced as such, and many of them different in sound to what the English scholar would expect, it is more in appearance than reality; its copiousness gives it a variety and harmony to be equalled by few, perhaps exceeded by none; it unites the expressive majesty of the Greek with the harmonious softness of the Italian; it is, therefore, particularly adapted for poetical expression. From the numerous gutturals and the frequent recurrence of the canine letter R, it has been termed rugged and incapable of expressing soft and melodious sounds; but these frequent gutturals, this repetition of R, and the assemblage of the most broad-sounding vowels and diphthongs render it capable of displaying one of the chief beauties of poetry, the sound corresponding with the sense; thus on thunder,

> Tân a dwr yn ymwriaw
> Yw'r taranau dreîgiau draw.
>
> The roaring thunder dreadful in its ire,
> Is water warring with aerial fire.

Yet, as a proof that it is capable of expressing a great degree of softness, take the following on the harp:

> Mae mil o leisian meluson
> Mal mel o hyd ym mola shon.
>
> Within the concave of the womb is found,
> The magic scale of soul -enchanting sound.

The laws of poetical composition were so strict among the Welsh (for the Cambrian Muse gloried in twenty-four ancient measures) that it must have cramped the genius of their Bards, had it not been for the extent of the language and its aptitude for alliteration, a figure they considered as a special beauty in poetical composition, thus,

> Gwyr a wna gwr yn wral:
> Gwr a wna gwyr yn ei ol.

Brave men with brav'ry will their leaders fire,
Brave chiefs their men with brav'ry will inspire.

To this they added the figure of adopting the sound so as to be an echo of the sense; and no poets, perhaps, were ever more distinguished for a masterly use of this beauty, nor any language better calculated for its exhibition. Athird was what Mr. Walters calls "*a peculiar ingenuity in the selection and arrangement of words, so as to produce a rhythmical concatenation of sounds in every verse.*" *Vid. Diss.* The most favoured measures seem to have been the triplet and tetrastich; Llewarch Hên has an Englyn rhiming every three lines, and each stanza com mencing with the same phrase. The hanes of Taliesin consists of eight tetrastichs, and Eyry Mynydd of Llywarch Hên of twelve octonary stanzas; so great was this syllabic or jingling rage, that *he* was considered the best poet who could reach the greatest monotonous extent. The cyngor of Taliesin has sixteen lines ending in *on*; and a Cywydd of Dafydd ap Gwilim has fifty-two, terminating in *af.*

Most of the printed books in the Welsh language are either translations or the works of moderns; the principal MSS. are preserved in the libraries of Wynnestay, Gloddaeth, Bodscallen, Corsygeddol, Gwedir, the Duke of Ancaster's, and the Archives of Jesus College, Oxford; but many of them have been lost and destroyed;

for Edward not only cruelly tried to exterminate learned men from amongst the Welsh, but also to destroy the means of information. Upon the conquest, many of the great and learned men were carried to the Tower and permitted to take with them their books and manuscripts to amuse them under confinement; but a pretence was soon found to seize upon them; the insurrection of Glyndwr gave an additional pretext for destroying them, and all that could possibly be collected were burnt by one Skolen, as recorded in this Englyn.

> Llyfran Cymrn au Llofrudd
> Ir twr gowyn aethantar gudd
> Ysceler oedd Yscolan
> Fwrw'r twrr lifran ir tan.
>
> Gutto'r Glyn. A. D. 1450.

The language is getting into disuse the gentlemen, educated in England, pretend not to speak it, and some have not scrupled to wish for its extermination; the examples of the higher classes is become contagious, and, ere long, this language and the manners ofthe Welsh will merge and be lost in the English. Their *music* is as varied and expressive as the language; much has been justly said in commendation of its peculiar beauties, and those who affirm that there is *a sameness in all the Welsh airs*, must have heard but very few specimens, or paid but little attention to the subject; a great simplicity marks the Welsh melodies, yet they are distinguished by features as varied as the country; invented by an enthusiastic and impassioned people, they partake of all the wildness of unrestrained originality: sprightly and vivacious, plaintive and energetic, they are characterized both by *Allegro* and *Penseroso*, and equally adapted for Lydian as for Doric measures; most ofthe tunes are very ancient, and preserved in the traditional recollection of the country;[2] they show their composers to have possessed genuine skill in music, and that they knew how to warm the imagination, and interest the heart. Whether the Muse delights in gay or mournful numbers, she may have her choice, and the expressive vibrations of the noble instrument the harp increases the pathos and solemnity. The vivacity of Joe Pulleine's Horn and Sir Watkin's Delight forms a fine contrast with the plaintive Dafydd ar Craig gwyn, and the solemn dirge of Morfa Rhuddlan. "*Ex uno disce omnes.*"

Of the Religious Order in the times of Druidism, there was a three-fold division into Vacerri, Beirdd, and Eubages; of these the second order was all that remained after the destruction of their altars and seminaries, and their final dispersion in Mona by Suetonius. (*Vid. Tacit. A. L. XIV.*) These continued to be had in reverence and enjoyed peculiar privileges for ages after the

---

2   Mr. Jones has performed a work deserving the praise of all amateurs in music; by collecting and publishing a number of these in his Musical and Poetical Remains ofthe Bards.'

abolition of Druidical worship.

> While other orders fell by turns disgraced,
> Their names dishonour'd, and their forms defaced,
> The Bards, in slaughter's desolating hour,
> Still held their office, and retain'd their power.
> On heights dispers'd, or wandering o'er the plain,
> They brought from hill and dale a list'ning train,
> Lur'd by soft numbers and the power of sound,
> Thy sons, informing Nature, pour'd around.

Such was the high estimation in which this order was held, that it was enacted by a law of Howel Dha, that whoever should strike a Bard must compound for the offence to the party aggrieved, one-fourteenth more than was necessary to be paid to any other person of the same degree. (*Vid. Leges Wall.*) Bede says, in his time they enjoyed great privileges, were respected by contending parties at war, obtained leave to pass free, and were received with honour and dismissed with donations, *Lib.* II .

The term is derived from Bar a Fury, and bears an analogy to the poetic fury and enthusiasm they fancied themselves inspired with. Diodorus Siculus and Marcellinus mention the Bards as composers of verse which they sung to the harp and other instruments of music, celebrating the praises of the brave and good; and lashing the vices of the cowardly an the bad with the severest satire. They were highly venerated by all the Northern nations, accompanied the armies into the field, animated them to the conflict by repeating the valourous deeds of their ancestors; and celebrated in plaintive strains the heroes that had fallen in battle.

> Vos quoque qui fortes animas belloque peremtas
> Laudibus in longum vates demittis in œvum
> Plurimi securi fudistis carmina Bardi.[3]
>
> —Lucan.

In the ages of Druidism, they were doubtless under mystic regulations; but for a series of years there are no authentic documents to elucidate the exact nature of their situation. Nennius, who wrote about the year 900, is the first who mentions them. He says that Talhaiarn was famous for poetry, and that Aneurin, Taliesin, and Llywarch Hên, flourished in the sixth century. Of these, only some fragments of the three latter are extant. If we judge of those that are lost by those that remain, they must be considered as men possessed of superior genius; and lament that works so calculated to instruct and please should have been so early consigned to oblivion. Those still remaining throw great light upon the manners and customs of the age in which they lived. (*Vide Evans Diss. de Bardis*). But many of these are with

---

3   Latin:

'You also, who recount in song the brave souls
Destroyed by war, in praises for ages long,
Have poured forth many songs, O Bards.' —Ed.

great difficulty understood, owing, in part, to the carelessness of transcribers, and more from the language becoming obsolete. Aneurin obtained the honourable distinction of Mychdeirn Beirdd, Monarch of the Bards; Taliesin, who resided at the courts of Maelgwyn Gwynedd and Urien Reged, was entitled Pen Beirdd, or Prince of the Bards; and Llywarch Hên had passed his youthful days in the court of Arthur, and had reigned, himself a Prince, over part of Cambria. There were other Bards that flourished about this period; the most eminent of which was Merddin Wyllt, who left a beautiful poem, called *Afallon*, or the Orchard. From the sixth to the tenth century, we meet with scarcely any of their writings; owing, probably, to the devastations of war, and the ravages occasioned by the civil dissensions among the Welsh themselves. The reform of this order of men was undertaken by Bleddyn, Prince of Powis and North Wales; and a statute was enacted to ascertain their privileges, and restrain their licentious manners. It prescribed the emoluments they were to receive, and the persons on whom they were imposed. This statute, which contains much curious matter, may be seen in the Welsh Chronicles. From this period, under the auspices of the Welsh Princes, many ingenious bards arose, distinguished for their talents, till the death of the last Llewelyn; when Edward, sensible that the bards had been the cause of the Welsh so long maintaining their independence, and fearing lest they might revive ancient ideas, and rekindle in the Welsh their native fire of freedom, proclaimed martial law; and commanded all the bards to be tried and hanged by it. Like the cruel Monarch of Macedonia, who, when treating with the Athenian States, demanded, as a condition of peace, that all the orators who had bravely excited their brother citizens to defend their birth-right should be delivered as *criminals into his hand.* This edict, more cruel than the proscriptions of the Roman Triumvirate, continued in force for several reigns; during which period this celebrated order was nearly exterminated; the genius of poetry was almost extinguished, and only employed in soothing the misery of the times, by obscure predictions of future prosperity; the ancient seat of music and poetry was deserted by the Muses, and was deprived of those fascinating arts, which softened the manners while they invigorated the genius of the people. There were three distinctions in the order: Bards, properly so called, were supposed inspired, and composed verse in a variety of measures; and like the Scalds of the North, retained the memory of numberless transactions that otherwise would have been lost. But what gave them the high rank, and brought them into estimation with the British nobility, was their skill in genealogy. They were the recorders of arms, and the comptrollers of honours; and flattered the vanity of the great by recounting the deeds of their remote ancestry.

This was the highest and most honourable division. The next was Clerwreu or Minstrels, who performed upon musical instruments, chiefly the harp and the crwth.[4] Thirdly, the Datceiniaid, or Singers; these accompanied the music with the voice, and were required to possess a competent knowledge of both sciences.

The election of bards was annual in an assembly of the princes and chieftains of the country, in which they were assigned precedence and emoluments suit able to their respective merits; but the bard most eminently distinguished for his talents was solemnly chaired, and had the badge of merit, or silver harp, conferred upon him.

This congress, called Eisteddfod, was usually held at one of the three royal residences, Caerwys, Aberfraw, or Mathraval; the Sovereign himself presiding in the assembly. Its being held in rotation, has induced some to assert that it was a *triennial* meeting. This was considered not only as an opportunity of displaying skill and talents, but also as a college of harmony, where genius was registered and degrees of honour conferred on musical merit. This assembly was held by special commission and authority from the princes of Wales during their independence, and subse-

---

4   The musical instruments in use among the ancient Welsh were the telyn or harp; the crwth or croud; the tabwrdd or tabret; and the corn buelm, cornet, or bugle-horn; with the pibgorn, or pipe. The harp, crwth, and pibgorn were the instruments delivered to the chief musicians, when they were invested; and on their death reverted to the Lord.

quent thereto from the Kings of England; with
out this examination and diploma granted none
could exercise the profession of bard or minstrel.
In these British olympics were collected, as in a
focus, the rays of music and poetry; here the varied genius of the principality, concentrated, displayed its captivating charms; here British bards
poured forth their animating strains, and minstrels tuned their fascinating harps to melody.

Andgave to song resistless powers to charm.

The last Eisteddfod, held by royal authority,
was in the reign of Elizabeth, the commission
bearing date 20th of October, 1567, was granted to Sir Richard Bulkley and others.[5] In consequence of this grant, an Eissteddfod was held
at Caerwys the 26th of May following; proper
notice having been given, and the sons of genius invited from their retired situations in every
part of the principality; at this meeting fifty-five
degrees were conferred, seven teen in vocal, and
thirty-eight in instrumental music. From this
period the Eisteddfod was neglected, and the
ancient Bard and Minstrel ceased to be considered as characters of importance; a spirited set
of men, however, associated under the name of

---

5   The original deed is in possession of the Mostyn family, together with the silver harp, which had from time immemori-
al been the gift of the ancestors of that family, to bestow on
the chief of the Faculty.

the *Gwyneddigion*,[6] in London, determined to revive a ceremony calculated to encourage a spirit of musical excellence, and preserve a knowledge of harmony's choicest instrument amongst their country men; and to deliver down a science in which their ancestors had shone so eminent, with increasing reputation, to posterity.

The ancient notice required of a year and a day was given prior to the meeting; the old town-hall was fitted up for the reception of the company, which was highly respectable; and the numerous attendance of the children of melody proved, that, however the spirit had been neglected and depressed, it was not extinguished among the inhabitants of North Wales. Some vein, says Jones, in his musical remains of the ancient minstrelsy, survives among our mountains. Numbers of persons of both sexes as semble and sit round the harp, singing alternately, pennyllion, or stanzas of ancient and modern compositions; the young people usually begin the night with dancing, and when tired assume this mode of relaxation; often, like the modern *improvvisatori* of Italy, they sing extempore verses, and those conversant in it readily produce a pennyll opposite to the last; the subjects are productive of mirth: sometimes

---

6   We learn that Mr. Owen Jones, of London, was the deviser and principal promoter of this meeting, and contributed largely towards the prizes bestowed on the occasion; a gentleman as highly distinguished for his liberality as his many other virtues.

they are jocular, sometimes satirical, but often of an *amorous nature,* and will bring to the recollection of the classic the dialogue between Horace and Lydia for, on these occasions, the fair are gene rally the *last to speak,* and terminate the contention not unlike Lydia:

> Tecum vivere amem, tecum obeam libens.[7]

They continue singing, without intermission, never repeating the same stanza (for that would forfeit the honour of being esteemed first of song) and, like nightingales, support the contest through the night. The audience usually call for the tune; sometimes a few only sing and sometimes the whole company; but, when a party of capital singers assemble, they rarely call for the tune, for it is indifferent to them what tune the harper plays; parishes are often opposed to parishes, and the mountains re-echo the melody of song. The following are specimens of this kind of extemporaneous composition, or pennyllion:

> Mi a i Llan Beris Ddydd full nesa,
> Oni ddaw Llan Beris yma;
> Llawer haws i mi fyrid yno,
> Nac i Llan Beris fawr symmudo.

> If cavern'd Llan beris can't easily move,
> Next Sunday I'll go there and find my kind love,

---

7   Latin: 'I would love to live with you, willingly to obey you.' —Ed.

Twice easier for me o'er the hills for to go,
Than for Peris to move from the valley below.

————————

Pe baer wyddva i gyd yn gaws
E fyddai 'n haws caell enllyn,
Amoel Eilian fara gwyn,
A'r Llynn yr gwrw melyn.

If Snowdon's high and airy head
Were turn'd to cheese, Moel Eilia bread,
And all the lakes to nut-brown ale,
T'would needless be to till the vale.

Dr. THOMAS.

The number of *Bards* was twenty, of Minstrels twelve, and of Datceiniaid eighteen; the first day was occupied in determining the merit for the cader or chair; the theses were "the love of our country, and the commemoration of the Eisteddfod;" many animated pieces were produced, but the decision was in favour of Robert ap Dafydd of Nantglyn; in the evening numerous extemporaneous effusions were poured forth, and, though there was a degree of excellence, yet they must remind the classical scholar of the poetaster in Horace, who could compose two hundred verses; *stans pede in uno.*[8]

On the second day the instrumental and vocal performers exhibited their respective powers, when Robert Foulks was declared Pencerdd Dafod, or chief vocal performer, and William Jones Gwydd the Pencerdd Dant, or chief player on the

————————

8   Latin: 'Standing on one foot.'

harp. This meeting must have been highly gratifying to the lovers of poetry and music; for in the
opinion of connoisseurs no contest for skill was
better supported than this at Caerwys. In various places we found that it had excited a spirit
of emulation, and we had the pleasure of hearing
instrumental performers that would not disgrace
the diplomas of universities; and we sincerely
wish, that an instrument so capable of expressing the powers of harmony as the harp may never
be disused, nor such genuine votaries of music
and poetry as the Welsh, ever languish for want
of protection. It has heen observed that mountainous scenery is peculiarly friendly to those
aërial and imaginary existences that constitute
the objects of *superstition*.[9] The constant variation in their appearance, added to the gloom
attendant upon lofty crags, hollow cwms, deep
ravines, lakes, dingles, caves, and torrents, must
have a strong tendency to affect the imagination;
fear is the offspring of ignorance, and unbound-
ed credulity the concomitant of fear; similar notions will produce similar manners, and equal
degrees of intelligence are generally marked by
a *coincidence of belief*. Hence the spirit of conjuration, so prevalent in Lapland, the second sight
of the Highlands, and the vagaries of the Aweny-
ddion, in Wales, (a word significant of poetical

---

9   Hence superstition sprung in elder time,
     Wild as the soil, and gloomy as the clime.
                                        RICHARD

426

raptures,) were derived from the same origin; these persons, when consulted, became inflamed with a high degree of enthusiasm, were, to all appearance, carried out of themselves, and seemed possessed of an invisible spirit, yet they did not immediately give a solution of the difficulty; but, by an inconsistent circumlocution with which they abounded, any person who observed the answer would, at length, by some turn or digression in the speech, receive, or fancy that he did, the required explanation.[10] From this state of extacy they were at last roused as from a deep sleep, and were compelled, by the violence of their friends, to return to their natural state; and it is said, that they did not recollect any thing that passed, or which they had uttered; if it happened that they were again consulted upon the same, or any other subject, they would deliver themselves in very different terms. This property of divining they fancied was bestowed upon them in their sleep, at which time, according to Gyraldus, it appeared to some as though new milk or honey was poured into their mouth; to others, as though a scroll of writing; and, on their waking, they publicly professed to be endued with these extraordinary gifts; but this kind of devotion is daily less in

---

10   The folly of divination and fortune-telling to the thinking mind must be obvious, and is more supported by the belief of the credulous than the arts of knavery; for, to the whole tribe of diviners may be appled the remark of Euripides,

"Μάντις δ ' ἀριϛΘ, ὁϛις εικάζει καλῶϛ."

repute and chiefly confined to the mountainous tracks. The belief of witchcraft is still strong, and many are the fatal and dire effects produced by the supposed hybrid beings.[11] We know so little of the Spiritual World, and the possibility of a connection with it, that it would border on presumption to assert, that no connection ever did or can exist; but it is certainly ridiculous to suppose, that a poor *decrepid old woman*, by entering into a supposed contract with the devil, should be able to change the course of nature; blight crops, inflict disease, raise storms, &c. and perform actions that bespeak Omnipotent Power; and, if it were not that the positive evidences were extremely strong, the many impostures and delusions that have been discovered, as well as the idle tales told, would be enough to demolish all faith in such a dubious crime; but the testimony of ages, the revealed will of God, is in favour of the existence of Witchcraft. It seems, therefore, the safest way, with the ingenious Addison, to allow there has been such a thing, but to refuse credit to the many modern instances of it. Down to the reign of James I. various statutes were passed, making witchcraft, conjuration, or sorcery, felo-

---

11   At every house you will perceive a horseshoe, cross, or some charm of defence against these venomous spirits; and it is usual to place on the Vigil of St. John sprigs of the *Hypericum*, thence called St. John's wort, at the entrance in the same manner the Druids were used to do *Veronica*. Its supposed virtue is couched in the title Cos gan Gythral, *i. e.* Demon's Aversion.

ny without benefit of clergy. During this period, while laws were enacted to perpetuate error, it is probable that many innocent persons, distressed with poverty and age, and disliked by the neighbourhood, fell the unfortunate victims; and this terror of *ancient females* was not removed till 9 Geo. II . c. 5.[12] Since that a pretence to divination is considered as a misdemeanor, punishable by pillory and imprisonment. The belief of those elvine beings called fais or *Fairies*, appears to have been ancient and general, not only from the Britons having reduced the notions respecting them to a kind of system, but because various allusions are made to them by the British Bards, under the common appellation *"The Spirits of the Mountains."* It is supposed they are fond of the southern sides of the hills and the deep recesses of the woods; of cleanliness, neatness of apparel, regular living, strict integrity, and devotedness to GOD; and that those who wish for their protection, or would avoid their ire, must pay attention to these things. To such characters they are esteemed friendly, and, to the opposite, exceedingly spiteful, troubling them with dreams, alarming them with noises, pinching them black and blue, carrying away their unbaptized children,

---

12 The learned Montesquieu, in his Spirit of Laws, ranks this crime with that of heresy, and judiciously observes, that we ought to be very circumspect in the prosecution of both, because the most unexceptionable conduct, the purest morals, and the constant practice ofevery duty of social life are not a sufficient security against the suspicion ofsuch crimes.

and confining them for a given period; and it is a custom with the ignorant to watch their children till after *baptism*, lest they should be stolen or changed. They are said also to maim cattle by throwing ugly weapons at them the stones called arrow-heads, found in these parts, are fancied to be elf-shots; and a species of fungus, growing on the lower parts of the trunks of trees, when reduced to a soft consistency by rains, is called Fairy's Butter. The description by those that pretend to have seen them is, that they are in the human shape, exceedingly diminutive, always clad in green, and when they are employed are often heard, as they are very noisy; their occupations over, they live a merry life, dancing hand in hand invisibly by moon-light, footing to lyric measures over the verdant turf, leaving their marks in darkened circles, alias fairy rings, over the green grass. Their vagaries are pleasantly alluded to by Brown in his pastorals:

————————————————Apleasant mead,
Where fairies often did their measures tread,
Which in the meadow made such circles green,
As if with garlands it had crowned been.
Within one of these rounds was to be seen,
A hillock rise, where oft the fairy queen
At twilight sate, and did command those elves,
To pinch those maids that had not swept the shelves;
And further if, by maiden's oversight,.
Within doors water were not brought at night,
Or if they spread no table, set no bread,
They should have nips from toe unto the head.

And for the maid that had perform'd each thing,
She in the water-pail bade leave a ring.

The re-appearance of departed spirits or *Ghosts* is generally believed. They are supposed to inhabit the deep cwms and glens amid the mountains, and to frequent old mansions, ruined castles, and especially the repositories ofthe dead; and the terror of them is so great, that no bribe will induce the common people to visit these places in the depth of the night; they are considered as the souls of persons departed, and permitted to return for some beneficial purposes, as to point out some hid treasure, help some to property of which they had been unjustly deprived, or lead to the discovery of some foul murder, that the perpetrators might be brought to justice, and those innocently accused cleared of the aspersion. Others again, are adjudged to walk in darkness for some venial fault; to this the inimitable Bard alludes in *Hamlet*:

              ——————————I am thy father's spirit,
Doom'd, for a certain time, to walk the night,
And for the day confin'd to fast in fires,
Till the foul crimes done in my days of nature
Are burnt and purg'd away.[13]

13 Persons who have been guilty of great oppressions, or acted contrary to the welfare of the country, are expatriated after they are dead; their spirits are supposed unable to rest, and are sent to reside on the borders of some lake or water-fall, amidst the wilds of the mountains. Thus the learned Sir John Wynne was esteemed by the people an oppressor, and

You will be told by those who pretend to have conversed with these ghosts, that some have lamented the hardness of their condition in being obliged to walk through cold and uncomfortable places, and requested the person's friendly aid to lead them to some other place, &c. &c.

That none, in the exercise of their rational powers, can, for a moment, credit the thousand ridiculous stories that are told and believed, is obvious; yet, to deny that such appearances have, on some particular occasions, been seen, would be to throw away the wisdom of antiquity with an unbecoming licence, and to oppose authorities that would undermine the most important truths, and invalidate evidence on which the principal part of our knowledge is built, and our best hopes founded. The misfortune of Superstition is, that it believes every thing it fears; and it is the curse of Infidelity to believe nothing it hates; the votary of the one has the testimony of antiquity on his side, and the votary of the other the countenance of fashion. To the humble inquirers after truth the declarations of the Scriptures will recur,

> That there are ministering spirits sent forth to minister to those that shall be the heirs of salvation, and others of an opposite cast wandering about in dry places, seeking rest, but finding none, and intent on mischief to the

they have sent his perturbed spirit to the adjacent cataract of Rhaiadr y Wenol.

human race, go to and fro on the earth, seeking whom they may devour.

To such the affirmative will appear the safest side of the question; the unreasonable credulity of the dark ages was undoubtedly a snare, and the extreme is equally so; the latter staggers the grand doctrine of the Soul's immortality, for those who deny there are spirits subsisting without bodies will, after that, with more difficulty believe the separate existence of their own.

Among superstitious or singular customs we remarked the following:—

On Christmas Eve, about three o'clock in the morning, most of the parishioners assemble in the church, and after prayers and a sermon, continue singing psalms and hymns till day-light, and if, through infirmity or age, any are disabled from at tending, they have prayers at home, and carols on the Nativity; this act of devotion is called *plygan*, or the *cock-crowing*.

Another very singular custom, I never could learn the *rationale* of is, that of a man on new year's day, dressing himself in blankets and other trappings, with a factitious head like a horse, and a party attending him, knocking for admittance, this obtained, he runs about the room with an uncommon frightful noise, which the company quit in real or pretended fright; they soon recover, and by reciting a verse of some ancient cowydd, or, in default, paying a small

gratuity, they gain admission. A similar custom is prevalent in the Highlands; (*Vid. Johnson,*) and, from Du Cange, we find it was a practice of Heathenism.[14]
Another custom, peculiar to this country is, the kindling of fires on All Saints eve on some eminence, and upon a stone near every habitation, when children, servants, masters, and mistresses, dance round and run through them with shouts and hollowings, throwing in, at the same time, fruits, nuts, stones, &c. by which they pretend to prognosticate as to their future success through the year; these are supposed by Rowland to be fires of rejoicing for the in-gathering of harvest, and that the Druids and ancient Britons sacrificed victims at this time, and about the vernal Equinox.

The *virgula divinatoria* is in high repute amongst the Welsh miners; what sympathy there is between a vein of coal or lead ore and a piece of hazle, it would be difficult to say, but constant recourse is had to this mode of detecting mineral strata. Though made of hazle it is no common instrument; it must be a fork cut in a planetary hour; for lead on Saturn's day and hour, because

14 "Ludi profani apud Ethnicos & Paganos solebant in Kalendis Januarii; belluarum, pecudum, & Vetularum, assumptis formis, hue & illuc discussare, & petulantius sese gerere: quod à Christianis non modo proscriptum, sed ab iis postmodum inductum; ut ea die ad calcandum Gentilium consuetudinem privatæ fierent Litaniæ & Jejunaretur. &c. *Vid. Gloss, du Cange.*

Saturn is the *significant of lead*; Jupiter must be in conjunction, sextile or trine, and the better if any reception happen; but if it happen at square or opposition the whole is marred; thus cut, it is laid by for use in a heap of wheat or barley: this is to be held by the forks with both hands and carried over the land supposed to contain the ore: over all the barren spots it appears unaffected, but no sooner does it impend over a vein than it presses strong down, and a similar at traction is discovered as between iron and the magnet; you will recognise in this the impious wands of the heathen, and smile at the continuance of the imposture; but how much are men the slaves of *nominal discrimination?* how often, while they condemn one absurdity are they the dupes of others still more absurd? A few years since a similar rod was used in France, and obtained credit, for discovering *springs of water*; and is it not in the memory of every one, when numbers experienced inchantment, both in France and England, *without any divining rod at all?* and believed themselves to be affected by an invisible agent which the inchanter called *Animal Magnetism?* But it required too much exertion of the imagination long to expect *effects without any visible causes.* Those who wish to dupe the public have been under the necessity of changing their *invisible* plan; and we are now furnished with divining rods again, under the pompous philosophic name of *Metallic Tractors.* There are persons who pretend to cure certain disorders, especially erysipelas, by breathing on the parts affected, and laving it with fasting spittle; but their qualifications are special and rare; their ancestors must have eaten of the flesh of an eagle, and they have certain in cantations delivered down to them by tradition.

The water for baptism used formerly to be brought from some Ffynnon Vair, or well of the Blessed Virgin; and, from that circumstance, it is still used from the font as a specific in *sore eyes*, &c. &c. As a relict of Druidism, it is believed that about Midsummer eve snakes congregate, and joining heads and hissing together a kind of bubble is formed on the head of one of them, which the other, by hissing, blows on till it comes off at the tail, when it hardens and resembles a glass ring, which whoever has the good luck to find, will prosper in all their future undertakings; they call them *gleiniau nadroedd*; they are evidently glazed rings, once in use among the Romans. Hydromancy, or divination by water, is still practised; Exorcism also is considered as a privilege concomitant with high learning; and every Oxford clergyman is supposed to possess the power of laying spirits, and preserving houses from being haunted.

These shadows of Religion, and indirect arguments for a future state were, in principle, nearly coeval with man; they flourished as iniquity increased, they took root downward and bore fruit upward, in the grosser ages of Judaism; they were notorious in the Grecian and Roman states, and volumes might be filled from their writers of ridiculous instances of general credulity, that controverted their right, while they preferred the claim for *enlightened nations*. The Druids interpreted omens and dealt in sorcery, and if they did not invent, handed many of them down to posterity. Several of the customs of their idolatry were long retained by our ancestors, intermingled with Christian rites; and notwithstanding the fulminations of the papal chair, superstition maintained its ground, and was making rapid advances in the days of *Gildas*.

During the dismal night of error, that covered the people again with thick darkness, after the promulgation of Christianity, the weeds of error sprang up, grew rank, and the nations of Europe were covered with the poisonous effluvia; the Romish priests did not fail to make use of these powerful engines to serve their avaricious purposes; they well knew that reputation was power, and they invented a thousand tales to instil into the minds of the people an idea of sanctity they never possessed; till, by shackling the mind with an influence at their own disposal, their unfortunate votaries became the constant dupes of hypocritical extortion. That they were the framers of some, and the modellers of many, no doubt can be entertained; for, as Brown facetiously observes, "*They* seem to have the most right to

437

inventions of this nature, whose brains are so fruitful of folly as to invent that Dunstan took the Devil by the nose with a pair of hot tongs till he roared again." *Antiq. Vulg.* Thanks to the great Author of Light and Truth, this night is past; the light of the Reformation has dispelled the darkness; yet, still here and there a few clouds disfigure the atmosphere of truth. Though no one can be a stronger advocate for Religion in its most perfect purity, or wish more strongly for the emancipation of the human mind from the worst of all slavery, *Superstition*; yet, must I question, whether good has been obtained by divesting the mind of all religious fear, under the name of Superstition? Especially when it is considered, that it had a tendency to recommend virtue and discountenance vice.

The philosophie religion that has nearly had its short-lived reign, is like the logic of the *Pyrrhonian School*, that pulls down every thing and erects nothing. Man must have some decisive principle on which to act, and some powerful motives to induce him to action. He must be persuaded that vice has the dread of punishment, and virtue the sanction of reward, before he will uniformly perform the relative duties of life.

Religion is the grand cement of society, the only sufficient guarantee of order and safety. If the people are so gross and blind as not to be able, without assistance, to look through Nature up to Nature's God; if their minds are not sufficiently spiritual to form just and adequate ideas of their real nature and indispensable obligations; shall we refuse them the necessary helps, because they are not compatible with *philosophic perfection?* If they cannot yet act from higher and juster motives, shall we therefore deprive them *of all?* Blot out every trace of hope and fear, and break even the *slenderest tie* that connects them with the *spiritual world?*

Recollecting the answer of the learned author of *The Evidences of Christianity,* (Addison,) to the unbeliever, "That, if Christianity *be* true, then Christians will have infinitely the advantage; and if it should *not,* they will then be equal with the Infidel" I cannot help concluding it safer to believe too much than too little; and that truth blended with error is far more eligible than error alone. Every lover of his country and his neighbour must feel his indignation excited when he sees a set of men under the usurped title of Philosophers, endeavouring to undermine religion, loosen the bands of society, and destroy all adequate motives for moral actions, under the plausible pretence of deliver ing mankind from the yoke of superstition!

Amidst all these superstitions, however, it appears the principles of religion are not lost; a considerable portion of devotional spirit occupies the bosoms of the lower classes of the Welsh. A disposition, which, while it contributes to their own comfort, administers no less to the happiness of society. And to this as a cause, must be referred the prevalence of moral excellence, the general spirit of subordination, respect to their superiors, and submission to the laws, discoverable through this happy country. Indeed it must be acknowledged, that the only foundation for solid morality, is *Religion*. A knowledge of the great duties it enjoins, and the obligations to perform them, imposed on beings who must give a final account of the talents they have received. The philosopher may make his calculations on the force of habit, and expatiate on the superior merit of suffering virtue; while the moralist boasts of the principles of truth and justice, exercised for their own reward. But the high morality contained in that golden sentence, "*Do unto others as You would they should do unto you,*" is only to be supported by the motives of the gospel, and only can be practised by the disciples of *the Saviour*.

Religion appears among this people to be what it really is, *the most important concern of man.* In the churches the service was performed with a degree of solemnity not generally observable in England; and the decorous behaviour of the congregations was a convincing proof in what high veneration they held the temples of Deity. The energy of the preachers, and the looks of the audience, plainly indicated that both were in earnest; and no one could help feeling a desire to join in the worship, though a stranger to the language in which it was performed.

How lamentable, said I, that divine truths should ever be delivered in an irreverent manner!!! And that the offices of religion should be performed without that *devoutness* such sacred and important ceremonies so justly demand!!! Perhaps more of this spirit was discoverable out of the church than in it; and without any disparagement to the clergy of North Wales, many of whom are highly respectable in their *official*, as well as social capacities, the reason is obvious. Some of the established clergy are not content with a dereliction of the great duties of their station, but by opposing those doctrines which, as ministers of the gospel, they ought to preach, they render the grand engine of reformation, the pulpit, unedifying; drive the inquiring mind to seek religious information elsewhere; and thus disperse and starve the flock they have sworn to collect and feed.

It is too notorious for the friends of the Church of England to deny that the late increase of the dissenting interest, (*as it is termed*,) so loudly complained of, has been occasioned by *the clergy themselves*. The dissolute lives of many, the careless ness and irreverence of others, have proved a stumbling block to the weak, and a just plea for the schismatic; while essential errors in the preaching of others has drawn the enlightened and conscientious part of the people, however reluctantly, from their parochial churches, and the bosom of the church; forced those seriously disposed, to look for more faithful teachers amongst less polished people; and to assemble in barns, and under hedges, for rational and devout worship: thus made dissenters by imperious necessity.

It is an aweful consideration, and well becomes the ostensible messengers of grace, and more especially the *Episcopal Guardians* of the Establishment, to pause—and seriously inquire into the causes of such defalcations; and, by a timely removal of the offence, to prevent the mischiefs of separation. It cannot be matter of wonder to an attentive observer, who marks how religion is made *a stalking-horse for interest and ambition*, if the Established Church should be neglected and despised. If the bees that have been regularly hived, are transformed into *drones*, and indolently neglect to sip the mellifluous flowers around them, is it surprising if the wilder insects of the woods take their stations and bear away the nectareous treasure? If the appointed shepherds neglect their important charge, suffer the ravenous wolf to disperse the flock, and remain careless whether the wanderers are restored to the fold; then will that August Being, whose purposes cannot be defeated, have recourse to other means for their accomplishment. He will call up men from the dunghill, to the dignified office of priesthood; give them popularity from usefulness; and thus put to open shame the more learned and regular of the function: "*Call them*

a people which were no people, and of these re-
puted stones, raise up children to Abraham."

In the towns and large villages, some building
is generally appropriated for the accommodation
of those who wish information on the interesting
theme. But it is common to see thousands assembling to hear a plain man expound the scriptures
on the hills, without any other shelter than the
azure canopy of heaven; and that in weather not
the most favourable for such exposure. And after
the service is over, as though the dew of heaven
was a medium, as it is an emblem, of spiritual
blessings, they are seen returning over the
mountains, many a long mile with the smile of
satisfaction on their brow, and chanting hymns
of praise, to their scanty board and lowly habitations; better satisfied with the dispensations of
Providence, and far better prepared to encounter
the difficulties, and perform the duties of their
arduous situations.

The idle and the luxurious, who prefer their
ease to attendance upon a place of worship, may
smile; but let it be remembered, that they *profess*
a belief in Christianity, as well as the poor Cambrian peasant; and then let it be asked, which gives
the most genuine proof of his sincerity—he who
prefers his indulgence, or he who trudges barefoot
for miles in spite of weather, to celebrate the praises of their common Creator? The former does not
reflect that the lap of ease is seldom the habitation
of virtue; nor the conduct of indifference, the ex-

pression of praise: while the latter considers every attention to religion, a privilege conferred on himself, and a tribute to his Maker.

Among the number of dissenters in North Wales, there are various distinctions, which perhaps exist more in *name* than *reality*: Rowlandists, or Calvinistic Methodists; Westleians, or the followers of the late John Westley; Independent Dissenters, including Presbyterians, Independants Particular, and General Baptists; and, according to some writers in the *Gentleman's Magazine*, a sect called *Jumpers*. *Vid. July and September*, 1799, *signed D. and M. B.*

The ridiculous tales related by many, shew their knowledge could be no more than report; and their descriptions are evidently the language of traduction. Friendly as I may be to the modest, chaste, and dignified mode of worship prescribed by the wisdom of the Established Church, and practised by all her serious and devout members; yet I cannot but observe, that indiscriminate censure, as well as indiscriminate praise, cannot be just; and, that brand ing any body of Christians with infamous conduct in general terms of abuse, savours strongly of illiberality, not to say *malignity*.

Had these persons made a proper inquiry, without observation, they would have learned that the *Jumpers*, vulgarly so called, are not a sect; that they belong to all persuasions, and are so *denominated* from their carrying their zeal to a height, that, when the preacher touches pathetically upon any subject alluding to the Saviour, more especially his unexampled love to men, and his vicarious sufferings for the guilty, the whole congregation begin exulting, and discover their deep obligation and their grateful sense of deliverance, by gestures, that may appear extravagant to those in the habit of thinking less warm upon the subject, or habituated to more temperate and modest expressions of joy. I have known a preacher think it prudent to suspend his harangues till the ferment of zeal has abated; but never witnessed any of those intemperate and indecent ebullitions of passion so frequently detailed by the enemies of religion.

A remark that struck me, has perhaps been made by many of the thinking part of mankind before, that at the aweful hour when he who is our Judge shall appear, it will be found superior wisdom to have exulted *rather more than appeared absolutely necessary at the name of the Saviour*, than to be found amongst the number of those that denied him.

It cannot but be regretted by the friends of order, that laxity of discipline is frequently the consequence of this spirit of independency in religion; and many from a love of novelty, dissent from the Established Church, and, from the love of distinction, take upon them the sacred office. Evils, doubtless, may arise from self-created priests, and self-instituted churches; and it might be desirable to place a barrier to these irregular proceedings. But it will probably baffle the wisest skill, and surpass all human power. Perhaps it will be the wisest plan to let the evil and the good remain together; the tares and the wheat, till the divine harvest shall arrive, when unerring judgement will separate the chaff from the wheat, and make a just distinction.

The high spirited bigot will feel perhaps offended at what he may deem an eulogium upon piety, *without the pale* of the Established Church: but to this I must put in a plea of toleration. I must ask for a tolerant spirit in the *individual* as well as in the State. A spirit that has placed another brilliant in the diadem of our unrivalled constitution, and given an unanswerable proof of the wisdom and moderation of the Establishment.

It is a right that every one is born heir to, to worship GOD in that way most congenial to the dictates of his own mind, within the bounds of decency. The State as it receives support from religion, is bound to support and protect it; but cannot, upon any pretence, dare to enforce or suppress it and every act of persecution on the score of religion, and every coercive restraint upon the exercise of rational devotion, is nothing less than an infringement upon the divine prerogative; calling in question the wisdom of GOD; and a violent stride upon His moral government of the world.

I am fully satisfied, that the power of truth will eventually triumph over the stratagems and exertions of error; and that the wisdom and goodness of GOD will be finally manifested, even by the *Divisions* that are permitted among the professors of Christianity.

With respect to the inhabitants of North Wales, I have seen so much positive virtue and holiness, so much resignation in distress, and patient suffering under the most trying afflictions, so amply convictive of the sincerity of their Christian profession, and so irresistibly conclusive that the spirit which possessed them must be divine, that I have no hesitation in declaring, I am still more convinced than ever, there are many good characters in every persuasion of Christians; and that the denomination is of very small importance, where the motives are pure, the demeanour holy, and the result happiness.

> If these are Christian virtues, I am *Christian*.
> The faith that can inspire this generous change,
> Must be divine, and glow with all its GOD.
> Friendship, and Constancy, and Right, and Pity,
> All these were lessons I had learn'd before;
> But this unnatural grandeur of the soul,
> Is more than mortal, and outreaches virtue:
> *It draws, it charms, it binds me to be Christian.*
>
> HILL's *Alzira.*

I am ever your's,

J. E.

FINIS

Index

G

Maen Hirion 99, 144
Maen Sigl 288
Maentwrog 147, 150, 156
Maes y Gaer 258
Maiden Castle 50
Mallwyd 55, 58, 64
Malvern Hills 354
March, Earl of. *See* Dunbar,
 10th Earl of March, George
Marcher Lordship of Chirk
 355
Maredudd ab Owain Glyndwr
 252, 329
Margam Forest 130
Margaret of Anjou 134
Margaret verch Evans 196, 199
Martin, Robert fitz 361, 362
Mary I 204
Mary II of England and Scot-
 land 368
Mason, George 187
Mathafarn 70
Matholwch, Lord of Cwl 334
Mathraval 349, 421
Matlock 118
Mawddach, River 112, 113,
 114, 115
Mawddach Waterfall 111, 113,
 114
Maw, River 111, 112, 119
Maw, Vale of the 111
Maxen Wledic 178
Meini Hirion 341
Melica Cœrulea 57
Menai Strait 181, 182, 184, 185,
 202, 208, 234, 235, 236,
 246, 248, 249, 251, 257
Mercia, Kingdom of 349
Merddin Wyllt 419

Meredith ap Evan 309
Mereudd ap Cynan ab Owain
 Gwynedd 110
Meredydd ap Bleydden 110
Meredyth, John 50
Merionedd 34
Merioneth 57, 71, 93, 100,
 131, 145, 151, 155, 164, 173,
 312, 316, 348, 354, 361,
 404, 405
Merionethshire 71
Merlin 225, 227, 268, 322
Merlinus Ambrosius 227
Micknant 152
Middleton, Sir Thomas 15, 32
Milton, John 44
Minera 350
minstrels 421, 425
Mnium jugermannia 102
Moel Dyfi 58
Moel, Elian 172
Moel Llyfni 202
Moel Mynydd Mawr 172, 202
Moel Orthrwm 111
Moel Siabod 202, 203, 219,
 224
Moelwyn Gwyn 157
Moelwyn yr Hŷdd 157
Moel y Golfa 13
Mold 350
Mona 132, 178, 195, 282, 416,
 452
Mona Antiqua Restaurata
 (Rowlands) 132, 178, 195,
 282, 452
Monmouth 43, 44, 361
Montalt, 1st Baron Montalt,
 Robert de 361
Montesquieu, Charles Louis

U

www.ingramcontent.com/pod-product-compliance
Lightning Source LLC
Chambersburg PA
CBHW030946150426
42814CB00033B/433/J